access to history

Italy: The Rise of Fascism 1896–1946

MARK ROBSON

FOURTH EDITION

Italy: The Rise of Fascism 1896–1946

MARK ROBSON

FOURTH EDITION

HODDER
EDUCATION
AN HACHETTE UK COMPANY

The Publishers would like to thank Robin Bunce, Nicholas Fellows, David Ferriby and Sarah Ward for their contribution to the Study Guide.

The Publishers would like to thank the following for permission to reproduce copyright material:

Photo credits: p13 http://it.wikipedia.org/wiki/Giovanni_Giolitti#/media/File:Giovanni_Giolitti.jpg; **p29** Library of Congress, 37463u; **p33** Topical Press Agency/Getty Images; **p34** http://en.wikipedia.org/wiki/Roberto_Farinacci#/media/File:Roberto_Farinacci_1930.jpg; **p36** Oscar Manello/Central Press/Getty Images; **p42** Hulton-Deutsch Collection/Corbis; **p52** Underwood & Underwood/Corbis; **p57** The Granger Collection/TopFoto; **p66** Topham Picturepoint; **p67** Corbis; **p73** Library of Congress, LC-USZ62-122356; **pp91, 93** Popperfoto/Getty Images; **p107** Bettmann/Corbis; **p108** Hulton-Deutsch Collection/Corbis; **p124** Kent Cartoon Archive/Solo Syndication; **p127** Bettmann/Corbis; **p128** Corbis; **p141** Underwood & Underwood/Corbis; **p146** Corbis; **p148** IMAGNO/Votava/TopFoto.

Acknowledgements: listed on page 186.

Hachette UK's policy is to use papers that are natural, renewable and recyclable products and made from wood grown in sustainable forests. The logging and manufacturing processes are expected to conform to the environmental regulations of the country of origin.

Orders: please contact Bookpoint Ltd, 130 Milton Park, Abingdon, Oxon OX14 4SB. Telephone: +44 (0)1235 827720. Fax: +44 (0)1235 400454. Lines are open 9.00a.m.–5.00p.m., Monday to Saturday, with a 24-hour message answering service. Visit our website at www.hoddereducation.co.uk

© Mark Robson
Fourth edition © Mark Robson 2015

First published in 1998 by
Hodder Education
An Hachette UK Company
Carmelite House, 50 Victoria Embankment
London EC4Y 0DZ

Impression number   10 9 8 7 6 5 4 3 2
Year   2019 2018 2017 2016

Cover photo © Mary Evans Picture Library
Produced, illustrated and typeset in Palatino LT Std by Gray Publishing, Tunbridge Wells
Printed and bound by CPI Group (UK) Ltd, Croydon CR0 4YY

A catalogue record for this title is available from the British Library

ISBN 978 1471838194

Contents

Dedication

Keith Randell (1943–2002)

The *Access to History* series was conceived and developed by Keith, who created a series to 'cater for students as they are, not as we might wish them to be'. He leaves a living legacy of a series that for over 20 years has provided a trusted, stimulating and well-loved accompaniment to post-16 study. Our aim with these new editions is to continue to offer students the best possible support for their studies.

CHAPTER 1

The death of Benito Mussolini

On 25 April 1945 Benito Mussolini, the *Duce* of Fascism, the leader of Italy for two decades, was informed that German forces in Italy had surrendered to the advancing British and US armies. His allies and protectors had abandoned him and now he would have to face the vengeance of his fellow countrymen. Angry, but defiant, he declared that he and 3000 loyal **blackshirts** would continue the war from the mountains of northern Italy.

Leaving Milan with a small band of followers and accompanied by his German SS bodyguard, Mussolini headed for the lakeside town of Como, intending to meet up with a much larger force of loyal Fascists. Arriving in Como on the evening of 25 April, the dictator could find no trace of these blackshirts. He moved on along the lakeside and then headed up the mountainside to the small village of Grandola. Here, at last, he found the main body of the Fascist forces. The *Duce* wanted to know how many men he now had at his disposal. Receiving no answer from the blackshirt commander he asked again:

> 'Well, tell me. How many?'
> 'Twelve', came the embarrassed reply.

Whatever illusions the *Duce* still had were shattered. The man who had once boasted of possessing an army of 'eight million bayonets' and an air force large enough to 'blot out the sun', the leader who had once claimed to have the support of over 95 per cent of Italians was left with no more than a dozen supporters.

With all hope lost, Mussolini was persuaded to join a German convoy heading towards the Austrian border. Donning a German helmet and overcoat he tried to disguise himself. A few miles further on a group of partisans – Italian anti-Fascist resistance fighters – halted the convoy and searched it. Peering into the back of a truck a partisan spotted a hunched figure:

> 'Aren't you an Italian?', he demanded.
> Mussolini paused then replied: 'Yes, I am an Italian.'
> 'Excellency', the man exclaimed, 'You are here!'

Recovering himself, the partisan arrested the former dictator and his mistress, Clara Petacci, and took them to a small farmhouse.

At about 4p.m. on 28 April a stranger burst into Mussolini's room calling out 'Hurry up, I've come to rescue you.' Taking them out of the house, he pushed Mussolini and his mistress into his waiting car and drove off. After a few

 **KEY TERMS**

Duce All-powerful leader. This was Mussolini's self-attributed 'title', which the regime encouraged people to use. It signified that he was not just prime minister, but also the effective dictator of Italy.

Blackshirts Armed Fascist militia.

minutes the car stopped and the couple were ordered out. Within seconds the *Duce* and Clara Petacci had been shot. Their executioner was a partisan authorised by his resistance group to kill the ex-dictator.

The bodies were put back into the car and then transferred to a removal van already loaded with the corpses of fifteen Fascists. Mussolini's body was slung on the top of the pile. The following day his and his mistress's bodies, now mutilated, were hung upside down from a garage roof in Milan's Piazzale Loreto to be mocked by jeering crowds.

Such was the ignominious end of the man who had dominated Italy for twenty years, the man who had claimed to have invented fascism, the man who had swept away the old Liberal regime, the man who had vowed to make his country 'great, respected and feared'.

The question of how Mussolini rose from obscurity to overthrow the Liberal system of government and create Europe's first Fascist dictatorship is the central theme of this book. To understand fully the rise of fascism and the nature of the Fascist dictatorship, it is important to examine both the circumstances in which Italy became a united country in 1870 and the weaknesses of the Italian state in the years immediately prior to the First World War. These themes are examined in Chapter 2.

The weaknesses of Liberal Italy 1870–1915

Mussolini and his Fascists rose to power in the years immediately following the First World War, replacing the old Liberal regime. However, the rise of fascism cannot be understood simply by examining the events from 1915 to 1922. This chapter considers the problems that faced Italy and its Liberal rulers immediately prior to the war, and shows that many of the factors which would help to cause the collapse of the Liberal regime in 1922 were already visible in the years leading up to Italian entry into the war in 1915. These problems and factors are addressed through the following themes in this chapter:

★ The unification of Italy 1815–70

★ Problems facing Liberal Italy 1870–1896

★ Growing challenges to Liberal political dominance 1896–1915

★ Liberal governments 1896–1915

★ Liberal Italy on the eve of the First World War

Key dates

1859–60	Kingdom of Piedmont seized most of northern Italy	**1870**	Italian troops seized Rome
			Unification of Italy completed
1861	Kingdom of Piedmont seized southern and central Italy, but with Rome remaining under the control of the Pope	**1895**	Italian Socialist Party founded
		1898	Army used to suppress widespread riots
		1911	Conquest of Libya expanded Italian Empire in Africa
	Kingdom of Italy established	**1912**	Universal male suffrage
	King of Piedmont became first King of Italy	**1915**	Italy joined First World War on the side of Britain and France

 ## 1 The unification of Italy 1815–70

▶ *How did the unification of Italy come about?*

In 1815 Italy, as the Austrian statesman Metternich pointed out, was only 'a geographical expression'. The country had not known political union for about 1500 years. It was a collection of relatively small, often quarrelling states. In the past, there had been great wealth in cities such as Florence, Venice and Rome, together with impressive cultural achievements, but the country had rarely been free from war or foreign domination. Indeed, while the likes of Leonardo da Vinci and Michelangelo were creating their great works of art during the 'Italian Renaissance' of the fifteenth and sixteenth centuries, Italy had been the battleground of Europe, as French and Spanish armies fought for supremacy.

In 1815 the states of the Italian peninsula were, for the most part, politically **reactionary** and economically undeveloped. The most determined reaction and abject poverty was to be found in the south, in the kingdom of the Two Sicilies. Central Italy was dominated by the Papal States, over which the Pope was not only the religious but also the political ruler. Further north were the small states of Tuscany, Modena and Parma, and the more economically advanced kingdom of Piedmont, based in Turin. Lombardy and Venetia, which contained the major cities of Milan and Venice, were ruled by the Austrian Empire.

Risorgimento

The period after 1815 witnessed an Italian literary and cultural revival, the *Risorgimento*, literally 'resurgence' or 'rebirth', which lamented Italian divisions and foreign domination, called for a new sense of Italian patriotism and demanded the political unification of the country. This movement particularly attracted students and the small professional classes, principally in the north. The kingdom of Piedmont was, however, the driving force behind unification.

In 1859 the Piedmontese statesman Camillo Cavour won French support for his expansionist ambitions. French arms forced Austria to cede Lombardy to Piedmont, while Tuscany, Modena, Parma and the Papal State of the Romagna were persuaded to give up their independence and join the kingdom of Piedmont. In the same year Garibaldi, the romantic adventurer and popular hero of the unification, invaded Sicily with 1000 armed men – his 'Red Shirts'. Despite the small size of his army, he had succeeded in conquering the kingdom of the Two Sicilies by late 1860. Garibaldi was then persuaded to hand over the state to King Victor Emmanuel II of Piedmont. At the same time a second part of the Papal States was annexed, leaving the Pope with only the area surrounding Rome.

In 1861 the kingdom of Italy was established as a **constitutional monarchy** based very closely on that of Piedmont. Italian support for Prussia in the Austro-Prussian war of 1866 led to the acquisition of Venetia from Austria. Finally, in 1870 Rome, the last independent territory in the peninsula, fell to Italian troops after the French had removed their soldiers from protecting the Holy City to fight in the Franco-Prussian war.

 **KEY TERMS**

Reactionary Hostile to parliamentary or democratic government, dismissive of individual freedoms and deeply suspicious of change.

Constitutional monarchy The king or queen is head of state but the prime minister is the head of the government. The monarch has the power to dismiss prime ministers but in practice leaves day-to-day politics in the hands of the prime minister and parliament. To stay in office and to pass new laws the prime minister needs the approval of the elected parliament.

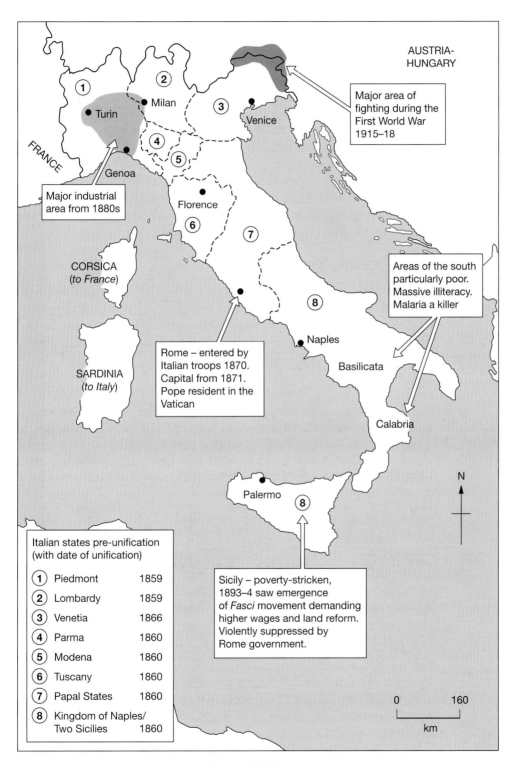

Figure 2.1 Italy: from unification to the First World War.

The following labels appear on the map:

AUSTRIA-HUNGARY

Major area of fighting during the First World War 1915–18

Major industrial area from 1880s

Areas of the south particularly poor. Massive illiteracy. Malaria a killer

Rome – entered by Italian troops 1870. Capital from 1871. Pope resident in the Vatican

Sicily – poverty-stricken, 1893–4 saw emergence of *Fasci* movement demanding higher wages and land reform. Violently suppressed by Rome government.

CORSICA (*to France*)

SARDINIA (*to Italy*)

FRANCE

Turin
Milan
Venice
Genoa
Florence
Naples
Basilicata
Calabria
Palermo

N

Italian states pre-unification (with date of unification)

1. Piedmont — 1859
2. Lombardy — 1859
3. Venetia — 1866
4. Parma — 1860
5. Modena — 1860
6. Tuscany — 1860
7. Papal States — 1860
8. Kingdom of Naples/ Two Sicilies — 1860

0   160
km

Problems facing Liberal Italy 1870–96

▶ *How serious were the problems faced by the Liberal rulers of Italy?*

The political unification of the states of the Italian peninsula was thus complete by 1870. With only two per cent of the population possessing the vote, the new state was to be dominated by the representatives of the wealthy and middle classes, and these were overwhelmingly Liberals. This **Liberal oligarchy**, as they have sometimes been referred to, saw themselves as an educated elite who would lead Italy forward to national unity, economic prosperity and great power status. They were, however, to find formidable obstacles in their path.

Lack of Italian identity

The long history of political division had done little to foster a sense of national identity among Italians. Only a very small proportion of Italians had played any role in bringing about unification and loyalties tended to be towards the family or the immediate locality rather than towards the Italian nation. To complicate matters, only about two per cent of the population actually spoke Italian. The great majority spoke dialects that were virtually unintelligible outside their local area. What was known as 'Italian' was simply the local dialect of Tuscany, the province centring on Florence. Liberal governments believed that if Italy was to become truly united and a great power in Europe then the public must view themselves as Italians rather than Sicilians or Piedmontese.

Hostility of the Catholic Church

The Catholic Church was a powerful force in Italian society, claiming at least the nominal allegiance of the vast majority of the population, and it was bitterly resentful of the new kingdom of Italy that had seized the Papal States and Rome from the Church. In retaliation, the Pope refused to recognise the Italian state and instructed loyal Catholics to boycott all elections. This ban was lifted in the 1890s but distrust between the Church and the Liberal regime remained a factor in Italian politics up to and beyond the First World War.

Economic weakness

Italy was still predominantly an agricultural country, with some 68 per cent of the population dependent on the land for at least part of their livelihood. Most peasants and farm labourers, particularly in the south, lived in poverty. Industry was also relatively undeveloped. Most enterprises were small scale, centring around workshops and skilled craftsmen. Heavy industry was at a disadvantage because of the lack of natural resources, principally coal and iron ore. There was some development in iron and steel and shipbuilding, but this was largely limited to military purposes and railways and was concentrated in the north. Economic underdevelopment meant the government received relatively little in taxes and made it more difficult for them to finance such projects as the expansion of schooling or the build-up of the Italian armed forces.

Weaknesses of the Liberal political system

The parliamentary system had been partly based on the British model but in certain vital respects it was very different: there were no clearly defined political parties and there was no **two-party system**. As the urban and rural poor did not the vote, politicians were drawn mainly from the professional, wealthy middle class and represented this narrow social class in parliament. These Liberals were not divided by ideology and, in fact, had relatively few major differences of opinion. Consequently, there seemed to be no necessity for formal political parties that might draw up policy, elect leaders and discipline dissenting members.

In the absence of well-organised parties, members of parliament, or deputies as they were known, clustered around prominent politicians and formed factions. A number of factions would agree to support each other and form a government, dividing up the ministerial posts between them. This was the politics of *Trasformismo*, where former political opponents might temporarily put aside their differences and come together in government. Of course, such alliances were fragile and when a leading politician felt aggrieved over an issue he would withdraw his faction's support and the government would fall. In fact, such was the turnover of governments that Italy had 29 prime ministers between 1870 and 1922.

To critics, these ever-changing governments indicated that Liberal politics was not about principle or the good of the nation; it was simply the pursuit of power for its own sake.

KEY TERMS

Two-party system A political system, as in Britain, where there are two dominant and distinct parties competing for power.

Trasformismo Different political factions forming a coalition government regardless of ideological differences.

3 Growing challenges to Liberal political dominance 1896–1915

▶ *Why did the Liberals face growing challenges to their political dominance?*

Context: political and economic crisis 1893–6

There was economic growth in the first twenty years of Liberal Italy but, by the early 1890s, the economy had fallen into depression, the result of foreign competition and trade disputes with France, Italy's main export market.

KEY TERM

Lire The Italian currency from 1861 to 2002. (Singular: lira.)

Companies and even banks began to go bust. One of these banks, the Banca Romana, had issued banknotes on behalf of the Italian state. On its collapse, it became apparent that it had printed and issued a large number of banknotes illegally – in effect it had literally printed its own money, to the tune of 60 million **lire**, for its own use. The public outcry caused by this scandal was increased still further when it was revealed that the bank had also lent large sums of money to leading politicians. These loans had been interest free. The prime minister, Francesco Crispi, had received 55,000 lire and his political opponent, Giolitti, had borrowed at least 60,000 lire. This was an enormous sum at a time when the annual income per person in Italy was under 2000 lire. This clearly smacked of corruption and lowered the reputation of Liberal politicians even further.

The economic depression of the early 1890s not only caused bankruptcies and a political scandal, but also led to protests and public disorder. The first signs of trouble appeared in Sicily, one of the poorest parts of the country. Workers, at first in towns but soon in the countryside as well, organised strikes and demonstrations to demand higher wages and lower rents. Crispi's government took fright, viewing these protests as a revolutionary subversive movement, perhaps sponsored by the Pope and hostile foreign powers. In January 1894 the government ordered the arrest of the workers' leaders. Sicily was placed under military rule and 40,000 government troops were despatched to restore order. Crispi feared that not only Sicily but also the whole of Italy was on the brink of revolt. To prevent this, opposition political groups were banned throughout the country and critical newspapers were censored.

Crispi's government survived this domestic crisis but a catastrophic defeat in foreign affairs destroyed both the government and the career of its leader. Crispi was determined that Italy should become a 'Great Power', the equal of Britain and France. By the 1880s these two countries were carving out empires in Africa, and many Liberals believed that Italy should have its share. Eritrea, in East Africa, was seized in 1890 and, in 1895, Crispi ordered Italian troops to occupy part of Ethiopia (known then as Abyssinia). War broke out and in the Battle of Adowa in March 1896 an Italian army was utterly defeated, leaving 5000 Italian soldiers dead.

This was a national humiliation which was etched into the Italian consciousness and only exorcised in 1936 when Mussolini's Fascists finally conquered Ethiopia (see page 121). Crispi's career came to an abrupt end. He had tried to make Italy a Great Power but had seen his army lose its first major campaign, the first European forces to be defeated by an African state in modern times.

The events of 1893–6 severely damaged the prestige and self-confidence of Liberal politicians and spurred economic depression, national humiliation and political corruption, which encouraged the growth of opposition movements that would challenge the Liberals' monopoly of power. These movements took the form of socialism, Catholicism and nationalism.

Socialism

Rapid industrialisation in northern Italy from the 1880s produced a sizeable working class who were attracted to **Socialist** ideas concerning pay, working conditions and the ownership of industry. A Liberal reform of 1881, allowing some 2 million more Italians to vote, provided an added incentive for Socialists to organise. The first determined attempt to create a single, united Socialist party was made by Filippo Turati, a middle-class lawyer, when, in 1891, he organised an Italian Workers' Congress in Milan.

At the Genoa Congress of 1892 the movement divided into two broad groupings. The first dedicated itself to revolutionary strikes and refused to participate in elections or parliamentary politics. The second and larger group also committed itself to workers' control of the state, but realised that this must be a long-term aim. It argued that in the meantime, and to achieve this ultimate goal, Socialists should work to extract better pay and conditions from employers, and should involve themselves in local and national politics, even if this meant dealing with the hated Liberals.

This more moderate group, including Turati, became the Italian Socialist Party (PSI) in 1895. By 1897 it had 27,000 members and ran its own newspaper, *Avanti!* In 1900 it received over 200,000 votes in the general election and secured 32 seats in the chamber of deputies, the lower house of the Italian parliament. According to its manifesto, these deputies were resolved to demand the introduction of **universal male suffrage**, an eight-hour day, income tax and women's rights. But despite the fact that socialism still had relatively little support by the turn of the century and had adopted moderate policies its emergence had provoked great fears. Such fears were particularly pronounced in the Catholic Church.

Catholicism

For the first decade or more after unification, the Catholic Church focused its hostility on the Liberal regime, but by the 1890s the Papacy had turned its attention to the rise of socialism. To the Church, socialism was a direct competitor for the hearts and minds of ordinary Italians, challenged the traditional social order and even rejected religion (see Source A).

SOURCE A

The Bishop of Verona writing to Catholics in his region, 1901, quoted in Martin Clark, *Modern Italy: 1871 to the Present*, Routledge, 2014, p. 177.

Socialism is the most abject slavery, it is flagrant injustice, it is the craziest folly, it is a social crime, it is the destruction of the family and of public welfare, it is the self-proclaimed and inevitable enemy of religion, and it leads to anarchy.

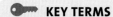

KEY TERMS

Socialist Socialists argue that the existing political and economic systems of Europe oppress the poor. They work to improve the political and economic status of the working class. Some believe that the existing political systems can be reformed peacefully; others argue that only violent revolution can bring about meaningful change.

Universal male suffrage The right to vote for all men over the age of 21, introduced in 1912.

Why was the Bishop of Verona, writing in Source A, so concerned about socialism?

To head off the danger of Socialist gains in parliament, the Church removed its ban on Catholics voting in general elections. By 1909 Catholics were even permitted to put themselves forward as candidates for election.

The Pope remained opposed to the formation of a Catholic political party that might rival his authority over the faithful, but the Catholics still presented a major challenge to the Liberal regime. Now that the Catholics were active participants in national politics, was it possible to ignore them, or must some form of accommodation be attempted? If there was to be co-operation, what would the terms be, and how could leading Liberals deal with the remaining **anticlericals** in their own ranks?

Nationalism

Nationalists, often middle-class intellectuals, were few in number but they found many supporters in the media. They accused Liberals of putting their own careers before the good of the country. In particular, they condemned the regime for failing to make Italy a great power, the equal of France or Britain. They demanded a larger Italian Empire in Africa and higher military spending. They also favoured **irridentism**, demanding that Italy seize those areas of the Austrian Empire where most of the population spoke Italian, namely South Tyrol, Trentino and Istria (see the map on page 33).

Nationalists argued that a more aggressive foreign policy would help to forge an Italian nation and reinvigorate Italian politics. It would be the Nationalists who would lead the calls for Italian entry into the First World War and who would be an early influence on fascism.

KEY TERMS

Anticlericals Those politicians, mainly Liberal, who opposed the claims of the Catholic Church that it deserved a privileged position within the Italian state. Liberals who were particularly anticlerical, and who demanded greater social reform, were known as Radicals.

Irridentism The demand that Italy seize from Austria those lands on its northern and eastern borders where a majority of the population spoke Italian.

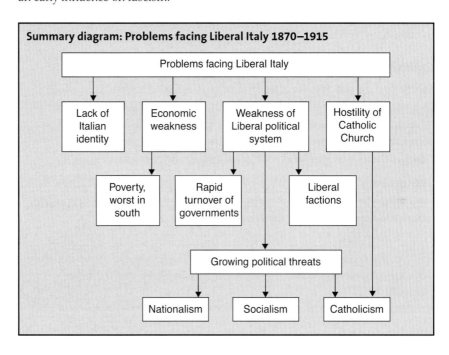

Summary diagram: Problems facing Liberal Italy 1870–1915

- Problems facing Liberal Italy
  - Lack of Italian identity
  - Economic weakness
    - Poverty, worst in south
  - Weakness of Liberal political system
    - Rapid turnover of governments
  - Hostility of Catholic Church
    - Liberal factions
- Growing political threats
  - Nationalism
  - Socialism
  - Catholicism

Liberal governments 1896–1915

▶ *What problems did Liberal governments face from 1870 to 1915?*

Crispi was forced to resign as prime minister after the defeat at Adowa in 1896 and peace was made with Ethiopia, but within Italy repression was maintained and even increased. The government viewed dissent as subversion and concessions as signs of weakness. This policy culminated in the traumatic events of 1898. The poor harvest of 1897, combined with high taxes on imported wheat, pushed up the price of food. Street demonstrations against high prices and shortages began in the south in early 1898 and by April had spread to most parts of the country. When the attempt to arrest some socialist newspaper sellers in Milan led to widespread rioting, the authorities thought that they had uncovered a socialist conspiracy. The army was brought in to suppress the riots, killing up to 200 people in the process. Martial law was declared in four provinces, all suspected subversives were arrested and the press was heavily censored. Thousands of people were jailed.

The repression worked in that the protestors were silenced, but the problem was not solved. Opposition did not disappear: it simply went underground. In fact, the methods used by the authorities only increased public disaffection. It became ever clearer to most Liberals that repression was not a viable long-term policy. By the beginning of the new century the voices of moderation were starting to be heard.

The most persuasive advocate of a new approach was Giovanni Giolitti, the man who was to dominate Italian politics for over a decade. Giolitti was convinced that Liberals had made the mistake of ignoring the plight of ordinary Italians. Indeed, he considered that the troubles of the 1890s had been partly of the Liberals' own making.

SOURCE B

Giolitti speaking in parliament in 1900, quoted in Franklin Hugh Adler, *Italian Industrialists from Liberalism to Fascism: The Political Development of the Industrial Bourgeoisie, 1906–34*, Cambridge University Press, 2002, p. 12.

The country is sick politically and morally, but the principal cause of its sickness is that the classes in power have been spending enormous sums on themselves and their own interests, and have obtained the money almost entirely from the poorer sections of society … I deplore as much as anyone the struggle between classes but at least let us be fair and ask who started it.

What is the message of Source B?

And, in 1901, Giolitti warned parliament:

> *The upward movement of the popular classes is accelerating day by day ... Let no one delude himself that he can prevent the popular classes from conquering their share of political and economic influence ... It depends chiefly on us, whether the emergence of these shall be a new conservative force, or whether instead it shall be a whirlwind that will be the ruin of our country's fortunes.*

Continued repression, then, would only fuel the 'struggle between classes' and create a Socialist movement dedicated to revolution. The only alternative was to demonstrate that government could be sympathetic to the demands of labour. Government should no longer be seen as the enemy of the urban worker and the rural poor. Moderate Socialists should be encouraged to play a constructive role in parliamentary politics, even to the point of being invited to join Liberal governments.

As minister of the interior from 1901 to 1903 and then as prime minister for all but three of the years from 1903 to 1914, Giolitti tried to put his philosophy into action. In the field of social reform he was responsible for passing laws forcing employers to grant one rest day a week and outlawing the employment of children under the age of twelve. Government expenditure on public works was increased, and had doubled from 1900 to 1907. Part of this money had gone to improving roads, farming and the quality of drinking water in the south. Taxes on food, which affected the poor relatively more than the rich, were reduced and the drug quinine was supplied free of charge to areas affected by malaria.

Giolitti's most controversial policy addressed the issue of labour disputes. Liberal governments recognised that workers had the right to strike but often viewed strikers as potentially revolutionary mobs to be dispersed by the police. This was particularly the case in the late 1890s when troops were frequently used to intimidate strikers. Giolitti, in contrast to his predecessors, was determined that the state should remain neutral in disputes between employers and employees. He thought that only if the government was seen to be neutral in strikes would workers support the Liberal state. This new approach was illustrated most vividly in 1904 when left-wing unions called a general strike. The strike received widespread support in the northern cities, but the government kept its nerve and refused to crush the strikers. After a few days the disorganised and uncoordinated strike collapsed. This defeat discredited extremists on the left, yet informed employers that they could no longer rely on the authorities to intimidate their employees into going back to work. Giolitti believed that employers should be prepared to negotiate with their workers.

To improve relations between the two sides of industry, the government encouraged the emergence of arbitrators. These arbitrators were independent officials who listened to the arguments of both employers and employees and then recommended a compromise. Employers began to be more conciliatory.

Giovanni Giolitti

1842	Born in Piedmont, northern Italy
1860	Graduated in Law
1882	Elected MP
1892–3	Prime minister
1901–3	Minister of the interior (equivalent of home secretary in the UK)
1903–5	Prime minister
1906–9	Prime minister
1911–14	Prime minister
1920–1	Prime minister
1928	Died

Giolitti was the dominant Liberal politician of the years 1896–1915. He was on the left of the party, believing that Liberal governments should help the poor through social reforms. He was a highly skilled politician who tried to win support by working with moderate Socialists and Catholics, and by increasing the numbers of Italians eligible to vote. He underestimated the Fascists after the First World War and offered them an electoral alliance in 1921.

Gradually, they conceded, for example, that workers could not be sacked without good cause or simply for going on strike.

Giolitti's policy certainly won the support of many moderate socialists, particularly those who sat in the chamber of deputies. Socialist MPs were prepared to support Giolitti's government, and effectively became part of his coalition. The prime minister also attempted to work with those moderate Catholics who feared socialism and favoured limited social reform. They were encouraged by Giolitti's willingness to drop a proposed law permitting divorce and they began to cast their votes in favour of those Liberals willing to stand up for Catholic interests, such as Church schools. This co-operation was particularly seen in local politics, where Catholics voted for sympathetic Liberals and even stood for election themselves. By 1911 Catholics were part of the governing coalitions in big cities such as Turin, Bologna, Florence and Venice.

Giolitti's grand design of a *Trasformismo* which would bring all men of goodwill together to protect the state seemed to be coming to fruition. Socialists and Catholics no longer appeared to be such subversive outcasts from Liberal Italy. However, Giolitti's coalition was very fragile and was to be destroyed by the consequences of a colonial war and the introduction of universal suffrage.

The Libyan War and the collapse of Giolitti's ministry

In September 1911 Italy invaded Libya, in North Africa. Giolitti hoped to overcome this outpost of the Turkish Empire quickly and establish an Italian colony there. Italy had harboured ambitions in North Africa since the early 1880s when the French had seized Tunis. In 1911 France seemed to be consolidating its control of Morocco and Algeria and, Italy feared, might turn its attention to Algeria's neighbour, Libya. Public opinion, whipped up by Nationalists and the press, would not stand for another humiliation and demanded intervention. Giolitti bowed to the pressure.

The war itself was relatively successful, certainly when compared to the Ethiopian campaign of 1896. The major Libyan towns and ports were taken within three weeks and Turkey formally ceded the territory to Italy in October 1912. Italian forces were still harried by Arab guerrilla groups, but the venture appeared a resounding success for the Liberal government.

In the event, however, the victory helped to destroy Giolitti's hopes of a grand *Trasformismo*. In the first place, the alliance between moderate socialists and Giolittian Liberals collapsed. The Socialist Party had condemned the war and moderate reformists lost their position as the dominant grouping within the party. More revolutionary socialists were now in the ascendant. Indeed, the socialist newspaper, *Avanti!* (*Forward!*), edited by a young firebrand named Benito Mussolini, now called for the abolition of private property and advocated violent strikes to overthrow the state. More conservative Italians were appalled, and many blamed Giolitti's conciliatory policy towards labour. They had hated his refusal to use force against strikers and insisted that such weakness had only encouraged socialist extremism. Some Italians began to listen to the Italian Nationalist Association, a grouping of businessmen, journalists and young, radical poets and painters, who condemned not just Giolitti, but the whole Liberal system. These Nationalists despised the manoeuvrings in parliament, accused the politicians of neglecting Italian interests, and demanded higher defence spending and colonial expansion. Italy must be a true 'Great Power' and in order to achieve this some form of **authoritarian state** would be necessary. The Nationalists secured few votes but their influence over conservative groups such as industrialists and landowners was out of all proportion to their numbers. Italian politics was **polarising**.

The difficulties faced by Giolitti-style liberalism were increased by the widening of the suffrage in 1912. Giolitti's reward to the victorious soldiers in the Libyan campaign increased the electorate from 3 million to 8.5 million. Now anyone who had completed their military service could vote, as could literate men at 21 years old and all men at 30 years old, whether literate or not.

In the 1913 general election, the first held under the new rules, it appeared as though nothing had changed. Of the 511 seats in the chamber, the various Liberal factions controlled 318, and could count on up to 70 votes from left-wing anticlerical Liberals known as Radicals. Against this, the Socialists could muster 78 seats – an increase of four per cent on their performance in the 1909 election – and the Nationalists only three seats. However, it became apparent that the Liberal majority had been achieved by arranging an electoral deal with the moderate Catholics.

The leader of the moderate Catholic group had agreed with Giolitti that Liberal candidates who promised to oppose divorce and favour religious orders and Church schools would receive Catholic votes. To ensure that they held their seats, 228 Liberal candidates signed a declaration that they would support such

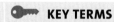
KEY TERMS

Authoritarian state
A state with a strong central government that is able and willing to ignore parliament and suppress dissent.

Polarising Moving towards extremes.

Catholic interests. Giolitti secured a majority, but it was clear that in the age of universal suffrage the number of committed Liberal supporters in the country would be too few to ensure future Liberal majorities in the chamber. It was somewhat ironic that the Liberal government now depended on the votes of Catholic groups. Dependent on Catholic support and with the Socialists totally opposed to co-operation, the trick of *Trasformismo* was becoming impossible to perform. Proof of this came in 1914 when the staunchly anticlerical Radicals withdrew their support from Giolitti's coalition. They had discovered the electoral deal that had been struck with the Catholics and they felt that they could no longer support an administration that was so apparently dependent on the old enemy, Catholicism. Giolitti promptly resigned. Within months, Europe was engulfed in the First World War, a war which would severely weaken liberalism in Italy.

 # 5 Liberal Italy on the eve of the First World War

▶ *How stable was the Liberal regime in the years leading up to the First World War?*

The positive view

Liberals argued that Italy had made huge progress under their rule and that the country was evolving into a strong and healthy democracy in the years immediately prior to the First World War.

National military service and the introduction of free primary education had helped to create a greater sense of Italian nationhood. Economic progress had been rapid, as evidenced by national income rising from 61 billion lire in 1895 to 92 billion lire in 1915, and by a six-fold increase in foreign trade in the 50 years up to 1913. Taxes on food had been reduced, and Liberal governments had spent money to improve roads, railways and the supply of drinking water.

In the field of foreign affairs, Italy had joined the **Triple Alliance** with Germany and Austria-Hungary, and built up an empire in East Africa. The conquest of Libya in 1911 had confirmed Italy as a Great Power.

Most importantly, according to the Liberals, Italy had a robust, stable political system. The vote had been progressively extended so that from 1912 there was effectively universal male suffrage. Giolitti, prime minister for most of the years from 1903 to 1914, had managed to co-opt both moderate Socialists and moderate Catholics into his governing coalition.

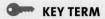 **KEY TERM**

Triple Alliance Military alliance between Italy, Germany and Austria-Hungary signed in 1882.

The regime was thus winning the support of the key groups within Italian society. The British historian G.M. Trevelyan, writing in the years before the First World War, illustrated this positive view: 'Nothing is more remarkable than the stability of the Italian kingdom and the building is as safe as any in Europe. The foundations of human liberty and the foundations of social order exist there on a firm basis.'

The negative view

This rosy vision of a successful Liberal Italy was firmly rejected by the Liberals' political opponents.

Socialist criticisms of Liberal Italy

Socialists condemned the regime as a cover for capitalist exploitation of the Italian working classes. Their argument was as follows. Wages were still very low and hours were very long when compared with the rest of western Europe. Welfare benefits, such as sickness and pension payments, also compared unfavourably. Any improvements in the life of the Italian worker had been wrung out of a state always too willing to use the army to crush strikers and opposing political groups. The wealth of the country had been squandered on imperialist adventures in East Africa and Libya. Severe poverty was still widespread. The fact that 5 million Italians had chosen to emigrate to the USA and South America in the period 1871–1915 confirmed the failure of liberalism to address the problem of poverty, let alone to solve it. For the Socialists, the question was not whether the Liberal regime would collapse, but how soon, and what methods would bring it about.

Nationalist criticisms of Liberal Italy

To the Nationalists, the regime was equally contemptible. It had lacked the will to make Italy a major force on the European scene. Liberal incompetence had led to a humiliating military defeat at the hands of the Ethiopians in 1896. For Nationalists, the vast emigration was also a national disgrace. These emigrants were men and women whose energy should have been employed to build up the Italian economy and fill the ranks of its armies. Liberalism, through its weakness, had only exacerbated the struggle between classes. The state had neither crushed socialism effectively nor provided a relevant alternative creed for Italian workers to believe in. Liberalism had never instilled an Italian 'national spirit', not least because its politicians lacked all principle. They were only concerned about their own careers and private interests and they made deals with anyone who could further their selfish aims. Giolitti himself was the epitome of such a lack of belief in public service. He had allied with Socialists and Catholics, and had shamelessly employed corrupt tactics to win general elections, using government officials to bribe or intimidate voters.

Catholic criticisms of Liberal Italy

Catholics were divided over liberalism. Many found it difficult to support a regime which in 1870 had trampled over the Pope's territorial rights in Rome. Furthermore, many believed the Liberals had neglected the problems of the poor Catholic peasantry, particularly in the south. Although governments during the Giolittian era had granted monies to southern provinces to improve irrigation and the supply of drinking water, the sums had proved woefully inadequate. Poverty remained a desperate problem, particularly in Sicily where 0.01 per cent of the population owned 50 per cent of the land, leaving a mass of landless peasants. From the late 1890s onwards southerners formed the majority of those 200,000 Italians emigrating overseas each year. This was proof of the seriousness of the 'southern problem'.

Catholic groups who looked towards social reform as a means of alleviating continuing poverty would form part of the Popular Party (the ***Popolari***) established after the First World War and they were determined not to be absorbed into the Liberal system. For them, the Liberals represented an urban educated elite who had little interest in or understanding of the real Italy.

Not all Catholics were fundamentally opposed to the Liberal regime, however. More conservative Catholics saw the regime as infinitely preferable to socialism. Liberalism might be far from ideal, but they feared that a Catholic political party in the hands of more radical reformers would be less willing than the Liberals to defend their property interests. In any case, the Pope was not yet prepared to permit the formation of a Catholic political party, a potential rival to his own authority.

 **KEY TERM**

Popolari Catholic political party founded in January 1919.

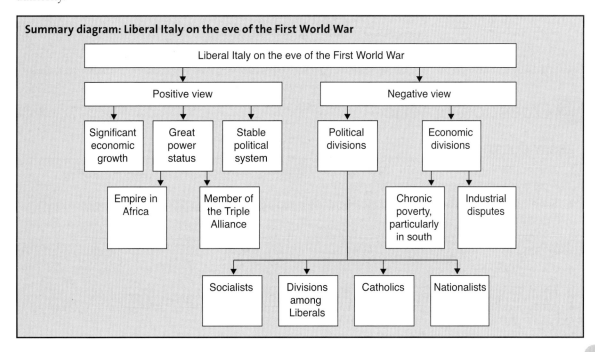

Summary diagram: Liberal Italy on the eve of the First World War

Chapter summary

The Liberal governments of 1870–1915 experienced economic problems and political scandals, and faced challenges to their political domination from Socialists, Catholics and Nationalists. There was economic progress, but the new industries were located in the north, and the south was still desperately poor. The Liberals, under Giolitti, introduced social reforms to help the poor and had widened the suffrage, but these reforms only spurred demands for further change.

In 1914 the Liberals remained in power but their basis of support was shallow and Socialist and Catholic opponents were growing in strength. The Liberal regime was in no immediate danger of collapse, but it was clear that the Liberal monopoly of power was over. The test for the Liberal political system was to see whether the practice of *Trasformismo* could bring moderate Catholics and Socialists into a Liberal coalition government, forming a new consensus which would narrow political divisions and marginalise the extremists: the revolutionary Socialists on the left and the Nationalists on the right. This, however, would be a very difficult task.

 ## Refresher questions

Use these questions to remind yourself of the key material covered in this chapter.

1 What problems faced the unified Italy in 1870?

2 Why did the Liberals dominate Italian politics in the years up to 1914?

3 What criticisms were made of the Liberal political system?

4 What did Socialists believe in?

5 Why did support grow for socialism?

6 Why did Catholics become more involved in politics?

7 What reforms did Giolitti introduce?

8 What criticisms did Nationalists make of Liberal politics and policies?

9 What were the consequences of the war in Libya?

10 Why did Giolitti's government collapse in 1914?

 ## Question practice

ESSAY QUESTIONS

1 'Liberal governments in the years 1896–1915 made little progress in solving the problems facing Italy.' Explain why you agree or disagree with this view.

2 'Socialism was the greatest threat to the Liberal regime in Italy in the years 1896–1915.' Assess the validity of this view.

3 How far was poverty the main reason for the growth of opposition to Liberal governments in the years up to 1915?

4 How significant were the governments of Giolitti in tackling the problems of Italy in the years 1900–14?

5 Assess the consequences of industrialisation in Italy in the years 1900–15.

6 Which of the following was the greater threat to Liberal governments 1900–15? i) Socialism. ii) Nationalism. Explain your answer with reference to both i) and ii).

SOURCE ANALYSIS QUESTIONS

1 With reference to Sources 1 and 2, and your understanding of the historical context, which of these two sources is more valuable in explaining why opposition to the Liberal governments grew in the years 1896–1914?

2 How far could the historian make use of Sources 1 and 2 together to investigate why groups opposed to the Liberals emerged in the years 1896–1914? Explain your answer, using both sources, the information given about them and your own knowledge of the historical context.

3 With reference to Sources 1, 2 and 3 (page 20), and your understanding of the historical context, assess the value of these sources to a historian studying the stability of the Liberal regime in the years 1896–1914.

SOURCE 1

Adapted from Benito Mussolini, *My Autobiography*, Paternoster Library, The Mayflower Press, 1928. Mussolini, at the time of writing in 1928, was dictator of Italy. In the following passage he is reflecting on politics just before the First World War.

Those years before the World War were filled by political twists and turns. Italian life was not easy. Difficulties were many for the people. The conquest of Libya had exacted its toll of lives and money in a measure far beyond our expectation. Our lack of political understanding brought at least one riot a week.

During one government of Giolitti I remember 33 [riots]. They had their harvest of killed and wounded and of corroding bitterness of heart … Riots and upheavals among day labourers, among the peasants in the Po valley, riots in the south. And in the meantime, above all this wasting away of normal life, there went on the tournament and the joust of political parties struggling for power.

SOURCE 2

Giolitti, Liberal prime minister on four occasions, 1892–1914, speaking to the Italian parliament in 1900, quoted in Franklin Hugh Adler, *Italian Industrialists from Liberalism to Fascism: The Political Development of the Industrial Bourgeoisie, 1906–34*, Cambridge University Press, 2002, p. 12.

The country is sick politically and morally, but the principal cause of its sickness is that the classes in power have been spending enormous sums on themselves and their own interests, and have obtained the money almost entirely from the poorer sections of society … When in the financial emergency of 1893 I had to call on the rich to make a small sacrifice, they began a rebellion [in parliament] against the government even more effective than the contemporary revolt of the poor Sicilian peasantry, and Sonnino who took over from me [as prime minister] had to find the money by increasing still further the price of salt and the tax on cereals. I deplore as much as anyone the struggle between classes but at least let us be fair and ask who started it.

SOURCE 3

Adapted from the writings of Antonio Gramsci, a former Socialist and a founder of the more radical Communist Party in 1921. In the following passage, written in the 1930s, Gramsci is analysing the leaders of the Liberal Party in the years up to 1914. Quoted in Q. Hoare and G. Nowell Smith, editors, *Selections from the Prison Notebooks of Antonio Gramsci*, Lawrence & Wishart, 2005, p. 90.

They [the leaders of the Risorgimento*] said that they were aiming at the creation of a modern State in Italy, and they in fact produced a bastard. They aimed at stimulating the formation of an extensive and energetic ruling class, and they did not succeed; at integrating the people into the framework of the new State, and they did not succeed. The paltry political life … the fundamental … rebelliousness of the Italian popular classes, the narrow existence of a cowardly ruling stratum, they are all consequences of that failure.*

CHAPTER 3

The rise of fascism 1915–22

Fascism was founded as a political movement only in 1919 and was insignificant until late in 1920. Nevertheless, by the end of October 1922 its leader, the former Socialist Benito Mussolini, had been appointed prime minister. Why did fascism rise to prominence so quickly? How important was Mussolini to its success? How far were the First World War and its consequences responsible for the rise of fascism? To what extent did Liberal failings enable the success of fascism? This chapter addresses these key questions under the following headings:

★ Italy at war

★ The economic and political effects of the First World War

★ Mussolini and the birth of fascism

★ The rise of fascism 1919–21

★ Mussolini seizes the initiative: May 1921 to October 1922

★ The March on Rome

The key debate on *page 43* of this chapter asks the question: To what extent was Mussolini's success the result of Liberal weakness?

Key dates

1915	May	Italy entered the First World War
1917	Oct.	Italian defeat at Battle of Caporetto
1918	Oct.	Italian victory at Vittorio Veneto caused Austria to sue for peace
1919	March	First meeting of Fascist movement
	June	Treaty of Versailles failed to award any German colonies to Italy
	Sept.	Treaty of St Germain with Austria Seizure of Fiume by Nationalist Gabriele D'Annunzio
	Nov.	Election: Socialists became largest party; Liberals unable to rule alone; Fascists failed to win any MPs
1920	Sept.	Occupation of the factories by 400,000 engineering workers
1920	Nov.	Fascist squad violence began
1921	May	Fascists gained 35 seats in general election
	Oct.	National Fascist Party organisation created
1922		Increasing Fascist violence
	July	Abortive Socialist general strike
	Oct. 27	Fascists seized key buildings in northern cities, the first move in the 'March on Rome'
	Oct. 28	Resignation of final Liberal government
	Oct. 29	Mussolini invited to become prime minister
	Oct. 30	Mussolini arrived in Rome. Fascists organised victory parade

1 Italy at war

▶ *What did Italy hope to gain by joining the First World War?*

▶ *Why did the conduct of the war lead to criticism of the Liberal regime?*

In August 1914 the Great Powers of Europe went to war. The Triple Entente of Britain, France and Russia faced Germany and Austria-Hungary, both members of the Triple Alliance. Italy, the third member of this alliance, remained aloof. Its membership of the Triple Alliance apparently committed Italy to support Germany and Austria-Hungary, but the government in Rome now declared the Alliance defunct. It claimed that Austria had broken the terms of the treaty by attacking Serbia without consulting Italy, and by seeking to expand its empire into the Balkans.

The great majority of Italians welcomed this decision. In fact, many Italians possessed an underlying hostility towards Austria-Hungary, a country that had resisted Italian unification by force in the 1850s and 1860s, and which still occupied territories inhabited by Italian speakers, notably the Trentino and Istria (see the map on page 32).

Intervention crisis

Most Italians were satisfied with neutrality: some Liberals, including former prime minister Giolitti, together with most Catholics and Socialists, and much of the army and big business, believed either that Italy was not ready for war or that war would be bad for Italian society and the economy. However, Liberals supporting Antonio Salandra, who had succeeded Giolitti as prime minister in 1914, had misgivings. They feared that victory for the Triple Alliance would only strengthen Austrian resistance to revision of its borders with Italy. Alternatively, if the **Entente powers** won, they would not be sympathetic to Italian ambitions in the Mediterranean if Italy had done nothing to bring about their victory. The government increasingly took the view that Italy must intervene in the war at some point and should negotiate with both sides in order to obtain the best terms for joining either the Alliance or the Entente. This policy was encouraged by the noisy demands of the Nationalist press that Italy must grasp its chance to become a great power.

Throughout the early months of 1915 negotiations continued. It became very apparent that, although Austria-Hungary would make some territorial concessions, these would not include the Italian-speaking areas of the Trentino or the city of Trieste. In contrast, the Entente promised Italy that it would receive not only the Trentino and Trieste but also other Austrian lands in the southern Tyrol, Istria and Dalmatia (see the map on page 32). The Italian kingdom would then dominate the Adriatic Sea. There was also the promise of further

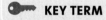 **KEY TERM**

Entente powers An alliance of Britain, France and Russia (Triple Entente).

colonies, as yet unspecified but probably in Africa or the eastern Mediterranean. Therefore, it was not surprising that Italy signed the Treaty of London with Britain and France, and entered the First World War in May 1915. It was a fateful decision. The war was to have traumatic consequences for Italy's society, economy and political system.

The impact of war 1915–18

Although the decision to join the war was hailed by crowds of ecstatic Nationalists, Italian intervention did not fire the imagination of the mass of the population. It was hard, for example, for a poor southerner to be enthusiastic about fighting for a few Italian-speaking areas on the country's north-eastern frontier. Catholics were made aware that, although their Church was broadly supportive of the war effort, it would not actively denounce the enemy, Catholic Austria. Italian Socialists openly condemned the conflict as a capitalist or 'bosses' war'. Even some Liberals, grouped around Giolitti, attacked the decision to fight.

Despite the absence of anything resembling war hysteria, 5 million men eventually served in the army, mainly as conscripts. Most of these conscripts came from rural areas, as much of the industrial working class was involved in producing war materiel and was therefore exempt from military service. The great majority of soldiers fought bravely, endured appalling conditions in the front line, and tolerated miserable rations and low pay. However, the expected victory did not materialise and, dogged by unimaginative leadership, the Italian army found itself in a murderous **war of attrition** on its Alpine northern border. The winter weather, the effect of stone splinters from the impact of high explosive shells, and the determination of many Italian commanders to maintain the offensive meant that casualties were heavy. On many occasions, thousands of lives were sacrificed in an attempt to gain a few hundred metres of mountainside.

Eventually, after two years of fighting, the Italian army cracked under a surprise Austro-German attack. At the Battle of Caporetto 700,000 Italians retreated in disorder for over 150 kilometres until the line was held at the River Piave. Around 300,000 Italians were taken prisoner. Recriminations abounded. Cadorna, the army's commander-in-chief, blamed the defeat on the supposed cowardice of the troops. He executed several thousand in retribution. Nationalists blamed the government for inefficiency in running the war and in supplying the troops. The government blamed Cadorna himself, and promptly sacked him.

Despite the arguments, the situation stabilised. As 1918 wore on, a shortage of food and munitions combined with general war-weariness to weaken the resolve of Austria-Hungary and Germany. In October, as Germany reeled from an Anglo-French offensive, the Italian army attacked the Austrians. In the fighting that ensued, casualties were heavy on both sides, with the Italians

 **KEY TERM**

War of attrition A war in which the commanders do not expect dramatic victories but hope to win by slowly wearing down their opponents over a period of months or years. High casualties are acceptable so long as the enemy's suffering is worse.

losing nearly 40,000 men killed or wounded. Finally, the Austrian will to resist collapsed and the Italian forces found themselves in possession of about 500,000 prisoners of war. The victory, to be known as the Battle of Vittorio Veneto, caused Austria to sue for peace. An **armistice** was signed on 3 November 1918.

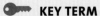

KEY TERM

Armistice Agreement to cease fighting.

 ## The economic and political effects of the First World War

▶ *How did the First World War make the problems of Liberal Italy worse?*

▶ *Why did the peace settlement undermine support for the Liberal government?*

The war ended with Caporetto avenged and Italy looking forward to enjoying the fruits of victory. However, Italians were to be disappointed. The war had enhanced their country's claims to Great Power status, but the eagerly anticipated territorial gains only partly materialised. Furthermore, the war had left Italy with severe domestic problems which would widen existing social and political divisions.

Economic problems

First, the human cost of the war had been enormous. A total of 650,000 men had died and a million more had been seriously wounded. In addition, the financial cost of keeping the soldiers armed and fed had placed a heavy burden on the Italian treasury. Huge sums had been borrowed from Britain and the USA: the national debt had increased from 16 billion lire in 1914 to 85 billion lire in 1919. However, these borrowings had proved inadequate to pay for the war and the government had resorted to printing money. This had a dramatic effect.

Inflation spiralled as ever-greater quantities of paper money chased ever-scarcer goods. Prices quadrupled during the war years. Inflation destroyed savings, hitting the middle classes in particular. Landowners relying on rents and state employees whose wages did not keep up with increasing prices also suffered. Nor did factory workers escape. The purchasing power of their wages fell by about 25 per cent between 1915 and 1918.

Industrialists, in contrast, did well out of the conflict. Providing their production was linked to the war effort, they were assured of a market. As inflation increased they simply raised their prices and a government desperate for military victory continued to buy their products. Large companies such as Pirelli tyres and Montecatini chemicals made huge profits while Fiat expanded to the point where it became the largest manufacturer of commercial vehicles in Europe in 1918. However, victory meant the end of easy profits. There was no longer any need for enormous quantities of rifles, artillery, trucks and the like. A government which, in 1918, had spent 23.3 billion lire more than it had collected in taxes could no longer afford to hand out lucrative contracts. Profits fell as government spending was cut back. Hard times lay ahead for industry.

Industrial disputes increased dramatically as the war came to an end and wartime discipline in the factories, enforced by the military, was relaxed. Workers who had resented the longer hours, the fall in real wages caused by inflation and the ban on industrial action vented their frustration. During 1919 over a million workers took part in strikes and the membership of Socialist **trade unions** shot up from a quarter of a million in 1918 to 2 million in 1920.

Unemployment rose as soldiers returning from the war were plunged into this deteriorating economic situation. The hoped-for prosperity was nowhere to be found. Industries whose profits were falling did not take on new workers. Unemployment increased to over 2 million during 1919. To the soldiers this seemed a very poor reward for their sacrifices.

The Socialist 'threat'

As the economy worsened, political divisions widened. The industrial workers flocked to the Socialist Party (Partito Socialista Italiano or PSI), whose membership rose from about 50,000 in 1914 to about 200,000 by 1919. The party had long abandoned the commitment to gradual reform that Giolitti had tried to encourage during the pre-war years. It now advocated revolution. Inspired by the Russian Revolution of 1917, Socialists called for the overthrow of the Liberal state. The goal, according to the party, was a 'Socialist republic' and the 'dictatorship of the **proletariat**' where private businesses and landed estates would be confiscated, and wealth shared. The 1919 congress made plain that to achieve this 'the proletariat must have recourse to the use of violence for the conquest of power over the **bourgeoisie**'.

Such extreme talk did not deter the voters. On the contrary, in the elections of November 1919, the first to be held under full universal male suffrage, the Socialists swept through the northern cities, securing 32.4 per cent of the national vote and winning 156 seats. The party dedicated to revolution was now the largest single group in the Italian parliament.

Many middle-class Italians were terrified. Their fears seemed confirmed when the new Socialist deputies interrupted the King's speech in parliament, shouting 'long live the Socialist republic', and then marched out singing the Socialist anthem, 'Red Flag' (*Bandiera Rossa*). Although this was empty posturing on the part of the Socialists – they had devoted no real thought to the question of how to bring about their revolution – many people feared that a **Bolshevik**-style seizure of power was imminent.

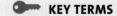 **KEY TERMS**

Trade unions Organisations, often Socialist, which seek to improve the pay and conditions of their members. Socialist trade unions represented several million factory workers and farm labourers.

Proletariat Industrial and rural working class.

Bourgeoisie The middle classes, owners of businesses.

Bolsheviks A group of very radical Socialists (often called Communists), led by Lenin, who seized power in Russia in 1917. They executed the Russian royal family and took control of all businesses.

In this state of fear, many conservative Italians were disgusted that the government appeared to be doing nothing to meet the threat. Instead of using the power of the state to crush strikes and to harass Socialists, the Liberal government of Francesco Nitti was urging industrialists to make concessions to workers. Shopkeepers had been alienated in June 1919 by what they saw as a government surrender to rioters who were protesting against the spiralling price of food. The government had set up food committees that had requisitioned supplies and set prices. The continuing inflation that had provoked the food riots was taken to be proof of government incompetence.

In addition, landowners were appalled by the government's failure to halt the spread of revolution to the countryside. Here, many peasants were occupying uncultivated land and farming it for themselves. Agricultural labourers were joining Socialist trade unions in ever-greater numbers, particularly in the province of Emilia Romagna, and were beginning to demand higher wages and guaranteed employment.

A 'mutilated victory'

It was not only over the issue of the supposed 'Socialist threat' that the right condemned the government. Nationalists, who had always considered the Liberals weak and incompetent at running the war, were now convinced that the government would fail to defend Italian interests at the Paris peace conference. They demanded that Italy should not only receive those territories agreed with the Entente in 1915 (southern Tyrol, Trentino, Istria and parts of Dalmatia), but also be given the city of Fiume on the border of Istria (see the map on page 32). The Treaty of St Germain, in 1919, did cede Austrian land in the south Tyrol and the Trentino, but when Britain and the USA refused to hand over Fiume because the city was vital to the economy of the new Yugoslav state, the Nationalists blamed Liberal weakness. When, in addition, it became apparent that Italy would be denied Dalmatia because so few Italians lived there, and would not share in the division of German colonies in Africa, Nationalists were outraged. To them, their country had been cheated. Italy's sacrifices had won only a **'mutilated victory'**, and liberalism was the culprit!

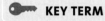 **KEY TERM**

Mutilated victory
The claim that Italy had been denied its rightful territorial gains in the peace settlement after the First World War.

Demobilised soldiers, struggling to adjust to civilian society and with work difficult to find, saw the peace settlement as a further humiliation. Many ex-officers, in particular, feared that the vibrant, expansionist Italy they had fought for was being undermined by weak government. Their Italy was falling into the hands of Socialist revolutionaries who had opposed the war from the start and who had done their best to sabotage the war effort. For such men, liberalism and the parliamentary system had proved abject failures. A powerful, dynamic Italy would have to be achieved by other methods.

Seizure of Fiume

In September 1919 the Nationalist intellectual Gabriele D'Annunzio led 2000 armed men into the city of Fiume and occupied it in defiance of the Italian government. Nationalists and many ex-soldiers hailed him as the embodiment of the Italy they wanted to create. D'Annunzio had shown to them that the way to achieve results was not to indulge in months of talking and negotiations, but rather to act decisively and not to be afraid to use force. Critics of the Liberal regime noted with satisfaction that the government lacked the will and the courage to use troops to end the occupation.

For over a year the flamboyant D'Annunzio ruled Fiume, drawing up fantastical constitutions for the city, while his armed supporters strutted through the streets. He became a public hero throughout Italy. His dramatic style, his eye for publicity and his high-volume denunciation of the government also made him something of a role model for another enemy of liberalism, Benito Mussolini. This ambitious journalist and politician, the leader of an insignificant political party when D'Annunzio marched into Fiume, was to become the first Fascist prime minister of Italy and, by 1925, would be the country's dictator.

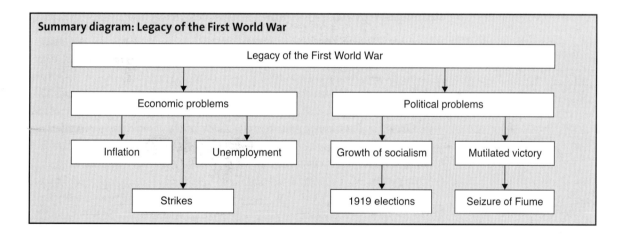

Summary diagram: Legacy of the First World War

Legacy of the First World War → Economic problems → Inflation, Unemployment → Strikes; Political problems → Growth of socialism, Mutilated victory → 1919 elections, Seizure of Fiume

3 Mussolini and the birth of fascism

▶ *What were the ideas behind the early Fascist movement?*

Benito Mussolini, the 36-year-old editor of *Il Popolo d'Italia* (*The People of Italy*), shared D'Annunzio's contempt for liberalism and hatred of socialism. Although a former Socialist, the war had convinced him that Italy needed a regime that would end the struggle between social classes and, unlike the Liberals, provide dynamic leadership for Italy both at home and abroad. Mussolini himself might provide this new dynamic leadership together with the more energetic and patriotic of the former soldiers. From July 1918 he began to claim that *Il Popolo* was the 'newspaper of combatants and producers'. By producers he meant soldiers, farmers and factory workers. He tried to contrast these with those he regarded as the parasitic groups in Italian economy: businessmen who had made vast profits from wartime contracts, Socialists who had opposed the war and Liberal politicians.

Creation of the Fascist movement

By early 1919 Mussolini believed that it was time to translate his rhetoric into action. Accordingly, in March, he called the inaugural meeting of a new movement, the *Fasci di Combattimento*, or 'Combat Groups'. Only about 100 people came to Milan for the meeting. They represented a wide range of political views, including nationalists, **republicans**, **anarchists** and radical poets and painters. They had little in common except a hatred of the Liberal state and a contempt for the class struggle rhetoric of the Socialists. Nevertheless, they did manage to draw up a political programme that contained both demands for an expansionist Italy and the following, leftist, statements of intent:

1 *A new National Assembly … [will be set up].*
2 *Proclamation of the Italian Republic [abolition of the monarchy]. …*
4 *Abolition of all titles of nobility. …*
9 *Suppression of all major companies, industrial or financial and of all speculation by banks and stock exchanges.*
10 *Control and taxation of private wealth. Confiscation of unproductive income (such as rent from the ownership of land or property). …*
12 *Workers to have a significant share of the profits of the businesses they worked in.*

Early failure

The early Fascist movement lacked the cohesion to form a disciplined political party. Indeed, when D'Annunzio occupied Fiume in late 1919, it was just another tiny grouping of radical agitators. What prominence Mussolini did have was due not to his self-proclaimed position as 'leader of fascism', but rather to his aggressive journalism in *Il Popolo d'Italia*. The proof of his movement's failure seemed to come in the general election of November 1919. Not only did Mussolini himself fail to become a deputy, polling only 5000 out of the 270,000 votes cast in Milan, but fascism performed dismally everywhere. Not a single seat was won in the new parliament and by the end of the year there were perhaps only 4000 declared Fascist supporters in the whole of Italy.

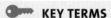
KEY TERMS

Republicans Those who want to abolish the monarchy.

Anarchists Oppose both a strong central government and capitalism, arguing that political and economic power should be held by workers and peasants, organised at a local level.

Benito Mussolini

1883 Born in Predappio, Romagna, the son of a devout Catholic schoolmistress and of a blacksmith with revolutionary views

1901–6 Primary school teacher, then worked briefly in Switzerland, before returning to Italy to become a journalist

1910 Editor of a small Socialist newspaper in the town of Forli, in his home province

1911 Jailed for attempting to stir up an insurrection against the war in Libya

1912 Released from prison and appointed editor of *Avanti!*, the Socialist Party's newspaper

1914 Resigned from *Avanti!* and set up a new paper, *Il Popolo d'Italia*. The paper claimed to be Socialist but it campaigned for Italian entry into the war. Expelled from Socialist Party

1915 Married Rachele Guidi

Conscripted into the army but only reached the rank of corporal

1917 Invalided out of the army after an accident during a training exercise

Took over editorship of *Il Popolo* once again. He blamed government defeatism and incompetence for the disaster of Caporetto, and claimed that Italy now needed a dictator who would direct the war effort with real energy

1919 Founded the Fascist movement

1922 Prime minister

1926 Prime minister and dictator of Italy

1943 Dismissed as prime minister by the King and arrested. Then freed by Nazi forces and installed as ruler of Salò Republic in northern Italy

1945 Captured and executed by Socialist resistance fighters

Mussolini came from a humble background in a small town in central-northern Italy. He did not excel at school, being noted more for his bullying nature. After a succession of minor teaching posts in village schools in which he showed little interest, and a brief period in Switzerland, Mussolini took up journalism. Taking up the cause of socialism, his writing was aggressive. He condoned the use of violence and condemned the Liberal state and those reformist Socialists who wanted to co-operate with it. He made it plain that revolution was the only policy for the Socialist Party to pursue. Mussolini's journalism got him noticed and by 1912 he was editing the Socialists' own newspaper, *Avanti!*

The outbreak of the First World War was to alter Mussolini's career dramatically. His Socialist Party condemned the war as an imperialistic struggle fought at the expense of the working classes of Europe, and demanded that Italy remain neutral. But Mussolini saw the conflict as an event which would shake society to its foundations and bring revolution closer. Mussolini, now expelled from the Socialist Party, set up his own newspaper, *Il Popolo d'Italia*. Accepting financial support from companies such as Fiat, he campaigned vigorously in favour of intervention in the war.

Throughout 1918 his paper sought to create a new political movement which would promote both nationalism and social reform. He was trying to appeal to the soldiers who had no wish to return to rural and urban poverty once the war was over. Contemptuous of both liberalism and socialism, Mussolini founded the Fascist movement in March 1919.

The movement appeared doomed. However, Mussolini was to be saved by the government's inability to convince conservative Italians that it could deal with the supposed Socialist threat. From near oblivion in December 1919, the Fascists became, within the space of one year, a powerful force on the political scene.

4 The rise of fascism 1919–21

▶ *Why did Liberal governments lose support and find it increasingly difficult to command a majority in the Italian parliament?*

▶ *What factors promoted the growth of fascism?*

Liberal problems in parliament

The elections of November 1919 had disappointed Mussolini but had also caused great difficulties for the Liberal government. Liberals and their allies could muster only about 180 of the 508 seats and they still lacked cohesion and party discipline. The **Chamber of Deputies**, designed to protect and promote liberalism, now contained a revolutionary Socialist Party holding 156 seats, and the Catholic Popular Party, the PPI, with 100 seats. The Liberal government led by the moderate Francesco Nitti did survive but it relied on support from Catholic deputies to maintain its fragile majority.

The PPI, or *Popolari* as it was known, had been founded in January 1919, when the Pope had finally lifted his ban on the formation of such a Catholic party. The *Popolari*, led by the Sicilian priest Don Sturzo, contained both conservative Catholics and Catholics determined to improve the lot of the peasantry. This was an uneasy coalition that found it easier to agree on what it opposed than what it stood for. It was reluctant to play a major role in government, but it was prepared to give its support to Liberal governments in return for concessions on policy. Despite this, the PPI remained deeply suspicious of liberalism and did not forget the Liberals' disputes with the Pope during the unification of Italy.

Nitti's government was discredited by Fiume (see page 26) in the eyes of much of the public and was disliked by both the left and the right, for its unwillingness either to grant major reform or to crush protest. It struggled on until June 1920. But, with *Popolari* support waning, Nitti's fragile majority was unsustainable and he quietly resigned. He was replaced by the veteran Liberal Giovanni Giolitti. Once again, the great exponent of *Trasformismo* (see page 7) attempted to appeal to both left and right – speaking of workers' entitlement to some say in management and at the same time planning to reduce the food subsidies that benefited the poor. Liberals, *Popolari* and even a handful of moderate Socialists joined his new coalition, but the majority of Socialists were implacably hostile. Although he was an anticlerical, the new prime minister still had to rely on Catholic support in the Chamber of Deputies to keep his government in power.

Socialist 'occupation of the factories'

Events outside parliament were to weaken Giolitti's government further. In September 1920 engineering workers, engaged in a dispute over wages, occupied their factories to prevent employers from locking them out. Within days, 400,000 workers from the northern cities were involved. The employers demanded that

KEY TERM

Chamber of Deputies The lower, but most important, house in the Italian parliament – similar to the British House of Commons.

the government intervene to crush the occupation. However, Giolitti followed the policy of neutrality he had adopted in pre-war industrial disputes and stood aloof. He was convinced that the use of force would lead to a bloodbath, and believed that the occupation would soon collapse of its own accord. This policy enraged industrialists, particularly when the prime minister urged them to make concessions to the strikers. When it became apparent that a number of factories were being used to produce weapons for the strikers, conservatives feared that the revolution was now at hand. Again, in their eyes, the government was failing to do its duty. Even though the occupation was disorganised and collapsed within one month, as Giolitti had predicted, employers and conservatives did not forgive him for what they saw as his complacency and cowardice.

Socialist advances in the countryside

In the countryside, landowners were also complaining bitterly about a Socialist threat. Agricultural strikes and land occupations were continuing to increase. In Emilia Romagna, the Po Valley, Umbria and Tuscany (see map on page 32), Socialist trade unions were expanding and, with close to a million members, were beginning to establish a stranglehold over agricultural employment. In Emilia, the unions demanded higher wages for agricultural labourers and guarantees that workers would not be laid off during quiet times of the year. Around Ferrara and Bologna a labourer could only gain employment through a job centre run by the Socialist Labourers' Union. If landowners resisted the trade unions' demands, their estates would face disruption and their farm managers might be subject to physical attack.

The power of the Socialists was shown not only in agricultural disputes but also in local elections, held in late 1920. The Socialists found themselves in control of 26 of the country's 69 provinces, mainly those located in north and central Italy. The Socialist Party was particularly strong in Emilia, where it controlled 80 per cent of the local councils. The urban middle classes feared that the Socialists would now raise local taxes on the better-off. Shopkeepers were concerned about the potential competition from the spread of Socialist-sponsored co-operative shops. These shops were designed to offer cheap prices to customers and, at the same time, to allow the shopworkers a say in the running of the business and a share of the profits.

Anti-Socialist reaction

Landowners and conservatives felt themselves an embattled class. Their political enemies and social inferiors seemed to be in the ascendancy and they thought they had been abandoned by the government. This sense of abandonment was intensified by the government's decision to allow agricultural labourers to keep the unused land they had illegally occupied.

By the end of 1920 the propertied classes in the provinces of northern and central Italy began to fight back. Desperate measures, including the use of violence, appeared justified in the face of revolution. In Emilia and Tuscany, in particular, frightened landowners and middle-class townsfolk began to turn to local Fascist groups, who shared their hatred of socialism and needed little encouragement to attack Socialists. November 1920 saw one of the first examples of Fascist violence when the inauguration of the new Socialist council in Bologna turned into a riot. These Fascist squads were often small and lacking in any coherent ideology, but they proved adept at burning down Socialist offices and beating up trade unionists. Their enemies might also find themselves being forced to drink litres of potentially lethal castor oil, a punishment that quickly became a trademark for Fascist thugs.

The violence continued through the winter and spring of 1920 to 1921, destroying over 80 trade union offices and leaving 200 dead and 800 wounded. By spring, Emilia Romagna and Tuscany had become strongholds of the Fascist squads. The police had looked the other way as *squadrismo* had crushed the Socialist power in these provinces.

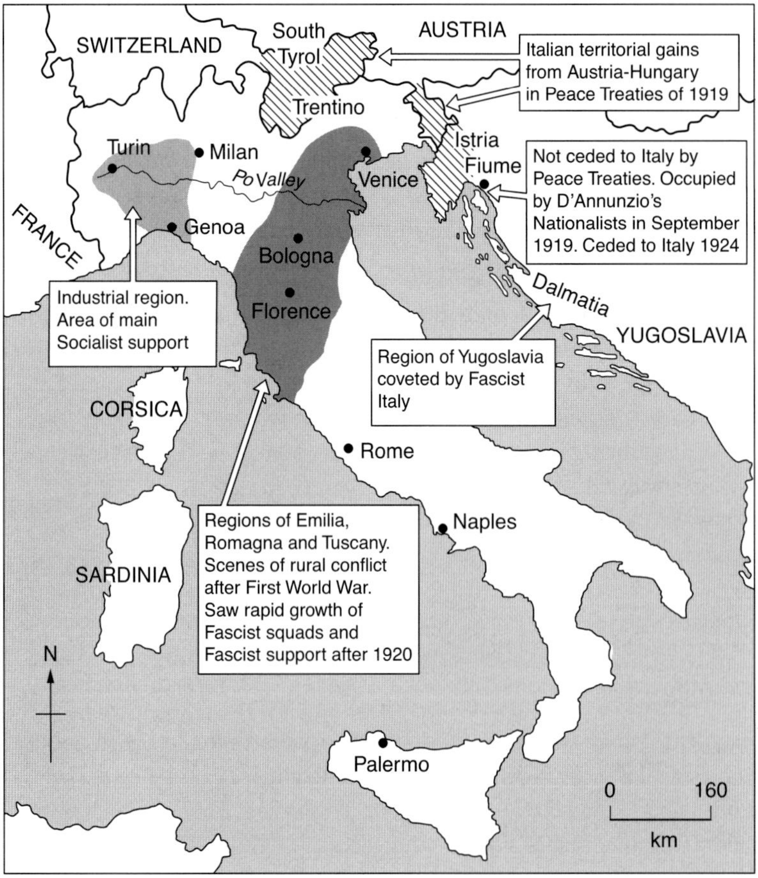

KEY TERM

Squadrismo The violent attacks of Fascist gangs, or squads.

Figure 3.1 Italy 1918–25.

SOURCE A

A carefully staged photo of blackshirted Fascist squads taken on 1 December 1922.

Look carefully at the photo in Source A: what message is it trying to convey about *squadrismo*?

Fascist supporters

In their early days the Fascist squads consisted mainly of middle-class students and demobilised soldiers, usually ex-army officers and more junior ranks, such as sergeants and corporals. But, as they proved their ability to intimidate the Socialists, the squads began to attract new followers. Many of the recruits were small farmers, farm managers and sharecroppers who, although far from rich, comprised the better-off peasantry. They were likely to be ambitious and anxious to buy their own land. Socialist talk of higher wage rates and **collectivisation** of land angered them.

At the end of 1921 the Fascist Party had probably a little over 200,000 active supporters. Roughly 50 per cent were ex-servicemen, but there were also landowners, shopkeepers, clerical workers and even teachers. There were workers in the squads but the leadership was overwhelmingly middle class. It was also apparent that fascism was a movement that attracted the young: almost ten per cent of members were students and 25 per cent were below voting age. For such people, the Fascists seemed an exciting contrast to the staid old men of Liberal politics.

Among the older generation, many people who had previously supported the conservative wing of liberalism now despaired of the seemingly ineffectual parliamentary system and saw fascism as a way of securing the disciplined state for which they longed. However, it would be wrong to conclude that fascism

> 🔑 **KEY TERM**
>
> **Collectivisation** Seizure of private land by the state. The land would then be reorganised into state-run farms or distributed to groups of peasants.

Roberto Farinacci

1892	Born in Isernia to a poor family
1909	Railway worker in Cremona. Attracted by socialism
1915–18	Enlisted as soldier. Began to write for *Il Popolo d'Italia*
1919	Attended first meeting of Fascist movement
	Organised Fascist squads in Cremona
1920–1	As **Ras** of Fascist squads in Cremona he attacked Socialists and their trade unions, and terrorised the local populace
1922	Appointed himself Mayor of Cremona
	Pressed Mussolini to march on Rome
1925	Appointed Fascist Party secretary
1926	Dismissed as party secretary
1935	General in the Fascist militia during war against Ethiopia
	Appointed to Fascist Grand Council
1943–5	Supporter of Mussolini's Italian Social Republic; a puppet regime under effective Nazi control
1945	Executed by Italian anti-Fascists

Farinacci's early career had similarities to that of Mussolini. Both came from humble backgrounds and were active Socialists. The First World War made them reject this socialism and convinced them that Italy needed a new, radical political movement that would sweep away liberalism. Farinacci was one of Mussolini's earliest supporters, and his squads in Cremona were among the most violent in Italy.

After Mussolini became prime minister, Farinacci pressed for the establishment of a dictatorship and continued use of violence against opponents. Appointed party secretary in 1925, his clamour for more radical policies contributed to his dismissal the following year. Although he no longer held a national position, Farinacci maintained great power over Cremona.

Returning to national prominence in the late 1930s he became pro-Nazi, advocating both **anti-Semitism** and Italy's entry into the Second World War. When mainland Italy faced an Allied invasion in July 1943, Farinacci, unlike many leading Fascists, continued to support Mussolini, and condemned the vote at the Grand Council of Fascism meeting which led to the sacking of Mussolini (see page 145)

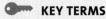 **KEY TERMS**

Ras Local Fascist leaders, usually with their own Fascist squads.

Anti-Semitism Hatred of Jews.

Coup d'état The violent overthrow of a government.

was hijacked by conservatives. The Fascist leaders in the provinces still thought of themselves as leading a revolutionary movement that would overthrow the state by force in a ***coup d'état***. Men like Roberto Farinacci, Italo Balbo and Dino Grandi remained dedicated to violent *squadrismo*.

Mussolini's control over Fascist *squadrismo*

Local Fascist leaders, such as the young and aggressive ex-army officer Italo Balbo in Ferrara and the equally callous Dino Grandi in Bologna, built up their own power base. Mussolini had not been the guiding hand behind the Fascist violence, but he soon saw the political opportunities *squadrismo* offered. He strove to put himself at the forefront of this *squadrismo* by reasserting his claim to be the sole and undisputed leader of the movement. There was reluctance on the part of the *Ras* to surrender their independence, but Mussolini seems to have been able to convince even the most ambitious of them that their success depended on his leadership. His was the dominant personality in the Fascist movement and his newspaper could publicise Fascist activities. He argued that, without his leadership, Fascism would lack all coherence as the various factions would fall out among themselves. With Mussolini as leader, fascism could be presented as a national movement with a vision of a new Italy. Mussolini, the journalist, could depict Fascist violence not as simple thuggery, but rather as a painful necessity if Italy was to be saved from radical socialism. *Squadrismo* would be portrayed as an anti-Socialist crusade.

SOURCE B

Mussolini speaking to the Fascists of Bologna in April 1921, quoted in Bernardo Quaranta di San Severino, translator and editor, *Mussolini as Revealed in His Political Speeches (November 1914–August 1923)*, J.M. Dent & Sons, 1923, pp. 138–9.

And, however much violence may be deplored, it is evident that we, in order to make our ideas understood, must beat refractory skulls with resounding blows. … But we … are violent when it is necessary to be so.

… Our punitive expeditions, all those acts of violence which figure in the papers, must always have the character of a just retort and legitimate reprisal; because we are the first to recognise that it is sad, after having fought the external enemy, to have to fight the enemy within … The Socialists had formed a State within a State … this State … is more tyrannical, illiberal and overbearing than the old one; … which we are causing to-day is a revolution to break up the Bolshevist State …

> In Source B, what did Mussolini mean when he claimed that the 'Socialists had formed a State within a State'?

Electoral breakthrough: May 1921

Although justifying and encouraging violent *squadrismo*, Mussolini was also careful to suggest to Liberal politicians that all this talk of violence and revolution might be little more than bluster. Giolitti was taken in; he claimed the Fascists were just 'fireworks: they'll make a great deal of noise but only leave smoke behind'. Giolitti saw fascism as just another political force that could be absorbed into the Liberal system. Mussolini did his best to encourage this belief. Persuaded that the self-styled leader of fascism was more an opportunist than an extremist, Giolitti offered an electoral alliance that he hoped would produce an anti-Socialist governing coalition.

Fascists and Giolittian Liberals co-operated during the general election held in May 1921. But despite this new air of respectability, the Fascist squads continued their work, killing about 100 Socialist sympathisers during the election campaign. Again, the police tended to turn a blind eye – this was what the 'Bolsheviks' deserved! However, the election results proved that the violence and intimidation had not deterred the voters. The Socialists remained the largest party in the Chamber, holding 123 seats, followed by the *Popolari* with 107. If Giolitti was disappointed that the Socialist vote had held up, Mussolini was satisfied with the progress that his party had made. The Fascists had secured seven per cent of the total vote and had won 35 seats. Mussolini was now a deputy.

SOURCE C

Why might Mussolini have chosen the Colosseum as the location for his speech in Source? What impression does the photo in Source C convey of Mussolini and his supporters?

Mussolini speaking in the Colosseum, Rome, in 1920.

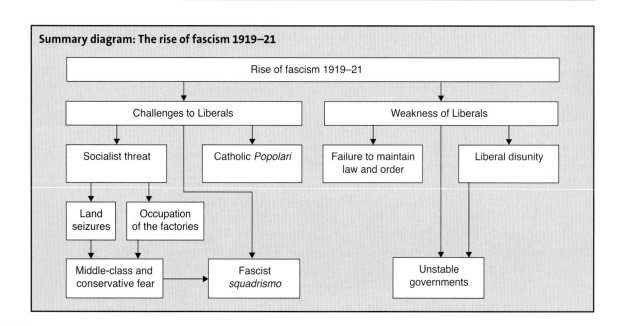

Summary diagram: The rise of fascism 1919–21

Rise of fascism 1919–21

Challenges to Liberals

Weakness of Liberals

Socialist threat

Catholic *Popolari*

Failure to maintain law and order

Liberal disunity

Land seizures

Occupation of the factories

Middle-class and conservative fear

Fascist *squadrismo*

Unstable governments

5 Mussolini seizes the initiative: May 1921 to October 1922

▶ *What tactics did Mussolini use to generate support from conservative groups and from Liberal politicians?*

▶ *How did Mussolini make use of Fascist violence to help his rise to power?*

The elections had given Mussolini what he wanted: an air of respectability and a foothold in parliament. He had no wish to be absorbed into liberalism, to be a junior partner in a coalition, as Giolitti had intended. Consequently, he announced that the Fascists would not, after all, support Giolitti's government.

Mussolini now saw the possibility of achieving real power. He had no master plan but he was an extremely astute politician. He knew that he needed to demonstrate to the Italian public, to industrialists, landowners and the middle classes in particular, that liberalism was finished as a political movement. Unstable, short-lived governments unable to maintain law and order or deal with the country's economic problems would provide proof of this. Mussolini also had to convince these crucial groups in society that only fascism could stop the Socialists and restore order and discipline to Italian society. Furthermore, he realised that for fascism to become acceptable to the middle classes and conservatives it must either abandon or play down any remaining ideas about radical economic and social reform. During 1921 and 1922 Mussolini skilfully took advantage of his opportunities to create such an impression.

Government instability

Governments following the elections of May 1921 were unstable. Giolitti did manage to form a coalition without Mussolini but it collapsed within a month. The *Popolari* had withdrawn its support when Giolitti proposed to introduce a tax which would have had the side-effect of hitting the Vatican's financial investments. Without the tacit support of this Catholic Party, with its 107 deputies in parliament, it was now virtually impossible for any government to survive, yet the *Popolari* was suspicious of the anticlerical traditions of liberalism and was willing to destroy any government that offended it.

To make matters worse, the Liberals were divided among themselves. Liberalism was still plagued by factions centred on prominent politicians, notably Giolitti, Salandra, Facta and Orlando, and these leaders actively disliked one another. In such circumstances it was not surprising that the three Italian governments between May 1921 and October 1922 were fragile and unable to introduce the decisive measures needed to cope with the industrial disruption and the collapse of law and order.

Collapse of law and order

The progressive collapse of law and order owed a great deal to Fascist actions. *Squadrismo* continued through 1921. Socialists were attacked, and not infrequently killed. Fascist violence even extended to parliament itself, most notoriously on the occasion when a Socialist deputy was beaten up on the floor of the chamber.

Mussolini increases his control over the Fascist movement

Mussolini's activities during the remainder of 1921 were directed towards making fascism a cohesive political force that could command more widespread support within Italian society. His attempt to organise fascism more effectively resulted in the establishment of the **National Fascist Party** in October 1921. Fascism was no longer just a movement, but a recognised political party. In the following month the party congress formally accepted Mussolini as the leader of the newly formed party. The Fascist Party was to be organised and run by men from Mussolini's own Milan faction, who were loyal to their leader. Mussolini had established more control over those Fascist squads that had so terrorised Socialists in the agricultural areas of Emilia and the Romagna. However, his control over this provincial fascism was by no means total, and there would be disagreements over the means to secure power. Yet he could now pose as the unchallenged head of a real political party.

Reassuring the Catholic Church and conservative Italians

In November 1921 Mussolini made a direct attempt to win over Catholics. He declared fascism to be opposed to divorce, in agreement with the *Popolari*, that the peasants deserved a better deal, and he prepared to settle the **Roman question** on terms acceptable to the Pope.

Mussolini also increased his efforts to appeal to conservatives: people who feared socialism, deplored the government's conciliatory policy towards workers and questioned its ability to restore order. He dropped the more socialist sounding policies espoused by fascism in 1919. In fact, the leader of fascism had begun to distance himself from such radical ideas during 1920, and it had not been coincidental that the 35 Fascist deputies elected in May 1921 were on the right of the movement. From 1921 Mussolini's speeches concentrated on what fascism was against, namely socialism and liberalism, but spelled out Fascist policies only in very broad terms, stressing its patriotism and commitment to strong government.

Such speeches were quite deliberate attempts to persuade the conservative classes that they had nothing to fear and much to gain from the victory of fascism. They also reflected fascism's lack of specific, detailed policies. Mussolini wanted a strong, expansionist Italy, hated socialism and democracy, and despised parliament, but he was principally concerned with winning power

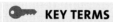

KEY TERMS

National Fascist Party Set up by Mussolini to unite the Fascist movement and to increase his control over local Fascist squads and their leaders.

Roman question The political dispute over the role of the Catholic Church in the Italian state, including the territorial claims of the Pope over Rome, and the issues of civil and church marriage and divorce.

SOURCE D

Mussolini speaking in the city of Udine in September 1922, quoted in Donald Sassoon, *Mussolini and the Rise of Fascism*, HarperCollins, 2007, p. 108.

Our programme is simple: we wish to govern Italy.

We must have a State which will simply say: 'The State does not represent a party, it represents the nation as a whole, it includes all, is over all, protects all.'

This is the State that must arise from the Italy of Vittorio Veneto. A State … which is not like the Liberal State … a State which does not fall under the power of the Socialists. …

We [also] want to remove from the State all its economic attributes. We have had enough of the State railwayman, the State postman and the State insurance official. We have had enough of the State administration at the expense of Italian taxpayers, which has done nothing but aggravate the exhausted financial condition of the country. [The new state will] still control the police, who protect honest men from the attacks of thieves … [and] the army that must guarantee the inviolability of the country and foreign policy.

> **?** Which passages in the speech in Source D are designed to appeal to Nationalists, and which to conservatives?

for himself and becoming dictator of Italy. Policy was completely subordinated to this end. In fact, it was advantageous to have little clear policy – no groups would be offended.

Fascist violence

Mussolini was concerned that the increasing Fascist violence, even if directed at Socialists, might go too far and provoke conservatives to demand that the authorities crush the Fascists and restore law and order. This was a real danger and it was clear to Mussolini that the police and army had the power to destroy his movement. That he managed to calm conservatives, yet avoid splits within his party was proof of his political skills. On the one hand, he encouraged the squads to continue their campaign of violence and suggested that he agreed with their plans for a violent seizure of power. On the other hand, when talking to conservatives, he disassociated himself from the worst excesses of Fascist violence. He would suggest that the perpetrators were renegades whom he would discipline, but would also imply that only he could curb these excesses. If conservatives wanted to avoid a violent conflict with fascism they should come to an accommodation with him. If they conceded some share of political power to fascism, he would ensure that the Fascists became a more respectable party.

This dual policy was followed throughout 1922. In the spring Fascist squads rampaged through north-central Italy attacking Socialist town councils and trade union property. In May the town council of Bologna was actually driven out of office. During July street fighting took place in most of the northern cities. During this time Mussolini talked to the various Liberal factions, stressing Fascist power but also suggesting that he was far from being a rabid revolutionary. He implied that he was interested in a parliamentary alliance that would bring the Fascists into government. In such circumstances the fragile government coalition lacked the political will to use the police to curb the violence of a party that might soon be joining them in office. In any case, the police were reluctant to intervene in the street fighting – they had no love for the Socialists and in some areas they had even loaned weapons to the local Fascist squads.

The general strike

At the end of July the Socialist trade unions called a **general strike** in an attempt to force the government to act against the Fascists. Mussolini made brilliant use of this opportunity to demonstrate that the left was still a threat and that only fascism could deal with it. As soon as the general strike was announced, he publicly declared that if the government did not stop the industrial action his Fascists would step in and do it for them. Almost as the strike began, Fascists took over the running of public transport and ensured that the postal system continued to function. If strikers protested they were beaten up.

The general strike proved a fiasco for the left. It had been poorly organised, and only attracted partial support from the workers. Even in those cities where the strike call was obeyed, the Fascist action limited its effect. Within days the strike had collapsed, leaving the Socialists in disarray. Mussolini could present his Fascists as the sole defenders of law and order. This was a crucial development. The Fascists' actions impressed the conservative middle classes, helping to convince them that fascism could be trusted with a share in government. From this point on the question was not whether the Fascists would enter the government, but rather on what terms.

6 The March on Rome

▶ *Why was Mussolini appointed prime minister?*

Mussolini launched himself into further negotiations with the Liberal factions, discussing which cabinet posts should be allocated to the Fascists. He did not disclose that his real ambition was to be prime minister. At the same time he was talking to the Fascist squads about organising a *coup d'état*. In fact, he was under great pressure to adopt such a policy – many Fascists had wanted to try to seize power at the end of the abortive general strike and it had taken all of Mussolini's authority to dissuade them. He believed that he could achieve power without a coup, but by considering such action he could keep his more radical supporters happy, and intimidate the Liberals into making concessions. At the beginning of October Mussolini increased the pressure by starting to organise a Fascist march on Rome.

The Fascist squads were organised into a militia and plans were drawn up to seize the major towns and cities of northern and central Italy. Around 30,000 Fascists would then converge on the capital and install themselves in power. If they met resistance they would crush it. Many Fascists genuinely believed that their coup was finally at hand. However, their leader saw the march as his ultimate piece of political blackmail. Mussolini seems to have been convinced that, under such a threat, the politicians would agree that he should become prime minister.

While going ahead with preparations for the march, Mussolini took care to reassure the members of the establishment that they need not fear a Fascist government. In particular, he stressed that fascism and the monarchy could work together, as the speech in Source E makes clear.

SOURCE E

Mussolini speaking in Naples on the eve of the March on Rome, October 1922, quoted in Bernardo Quaranta di San Severino, translator and editor, *Mussolini as Revealed in His Political Speeches (November 1914–August 1923)*, J.M. Dent & Sons, 1923, pp. 175–6.

There is no doubt that the unity of Italy is soundly based upon the House of Savoy [the royal family]. There is equally no doubt that the Italian Monarchy … cannot put itself in opposition to the new national forces. It did not manifest any opposition … when the Italian people … asked and obtained their country's participation in the war. Would it then have reason to be in opposition to-day, when Fascismo does not intend to attack the régime, but rather to free it from all those superstructures that overshadow its historical position and limit the expansion of the national spirit?

The Parliament … and all the paraphernalia of Democracy have nothing in common with the monarchy. Not only this, but neither do we want to take away the people's toy – the Parliament. We say 'toy' because a great part of the people seem to think of it this way. Can you tell me else why, out of eleven millions of voters, six millions do not trouble themselves to vote? … But we will not take it away.

How is Source E evidence of Mussolini's determination to appeal to more conservative Italians?

Mussolini realised that the attitude of the King was critical. As commander-in-chief he could order the army to crush fascism if he so wished.

By the final week of October preparations were complete. On the night of 27 October Fascist squads seized town halls, telephone exchanges and railway stations throughout northern Italy. In the early hours of 28 October the government of Luigi Facta finally found the courage to act, and persuaded the King to agree to the declaration of a state of siege. Police and troops prepared to disperse the Fascist gangs converging on Rome by road and rail. However, by 9a.m. King Victor Emmanuel had changed his mind. He now refused to authorise the declaration of martial law that would have sanctioned the use of force against the Fascists. This would prove to be a fateful decision: it was a sign that the King lacked confidence in his government and was anxious to avoid a violent showdown with Mussolini's Fascists.

It is still uncertain why Victor Emmanuel made this decision. He may have overestimated the number of Fascists marching on Rome and feared a civil war; he may have feared that his cousin, the Duke of Aosta, a known Fascist sympathiser, was waiting to depose him if he acted against Mussolini. Probably, more plausibly, the King had little love for the existing Liberal politicians and, believing Mussolini's protestations of loyalty, considered that Fascists should be brought into the governing coalition. Their nationalism, their anti-socialism and their energy might breathe new life into the regime. Victor Emmanuel certainly did not realise that his decision would open the way for a Fascist dictatorship.

On hearing of the King's refusal to declare martial law, Facta's government resigned. Victor Emmanuel then approached Salandra, a veteran conservative Liberal, and asked him to form a new government. Salandra attempted to negotiate with the Fascists, offering them a few cabinet posts, but it soon became apparent that Mussolini would accept nothing less than the post of prime minister for himself. With other Liberal leaders also opposed to a Salandra premiership – a sign of the continuing faction fighting – the King realised that he needed to find a different man to head the government. In the apparent absence of any other viable candidate, Benito Mussolini was asked, on 29 October, to become prime minister of Italy.

SOURCE F

> What impression is the photo in Source F intended to convey about the Fascist Party and Mussolini's position within it?

Mussolini with Fascist *Ras*, photographed in Rome in 1922.

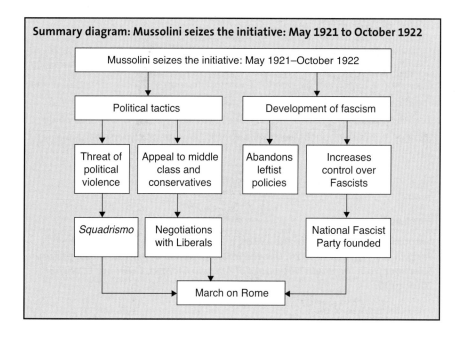

Summary diagram: Mussolini seizes the initiative: May 1921 to October 1922

⑦ Key debate

▶ *To what extent was Mussolini's success the result of Liberal weakness?*

Since the 1930s there has been continual and often acrimonious debate about the rise of fascism. Was it simply the weakness of the Liberal political system and the mistakes of Liberal politicians which enabled Mussolini first to become prime minister and then to create a dictatorship? Or should the Socialists shoulder much of the blame? How significant were Mussolini's political skills, and how much public support could fascism command by October 1922? This section explores some of the major contributions to the debate.

Was fascism an aberration?

To Renzo de Felice, the most prominent Italian historian on the period, fascism was something of an aberration, an unfortunate episode separating Liberal Italy from the democratic Italy of post-1945. The **Liberal historian** Benedetto Croce, writing in the 1930s and 1940s, was one of the first to describe fascism as a 'momentary contagion'. For him and his fellow Liberals, the rise of fascism had nothing to do with any failings of the Liberal regime, but was the result of the shock of the First World War and the Russian Revolution, with their dire social and economic consequences. To such writers, the pre-Fascist regime had represented progress and freedom.

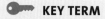 **KEY TERM**

Liberal historian One who sympathises with the Liberal regime, arguing that Italy, prior to fascism, was maturing into a stable, parliamentary democracy.

Failure of the state

To those on the left this was sentimental nonsense. For them, fascism was the result of the utter failure of the new Italian state. The Liberal regime had been foisted on the Italian people, made no attempt to represent or involve the masses in political life, and far from upholding political liberties, willingly employed repression against popular protest. Politics was the preserve of a wealthy elite dedicated not to the public good, but rather to the pursuit of personal power and financial gain.

This interpretation was summed up by the **Marxist historian** Antonio Gramsci, writing in the 1930s.

KEY TERM

Marxist historian
One who broadly subscribes to the views of Karl Marx, arguing that Liberal regimes are a guise for the exploitation of the working class and that such regimes will be overthrown once the working class realises and exerts its political strength.

EXTRACT 1

Antonio Gramsci, writing in the 1930s, is analysing the leaders of the Liberal Party in the years up to 1914. Quoted in Q. Hoare and G. Nowell Smith, editors, *Selections from the Prison Notebooks of Antonio Gramsci*, Lawrence & Wishart, 2005, p. 90.

They [the leaders of the Risorgimento] said that they were aiming at the creation of a modern State in Italy, and they in fact produced a bastard. They aimed at stimulating the formation of an extensive and energetic ruling class, and they did not succeed; at integrating the people into the framework of the new State, and they did not succeed. The paltry political life … the fundamental … rebelliousness of the Italian popular classes, the narrow existence of a cowardly ruling stratum, they are all consequences of that failure.

Few modern historians would go so far in their condemnation of the Liberal regime, but most would agree that the political system was unstable by 1914 and that the war only worsened the problems.

Mass appeal of fascism

One of the most recent biographers of Mussolini completely rejects the Marxist interpretation.

EXTRACT 2

From Nicholas Farrell, *Mussolini: A New Life*, Phoenix, 2004, pp. 124–5.

Mussolini did not seize power. That was the Fascist version of history. He was given power by the King. Nor was Fascism a bourgeois counter-revolution against the working class. That was the Marxist version of history … Fascism was not, as the Left insisted, the creature of big business. It had mass appeal: in October 1922 membership stood at 300,000 and a year later at 783,000 … To many Italians exhausted by three and a half years of war followed by four years of virtual civil war – two years of 'red violence', the two years of 'black' violence – Mussolini represented the best chance of a return of order but also the best chance, if not of revolution, of resurrection.

The suggestion that fascism had mass support prior to October 1922 is highly controversial and several historians have emphasised other reasons for Fascist success. These are explored in the following sections.

Fear of socialism

Alexander De Grand, a leading US historian, has argued that the First World War worsened class conflict, and that fascism grew out of the reaction to the rapid rise of socialism. When the Socialists became the largest political party in parliament in 1919, the rich and the middle classes were terrified. As Liberal governments appeared to have little answer to the Socialist strikes and land seizures, Italians with more conservative views began to look for a more dynamic response that would restore law and order and protect their interests. This response took the form of anti-Socialist violence in the towns and countryside of central-northern Italy. De Grand stresses the importance of these violent Fascist squads in generating new recruits for fascism and in establishing the credibility of the Fascist movement.

Role of Mussolini

Denis Mack Smith, the most prominent British writer on modern Italian history, accepts the importance of violent *squadrismo*, but emphasises the key role of Mussolini in making political capital out of this disorder. For example, his *Il Popolo d'Italia* took every opportunity to exaggerate the Socialist threat and to depict Fascists not as violent thugs, but as selfless individuals devoted to creating their vision of Italy, an Italy of peace and stability, an Italy of social harmony, an Italy respected in the world. This image proved attractive to some Italians.

Mussolini's astute political skills were seen in his realisation that the route to power lay through winning conservative support. Consequently, he abandoned the radical programme set out in 1919 and took care to appear as a moderate when talking to Liberals. He avoided committing himself to any clear policy programme and altered his message according to the audience he was addressing. Mussolini would speak to Fascists of his determination to transform Italian society radically, yet tell Liberals that his real goal was simply to destroy socialism and to inject some energy into the political system. Mussolini's ability to reassure Liberals proved vital in securing his appointment as prime minister in October 1922.

Liberal failings

Mack Smith does not accept the argument of Marxist historians, such as Gramsci, that the rise of fascism was simply the deliberate attempt of Liberals, and their conservative and big business allies, to crush the growing power of the Italian working class. For him, liberalism after 1918 was characterised by weakness and division. The arrival of mass democracy meant that parliament was no longer dominated by Liberals, yet the Liberal leaders tried to maintain the old style of politics. There was still no coherent Liberal party. There was just a series of factions based around prominent personalities. The Liberal governments of the post-war years were, in consequence, particularly fragile coalitions unable and often unwilling either to grant reform or to direct the forces of the state (the police and the army) to uphold the law. Governments lost control of events and politics began to take to the streets.

Unable to form stable coalitions, fearful of the Socialist threat and unsure of how to respond to the growing disorder, many Liberals allowed themselves to be convinced that only a Fascist presence in government could crush the Socialists, revitalise parliament as an institution and restore confidence in the regime. Thus, when Mussolini was appointed prime minister in October 1922 they were not dismayed: in their naivety they believed that Mussolini could be transformed into a 'normal' politician.

Martin Clark does not dismiss Liberal failings but argues that the Liberals should not be judged too harshly and that the Fascist rise to power was not at all inevitable.

EXTRACT 3

From Martin Clark, *Modern Italy 1871–1982*, Routledge, 2014, pp. 221 and 260.

Although it is right to stress the longer term causes of Mussolini's victory – mutilated victory, rural class conflicts – there was nothing inevitable about it … If Giolitti had not made Fascism respectable in May 1921 (offering an electoral pact), if the Popolari *had not been so opposed to a new Giolitti government, if the Socialists had not called a general strike in August 1922, if the King had not been worried by his cousin's Fascist sympathies, all might have been different. And the idea of 'absorbing' the Fascists … , allowing them a few posts in someone else's government was not foolish. It might have worked … Fascism was not inevitable, nor was it bound to succeed.*

? How far do the historians quoted in Extracts 1–3 agree or differ in their interpretation of the reasons why Mussolini rose to power?

Chapter summary

By 1914 Liberal governments were facing challenges from Socialists, Catholics and Nationalists. Italy's experience in the First World War only strengthened these challenges, particularly from the Socialists. A growing working class turned increasingly to the Socialist Party. Many middle-class and conservative Italians convinced themselves that the Socialists were planning a revolution, and expected Liberal governments to suppress Socialist-led strikes and land seizures. The Liberals, however, appeared to do little. Their failure to secure as much land for Italy as expected in the peace settlement after the First World War, the notorious 'mutilated victory', only confirmed this image of weakness.

Mussolini's Fascists burst on to the political scene in late 1920 when squads attacked Socialists in rural northern and central Italy. As violence spread the atmosphere of crisis deepened. Mussolini presented himself and his movement as a new, dynamic force which could save Italy from socialism and restore Italy to greatness. Abandoning many of his earlier left-wing ideas, Mussolini began to reassure key conservative groups such as landowners, industrialists, many Liberals and the Catholic Church that he could be entrusted with share of political power. By the summer of 1922 it was widely accepted that the Fascists would soon join a Liberal-led government. Pressurised by his own Fascists and determined to lead his own government, Mussolini planned his 'March on Rome'. Threatening to take power by force, Mussolini effectively blackmailed the King into appointing him prime minister and the Liberals into offering him their support. Neither the King nor the Liberals imagined that within four years Mussolini would have transformed Italy into a dictatorship.

 Refresher questions

Use these questions to remind yourself of the key material covered in this chapter.

1 Why did Italy enter the First World War in 1915?

2 How did the First World War create economic problems for Italy?

3 Why did support for socialism grow as a result of the First World War?

4 In what ways did the First World War weaken support for the Liberals?

5 What was the 'mutilated victory'?

6 What were the policies of fascism in 1919?

7 How and why did Mussolini change Fascist policies from 1919 to 1922?

8 Why was it difficult for the Liberals to form stable governments from 1919?

9 What actions of the Socialists in the years 1919–21 terrified many conservative Italians?

10 What was *squadrismo*?

11 Who were Fascist supporters?

12 How did fascism gain support from powerful groups 1921–2?

13 What was the March on Rome?

14 Why was Mussolini appointed prime minister?

Question practice

ESSAY QUESTIONS

1 'Italian democracy collapsed in 1922 because the conservative elites feared socialism more than they feared fascism.' Explain why you agree or disagree with this view.

2 'The post-war crisis in Italy in the years 1919–21 exposed the deep-rooted failings of the ruling elites since 1900.' Assess the validity of this view.

3 How far did Fascist ideology change in the years 1919–21?

4 How far was fear of the left responsible for the rise of Fascism in the period 1919–22?

5 Assess the consequences for Italy up until to 1920 of its participation in the First World War.

6 Which of the following was the greater problem for Italian governments 1918–22? i) Agrarian unrest. ii) The seizure of Fiume by D'Annunzio. Explain your answer with reference to both i) and ii).

INTERPRETATION QUESTIONS

1 Read the interpretation and answer the question that follows. 'Of all the factors that made fascism possible, the First World War was the most important.' (From D. Sassoon, *Mussolini and the Rise of Fascism*, Harper Press, 2007, p. 29.) Evaluate the strengths and limitations of this interpretation, making reference to other interpretations you have studied.

2 Read the interpretation and answer the question that follows. 'Fascism obtained power not through revolution but as the result of Mussolini's compromises with conservatives and liberals.' (From M. Blinkhorn, *Mussolini and Fascist Italy*, Methuen, 1984, p. 44.) Evaluate the strengths and limitations of this interpretation, making reference to other interpretations you have studied.

SOURCE ANALYSIS QUESTIONS

1 With reference to Sources 1 and 2, and your understanding of the historical context, which of these two sources is more valuable in explaining why support grew for fascism in the years 1920–2?

2 With reference to Sources 1, 2 and 3, and your understanding of the historical context, assess the value of these sources to a historian studying the rise of fascism from 1920 to 1922.

3 Why is Source 2 valuable to the historian for an enquiry into the reasons why support grew for fascism in the years 1920–2? Explain your answer using the extract, the information given about it and your own knowledge of the historical context.

4 How much weight do you give the evidence of Source 3 for an enquiry into appeal of fascism 1920–2? Explain your answer using the extract, the information given about it and your own knowledge of the historical context.

5 How far could the historian make use of Sources 1 and 2 together to investigate the reasons for the Fascist rise to power in the years 1920–2? Explain your answer, using both sources, the information given about them and your own knowledge of the historical context.

SOURCE 1

From Angelo Tasca, a former Communist, writing in 1938 about the rise of fascism 1920–2, quoted in J. Whittam, *Fascist Italy*, Manchester University Press, 1995, p. 150.

Out of 280 villages in Emilia 223 were in Socialist hands. The landowners were powerless before the all-powerful workers' trade unions. In the countryside the prizes of public life were almost entirely denied to the whole middle class who were not members of the Socialist organisations. The country landowner who for years had been head of the village, was ousted [from his position]. On the land he had to reckon with the [Socialist] league which controlled employment, in the market with the Socialist co-operative which fixed prices … Profit, position, power were lost to him and his children. Hatred and bitterness were welling up, ready at any moment to overflow … The old ruling classes felt that they were being swept away to make room for the new social structure.

SOURCE 2

From an article in the Liberal newspaper *La Stampa* in May 1921, describing a Fascist crowd, quoted in J. Hite and C. Hinton, *Fascist Italy*, John Murray, 1998, p. 48.

[Ex-army officers] who have sought and not found employment; it is a mixture of hope and desperation; [there are] public sector employees scarcely able to eat; swarms of shopkeepers hit by the slump, who detest with a deadly hatred the trade union run shops; students and young graduates with no jobs … convinced that their misfortunes were due to the sinister plots of old politicians; adolescents aged 16–19 made bitter by bad luck which made the war finish too soon … because they wished to do great deeds; and bands of ex Socialists who had become war enthusiasts in 1915 …

SOURCE 3

From Italo Balbo, a Fascist leader in Ferrara, writing in 1932, quoted in N. Farrell, *Mussolini: A New Life*, Phoenix, 2004, p. 101.

When I came back from the war, just like so many, I hated politics and politicians, who in my opinion had betrayed the hopes of the combatants, reducing Italy to a shameful peace and systematic humiliation of any Italians who supported the cult of heroes. Fight, combat, to come back to the country of Giolitti, who offered every ideal as an item for sale? No. Better to deny everything, to destroy everything, so as to rebuild everything from scratch. Many in those days turned to Socialism. It was the ready-made revolutionary programme and, apparently the most radical … It is certain, in my opinion, that, without Mussolini, three-quarters of the Italian youth which had returned from the trenches would have become Bolsheviks.

CHAPTER 4

Mussolini: from prime minister to dictator 1922–8

Mussolini became prime minister in October 1922, but was still far from being the 'all-powerful' dictator of Italy. Over the next six years he would:

● Increase his power over government, parliament and the Fascist movement

● Reform election law to guarantee a Fascist majority in parliament

● Create his dictatorship, removing free elections, political opposition and the power of parliament

This chapter will examine the key issue of whether the dictatorship was created through the skill of Mussolini or was the result of the weakness and ineptitude of non-Fascist politicians. This issue is addressed through the following themes:

★ Mussolini's increasing power 1922–4

★ Electoral reform

★ The creation of the Fascist dictatorship 1924–8

Key dates

1922 Oct.	Mussolini appointed prime minister in a coalition government	
Nov.	Parliament gave Mussolini the right to rule by decree for a twelve-month period	
Dec.	Creation of the Grand Council of Fascism strengthened Mussolini's control of Fascist movement	
1923 Jan.	Fascist squads converted into a national militia	
July	Acerbo law changed the electoral system to ensure that the most popular party won a majority of MPs	

1924 April	First general election under the Acerbo law gave Fascists a majority in parliament
June	Murder of Matteotti, a leading Socialist, by Fascist thugs created a crisis for Mussolini and led to the emergence of a dictatorship
July	Press censorship introduced
1925 Jan.	Mussolini announced intention of creating a dictatorship
Dec.	Opposition political parties and free trade unions banned
1926 Jan.	Mussolini gained the right to make laws without needing the approval of parliament

Mussolini's increasing power 1922–4

▶ *What tactics did Mussolini use to increase his power?*

On 30 October 1922 Mussolini arrived in Rome and was appointed prime minister of Italy. His Fascist blackshirts were now permitted to enter the city and they paraded in triumph before their leader.

Mussolini held the top political post in the land, but his dream of complete, unchallenged personal power was still a long way from realisation. Although many of his blackshirts believed that the Fascist revolution was about to begin, their leader showed caution. He had a more realistic appreciation of the limits of Fascist power. Mussolini was aware that a completely Fascist government was not yet possible: fascism and its supporters did not have a majority of MPs in parliament and the King, no doubt supported by the army, would probably not allow him to do away with parliament. The new prime minister would have to construct a coalition government.

Mussolini's first government contained fourteen senior ministers, of whom only four were Fascists, the majority being Liberals and *Popolari*. This reassured those conservatives and Liberals who saw Fascism simply as a useful tool with which to crush the left. They had supported the Fascist entry into government on these grounds and believed that once the Socialists had been destroyed they could either absorb fascism into the regime or dispense with it altogether. Many thought that since fascism lacked a coherent ideology and a clear set of policies it was unlikely to last for long.

Mussolini's strategy

Mussolini was determined to be no one's pawn. Fascists might be a minority in the governing coalition but he held not only the post of prime minister but also the powerful position of minister of the interior, which gave him control of the police. He was also minister of foreign affairs. Above all, Mussolini was determined not to lose the momentum built up by the 'March on Rome' (see page 40). He was not yet able to secure supreme power, but he continued to use the threat of Fascist violence to intimidate parliament. At the same time he attempted to persuade MPs that, if they granted him near-dictatorial powers, they would be acting both in their own interests and in the interests of Italy itself.

Mussolini tried to convince MPs that the breakdown of law and order was so serious and the threat of a Socialist revolution so great that extraordinary measures were needed to deal with the situation. He argued that, once the condition of the country had been stabilised, he would give up his special powers and revert to normal parliamentary rule. Of course, the Socialist threat

SOURCE A

What impression does Source A give of Mussolini's first government?

Mussolini (at the head of the table) at his first cabinet meeting on 16 November 1922.

was nearly non-existent and the collapse of law and order was largely the result of Fascist violence, but conservatives and Liberals remained mesmerised by the supposed danger from the left. They also genuinely believed Mussolini's assurances that any new powers they granted him would only be temporary.

Most MPs would remain convinced, until at least late 1924, that Mussolini could be 'transformed' into a respectable, even traditional, prime minister and that his movement could be found a place within the regime. This was to prove a fatal miscalculation. By the time these politicians realised their error it was already too late: the dictatorship was largely in place, parliament was increasingly an irrelevance, and open opposition was extremely hazardous.

Rule by decree

The new prime minister took immediate action to increase his power, demanding that parliament grant him the right to rule by decree for twelve months. This would mean that he could effectively create new laws without consulting parliament. Mussolini justified this demand by stating that only a strong government could take the stern measures that were necessary to restore law and order and to put the country back on its feet. To convince parliament to give him these extraordinary powers, he delivered the speech quoted in Source B.

SOURCE B

Mussolini speaking in parliament, 16 November 1922, quoted in Bernardo Quaranta di San Severino, translator and editor, *Mussolini as Revealed in His Political Speeches (November 1914–August 1923)*, J.M. Dent & Sons, 1923, pp. 208–9.

… I am here to defend … the revolution of the 'black shirts' … With three hundred thousand young men, fully armed, … [prepared] to obey any command of mine, I could have punished all those who have slandered the Fascisti … I could have shut up Parliament and formed a Government of Fascisti exclusively; I could have done so, but I did not wish to do so, at any rate at the moment. …

I have formed a Coalition Government … in order to gather together in support of the suffering nation all those who, over and above questions of party … wish to save her.

… I thank all those who have worked with me … [and] I pay a warm tribute to our Sovereign [King], who, by refusing … to proclaim martial law, has avoided civil war and allowed the fresh and ardent Fascista … to pour itself into the sluggish main stream of the State. …

Before arriving here we were asked on all sides for a programme. It is not, alas! programmes that are wanting in Italy, but men to carry them out. All the problems of Italian life – all, I say – have long since been solved on paper; but the will to put these solutions into practice has been lacking. The Government to-day represents that firm and decisive will.

The MPs gave Mussolini a massive vote of confidence and granted him emergency powers for the twelve-month period. Only the Socialists and Communists opposed the motion; prominent Liberals including Giolitti, Salandra and Facta proclaimed their support for this decisive new prime minister.

Grand Council of Fascism

Mussolini now moved to consolidate his position. In December he tried to increase his authority over his own party by establishing the **Grand Council of Fascism**.

Mussolini gave himself the right to make all appointments to the Grand Council to ensure that he alone controlled Fascist policy. In the following month he reduced the influence of provincial Fascist leaders still further by converting the Fascist squads into a **national militia** paid for by the state. He now possessed a private army of over 30,000 men, which he continued to use to intimidate potential opponents.

> In what ways was the speech in Source B both threatening and reassuring to Liberals and Italian conservatives?

> **KEY TERMS**
>
> **Grand Council of Fascism** The supreme body within the Fascist movement, which discussed policy proposals and made all key appointments within the Fascist Party.
>
> **National militia** Fascist squads were converted into a national militia, giving them legal status. This blackshirted militia was under Fascist Party control.

Support from powerful groups

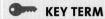
Mussolini encouraged Fascist violence to deter potential opponents, but he also actively courted influential groups. By early 1923 he had persuaded the employers' organisation, **Confindustria**, to support his premiership.

Mussolini's government's decision not to attack widespread tax evasion had helped to convince industrialists that the new prime minister was no dangerous radical.

Mussolini even managed to gain some support from the Church by confirming that he intended to ban contraception and to make religious education compulsory in state schools. In response, the Pope began to withdraw support from the *Popolari*, to the point of instructing its leader, the priest Don Sturzo, to leave Italy. By mid-1923 the *Popolari* had been dropped from the governing coalition and had lost the backing of conservative Catholics. Its political significance was now effectively at an end.

Within a year of becoming prime minister, Mussolini's reassurances, concessions, and threats had generated vital support from Liberals, conservatives, the Church and business. Most had convinced themselves that here was a man who could destroy socialism and inject energy and dynamism into Italian politics. Above all, they believed that Mussolini could be influenced and perhaps even controlled, a prime minister content to share power rather than one who wanted to monopolise it for himself.

 # Electoral reform

▶ *How did electoral reform work to Mussolini's advantage?*

Now that he was confident of the solid support of conservatives, many Catholics and the majority of Liberals, Mussolini moved to change the electoral system. He intended that this change would make his Fascists the biggest party in parliament.

Acerbo law

Mussolini proposed that the political party winning the most votes in a general election (provided it polled at least a quarter of the votes cast) should get two-thirds of the seats in the Chamber of Deputies. This was a revolutionary idea. Mussolini defended it by stating that the reform would produce a government which could count on the support of a large majority of MPs and which could then deal decisively with Italy's problems. There would be no more weak coalition governments where the different parties in government could not agree what to do. It was these coalitions, so Mussolini claimed, that had plagued Liberal Italy and helped to bring the country to its knees.

Mussolini neglected to point out that if his proposal became law the Fascists and their supporters would be the ones with the large majority of MPs and it would become virtually impossible to vote them out of power. Given the command, the Fascist squads would smash up the offices of hostile newspapers and would physically prevent opposition voters from reaching the polling booths. As Mussolini was minister of the interior, he could instruct the police to stand aside as Fascists caused havoc. The potential to fix elections was increased by the fact that he had promoted Fascist sympathisers to important positions in local government.

When this '**Acerbo law**' was debated in parliament in July 1923 it secured an overwhelming majority. The fact that armed blackshirts had roamed the chamber during the debate undoubtedly intimidated MPs, but the support for Mussolini's proposal was not simply the result of fear. Many MPs genuinely approved of the repressive actions taken by the government against what they still viewed as the dangerous, revolutionary left. They were prepared to turn a blind eye towards arrests and beatings of Socialists. Other MPs welcomed the end of those seemingly impotent coalition governments that Italy had experienced since the end of the war.

The most important factor in gaining the support of Liberal MPs was their continuing belief that Mussolini and his Fascists were not enemies of parliamentary government and that 'normality' would be restored as soon as circumstances permitted. Mussolini had assured the chamber on more than one occasion that he had no desire to dispense with parliament. The fact that he was the head of a coalition government and was prepared to discuss an electoral alliance with conservative groups seemed proof of his good faith. Giolitti and Salandra, the two most prominent Liberals, both pledged their support for the reform.

1924 Election

The new Acerbo law was put into practice in April 1924. In the general election of that month the Fascists campaigned with right-wing Liberals including Salandra. The Fascists and their allies secured 66 per cent of the vote. Fascist MPs increased from 35 to 374, giving the party a clear majority in the 535-seat chamber. Mussolini had certainly grown in public popularity, but widespread blackshirt violence and Fascist **ballot-rigging** had contributed significantly to the party's vote. Yet, despite the intimidation, the opposition parties – principally the Socialists and Communists – had still managed to attract 2.5 million votes. The resilience of support for opposition parties was illustrated by the fact that the two major cities in the north – Milan and Turin – both failed to produce Fascist majorities.

KEY TERMS

Acerbo law Mussolini's July 1923 reform of elections to guarantee a Fascist victory.

Ballot-rigging Fixing the result of an election by such illegal measures as destroying votes cast for opposition parties or adding fraudulent voting papers.

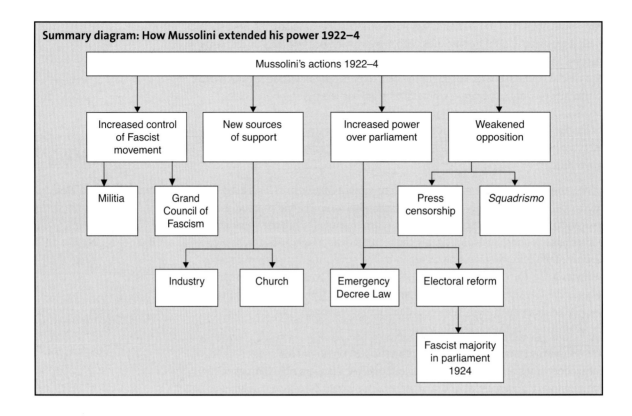

Summary diagram: How Mussolini extended his power 1922–4

3 The creation of the Fascist dictatorship 1924–8

► *How was Mussolini able to make himself dictator?*

It now seemed that Mussolini had control of parliament, but he still did not possess the powers of a dictator. Parliament was still needed to approve laws, opposition parties still existed and the King could still sack his prime minister. It was unclear whether Mussolini would try to establish a dictatorship or how he would do it. In the event, the murder of a prominent opponent would threaten Mussolini's very survival but also pave the way to a Fascist dictatorship.

Murder of Matteotti

When parliament reopened, opposition MPs tried to publicise illegal Fascist actions at the polls. Their most prominent spokesperson, the Socialist Giacomo Matteotti, produced evidence detailing Fascist violence and terror during the election campaign. On 10 June 1924, within days of these allegations being made, Fascist thugs abducted Matteotti in broad daylight and stabbed him to death. This brutal murder shocked not only Mussolini's political enemies but also many pro-Mussolini Liberals who thought that the Fascists had finally gone too far. Mussolini denied all knowledge of the crime but the chief suspect was the personal assistant to Mussolini's press secretary. As evidence linking the prime minister to the murder began to appear in the press, public opinion began to turn against him and crowds protested in the streets.

At this point, opposition MPs walked out of parliament and set up their own breakaway parliament. These MPs, mainly Socialist, Communist and dissident *Popolari*, hoped that their '**Aventine secession**' (named after a similar event in ancient Rome) might encourage the King to dismiss Mussolini. The Fascist leader's position appeared vulnerable. In response, Mussolini put more blackshirts on the streets to deter opposition, but also distanced himself from the crime, ordering the arrests of the Fascist suspects. By appointing a conservative as minister of the interior in charge of the police, Mussolini tried to create the impression that he wanted an open and fair investigation into the murder.

Mussolini's actions perhaps reassured the King, who refused to contemplate his dismissal – he avoided reading a report which directly implicated Mussolini in the murder! Victor Emmanuel feared that sacking the prime minister would only strengthen the revolutionary left and might lead to civil war. He was encouraged in this belief by leading Liberals and conservatives who saw the affair not as an opportunity to dispose of the Fascist leader, but rather as a chance to increase their influence over the weakened prime minister. Giolitti and Salandra, for example, still supported Mussolini's premiership. For such men there appeared at that moment to be no viable acceptable alternative to the Fascist leader.

 KEY TERM

Aventine secession Anti-Fascist MPs walked out of parliament in protest against Fascist violence, hoping that this would encourage the King to sack Mussolini.

SOURCE C

An Italian newspaper's view of the Matteotti affair at the time.

What is the message of the cartoon in Source C?

Destruction of democracy

Mussolini moved to suppress any further opposition. In July 1924 he introduced **press censorship** and in the following month banned meetings by opposition political parties. But, despite the government's efforts, the controversy raised by the Matteotti affair did not disappear. Those Liberal leaders who had previously supported the government joined the opposition in November in protest against press censorship. Eventually, in December 1924, leading Fascists, exasperated by the uncertainty created by the affair and frustrated by the government's lack of radicalism, presented Mussolini with an ultimatum. If he did not end the Matteotti affair immediately and move decisively towards the establishment of a dictatorship, they would withdraw their support.

The prime minister bowed to their demands and, in a speech on 3 January 1925, told parliament that he accepted responsibility for all Fascist actions up to that date (see Source D).

SOURCE D

From Benito Mussolini, *My Autobiography*, Charles Scribner's Sons, 1928, pp. 231–3.

… I declare here before … all the Italian people, that I assume … responsibility for everything that has happened. … If Fascism has only been castor oil or a club, and not a proud passion of the best Italian youth, the blame is on me! If Fascism has been a criminal association, … the responsibility for this is on me, because I have created it with my propaganda …

Italy … wants peace, wants quiet, wants work, wants calm; we will give it with love, if that be possible, or with strength, if that be necessary.

Mussolini was signalling that he would now take the measures necessary to give himself much greater personal power. His speech was cheered in the chamber. With a clear majority in parliament and confident that the King would not move against him, Mussolini created his dictatorship. What opposition there was in the chamber proved no threat: it was divided, lacking in leadership and compromised by its earlier support for fascism.

In January 1925 the prime minister established a committee to reform the constitution. In December the *Leggi Fascistissime* were passed, banning opposition political parties and **free trade unions**.

Press censorship was tightened, a new secret police force was set up and a special court was established to try political crimes. Fascist control of local government was increased by replacing elected mayors with nominated officials, known as *podestas*.

KEY TERMS

Press censorship
Newspapers are no longer permitted to criticise the government.

Leggi Fascistissime
Fascist laws which banned all opposition parties and organisations.

Free trade unions Trade unions which represent the interests of workers, and which are independent of government control.

? Why did the speech quoted in Source D receive huge applause in parliament?

In January 1926 Mussolini was granted the right to issue decrees carrying the full force of law. He could now make laws without consulting parliament, which meant that his personal rule was enshrined in law. By the end of the year parliament had even lost the right to debate proposed laws or criticise the government.

Final touches to the dictatorship were added in 1928 when the King lost the right to select the prime minister. In future, a list of possible candidates would be drawn up by the Grand Council of Fascism, a body appointed and controlled by Mussolini, and the King would have to make his selection from this list.

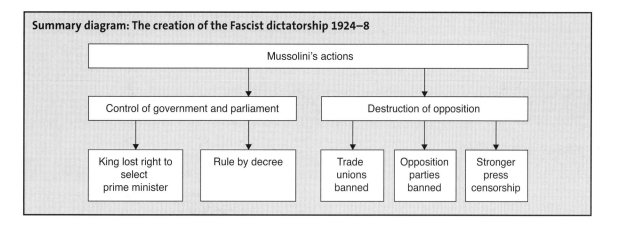

Summary diagram: The creation of the Fascist dictatorship 1924–8

Chapter summary

When the King appointed Mussolini prime minister neither he nor the conservative elites –the Liberals, the Church, landowners and industrialists – imagined Italy becoming a Fascist dictatorship. Mussolini himself had no clear plan and was aware that his Fascists were a minority in both government and parliament.

Over the next four years Mussolini manipulated the Liberals into voting for the Acerbo law and press censorship. He played on their fear of socialism, threatened them with Fascist violence and, at the same time, suggested that he would be happy to co-operate with them in governing Italy. The Matteotti crisis of 1924 could have led to the fall of Mussolini but the Aventine Secession showed continuing Liberal divisions, and no concerted attempt was made to persuade the King to sack him as prime minister. When, in January 1925, Mussolini announced his intention to create a dictatorship there was no one with the will to try to stop him.

Refresher questions

Use these questions to remind yourself of the key material covered in the chapter.

1 What factors limited Mussolini's power on becoming prime minister in October 1922?

2 How did Mussolini persuade parliament to vote for rule by decree and for the Acerbo law?

3 Why was the Acerbo law so important in increasing Fascist power?

4 Why did the murder of Matteotti create a crisis for Mussolini?

5 Why did Mussolini survive the Matteotti affair?

6 What prompted Mussolini to announce his creation of a dictatorship in January 1925?

7 What actions did Mussolini take in the years 1925–8 to create his dictatorship?

Question practice

ESSAY QUESTIONS

1 'Mussolini was able to consolidate his dictatorship in the years 1922–6 because of the mistakes of the Liberals.' Explain why you agree or disagree with this view.

2 'It was violence, and the fear of violence, that enabled Mussolini to consolidate his power between October 1922 and 1929.' Assess the validity of this view.

3 To what extent were Mussolini's political skills the main reason why he survived the Matteotti affair?

4 How significant was fear of the left in enabling Mussolini to create his dictatorship 1922–8?

5 'Liberal weakness was the most important factor in enabling Mussolini to create his dictatorship 1922–6.' How far do you agree?

6 Which was the more important factor in Mussolini's consolidation of his dictatorship 1922–6? i) Fear of socialism. ii) The Matteotti crisis. Explain your answer with reference to both i) and ii).

INTERPRETATION QUESTION

1 Read the interpretation and then answer the question that follows: 'Mussolini survived the Matteotti crisis because of the decisive voices of the Church and industry.' (From E. Wiskemann, *Fascism in Italy*, Macmillan, 1969, p. 16.) Evaluate the strengths and limitations of this interpretation, making reference to other interpretations you have studied.

SOURCE ANALYSIS QUESTIONS

1 With reference to Sources 1 and 2, and your understanding of the historical context, which of these two sources is more valuable in explaining why Mussolini succeeded in consolidating his Fascist regime between October 1922 and 1926?

2 With reference to Sources 1, 2 and 3, and your understanding of the historical context, assess the value of these sources to a historian studying Mussolini's consolidation of his dictatorship in the years 1922–6.

3 Why is Source 2 valuable to the historian for an enquiry into the reactions of Liberal politicians towards the consolidation of Mussolini's dictatorship? Explain your answer using the source, the information given about it and your own knowledge of the historical context.

4 How much weight do you give the evidence of Source 1 for an enquiry into the reasons why Mussolini was able to consolidate his dictatorship in the years 1922–6? Explain your answer using the source, the information given about it and your own knowledge of the historical context.

5 How far could the historian make use of Sources 1 and 2 together to investigate the reasons why Mussolini was able to consolidate his dictatorship in the years 1922–6? Explain your answer, using both sources, the information given about them and your own knowledge of the historical context.

SOURCE 1

Adapted from an editorial in a British newspaper, *The Times*, 31 October 1923, reviewing the first year of Italy under Mussolini's rule. Quoted in J. Hite and C. Hinton, *Fascist Italy*, John Murray, 1998, p. 75.

Italy has never been so united as she is today. Fascism has abolished the game of parliamentary chess; it has also simplified the taxation system and reduced the financial deficit to manageable proportions. It has vastly improved the public services, particularly the railways. It has reduced the large bureaucracy without any very bad results in the way of hardships or unemployment. It has pursued a vigorous and fairly successful colonial policy. It has given to Italy national security and national self-respect. Fascism has had a great deal of courage, very considerable wisdom and immense good luck. It deserves the sincere birthday greetings of the world.

SOURCE 2

Adapted from a speech by Vittorio Orlando, 16 January 1925. Orlando held several government posts before the First World War and was prime minister from 1917 to 1919. At first, he had supported Mussolini's government. Quoted in J. Hite and C. Hinton, *Fascist Italy*, John Murray, 1998, p. 80.

It is claimed that the country is calm. Well, if you are willing to be content with that kind of calm! During the last two years we have gone through various phases of government! There was what I would call the private violence of the Fascist party and organisations. This violence was deplored even by the Government. Then there followed governmental restrictions on personal freedom, with the justification that this was the way to deal with the aforementioned violence. And thus repression from the Government took over from the Fascist party. But now we have both evils: governmental repression and continuing party violence.

SOURCE 3

Mussolini speaking in parliament, 16 November 1922, quoted in Bernardo Quaranta di San Severino, translator and editor, *Mussolini as Revealed in His Political Speeches (November 1914–August 1923)*, J.M. Dent & Sons, 1923, pp. 208–9.

… I am here to defend … the revolution of the 'black shirts' … With three hundred thousand young men, fully armed, … [prepared] to obey any command of mine, I could have punished all those who have slandered the Fascisti … I could have shut up Parliament and formed a Government of Fascisti exclusively; I could have done so, but I did not wish to do so, at any rate at the moment. …

I have formed a Coalition Government … in order to gather together in support of the suffering nation all those who, over and above questions of party … wish to save her.

… I thank all those who have worked with me … [and] I pay a warm tribute to our Sovereign [King], who, by refusing … to proclaim martial law, has avoided civil war and allowed the fresh and ardent Fascista … to pour itself into the sluggish main stream of the State. …

Before arriving here we were asked on all sides for a programme. It is not, alas! programmes that are wanting in Italy, but men to carry them out. All the problems of Italian life – all, I say – have long since been solved on paper; but the will to put these solutions into practice has been lacking. The Government to-day represents that firm and decisive will.

CHAPTER 5

Mussolini and the Fascist political system

This chapter examines the nature and extent of Mussolini's dictatorship. Is it more accurate to describe Italy 1922–43 as a Fascist dictatorship or a personal dictatorship? How far did Mussolini change the way government worked and how powerful were the Fascist Party and other Fascist leaders? Why was there not more opposition to fascism? These issues are examined under the following headings:

★ Mussolini's aim: personal dictatorship

★ Propaganda and the cult of personality

★ Mussolini and government

★ Mussolini and the Fascist Party

★ Relations between party and state

★ Popular support and opposition

The key debate on *page 78* of this chapter asks the question: How popular was Mussolini's Fascist regime?

Key dates

1925	Final congress of the Fascist Party: Mussolini banned internal arguments	1928	All appointments in Fascist Party made by party headquarters in Rome, controlled by Mussolini
	Vidoni Palace Pact outlawed independent trade unions		
1926	Mussolini able to make laws without the consent of parliament	1929	Lateran Agreements improved relations between fascism and Catholic Church
	Parliament lost right to debate proposed laws or to criticise the government	1933	Hitler became chancellor of Germany
	Opposition newspapers suppressed	1939	Parliament replaced by the Chamber of Fasces and Corporations
	Cult of personality underway		

Mussolini's aim: personal dictatorship

▶ *To what extent was Mussolini's rule a 'personal dictatorship'?*

By 1926 Mussolini had achieved his ambition of becoming dictator of Italy. He could make laws simply by issuing decrees. Parliament was under his full control – no longer a forum for debate, but simply a theatre in which his decisions could be applauded by Fascist supporters and sympathisers. With Liberals and *Popolari* divided and leaderless, and the Socialists under constant physical attack, organised political opposition did not exist. Of course, technically, Mussolini could still be dismissed by the King, but the 'March on Rome' and the Matteotti affair (pages 40 and 56) had proved that Victor Emmanuel was not prepared to stand up to his prime minister. Furthermore, providing the King remained in fear and awe of the Fascist leader, Mussolini need not worry about the armed forces, as they were very unlikely to break their pledge of loyalty to the monarch.

 **KEY TERM**

Personal dictatorship
A regime where a single person, rather than a team of ministers or a political party, holds total power. This individual is able to make their own laws and arrest opponents at will.

With his position secure, Mussolini now set out to create his Fascist state. This state was to be a **personal dictatorship**, for the prime minister's central goal was to maintain and increase his own personal power. In pursuit of this aim he encouraged a cult of personality that stressed his genius, his power and his indispensability as leader of the nation. He attempted to consolidate his position by seeking a constructive working relationship with powerful interest groups, notably the Church, industrialists and the armed forces.

Mussolini's pursuit of personal power took priority over the desire to impose Fascist ideas on all aspects of Italian life. This policy disappointed many in the Fascist Party who hoped that the Fascist revolution would sweep away interest groups and create a state in which the party controlled all areas of government. Their leader still talked of revolution, but he was determined that the party should be his servant and not his master. Mussolini would decide what powers the party should possess, what Fascist policy should be, and how and when it should be implemented.

The Italy that Mussolini created was one in which he alone possessed ultimate power. Interest groups, the old institutions of government and the Fascist Party all competed against each other for authority, but they looked to Mussolini to adjudicate their disputes and to make the final decisions. Without him government could not function and the regime would collapse.

Propaganda and the cult of personality

▶ *What was the purpose of Fascist propaganda?*

▶ *What was the cult of personality? How successful was it?*

Mussolini had first come to national attention as the editor of a propagandist newspaper, *Il Popolo d'Italia*, and was determined to use propaganda to build up support for his regime and to deter opposition. Unsurprisingly, he was anxious to control the news. In 1926 opposition newspapers were suppressed, and journalists and their editors made aware that they could be arrested if they published anything derogatory towards the regime. Mussolini's own press office issued 'official' versions of events which newspapers were expected to publish without question.

Radio and cinema were also to be tools for Fascist propaganda. There were perhaps only 40,000 radio sets in the whole of Italy in the mid-1920s, but from 1924 the radio network was run by the state. News bulletins continually praised Mussolini and broadcast his speeches in full. Radios were given to schools and by the 1930s the party was trying to ensure that even those living in rural areas could at least listen to communal radios in their villages. The regime was slow to make propagandist feature films, and US Hollywood films always dominated Italian cinema screens, but each of these films would be preceded by a short newsreel which gave a Fascist version of current events.

Cult of personality

The media were to play a crucial role in creating the cult of the *Duce*, as Mussolini was increasingly known. The cult was intended to build popular support for the dictator and to overawe potential opponents by stressing his supposed superhuman talents. He was to be portrayed not as just another politician but as Italy's saviour, a man chosen by destiny to save the country from the Socialist menace and corrupt democratic politicians and to restore Italian greatness. He was portrayed as the new Caesar: a man of genius, a man of action, a man of culture, a statesman of world renown dedicated only to the revival of Italy.

By 1926 the regime was using all the methods of propaganda at its disposal to convey its message. Government-controlled newspapers stressed Mussolini's benevolence and took particular pride in quoting the opinions of foreign admirers, particularly if they were leading statesmen. The British foreign secretary, Austen Chamberlain, was thus widely reported as saying that Mussolini was 'a wonderful man working for the greatness of his country', while Winston Churchill's opinion in 1927 that the *Duce*'s 'sole thought was the lasting well-being of the Italian people as he sees it' received similar publicity.

SOURCE A

Study Source A. Why would Mussolini want to associate himself with memories of ancient Rome?

Mussolini viewing a statue of Julius Caesar that had been installed in the recently excavated Roman Forum in 1932.

Mussolini's supposed dedication to duty led to stories that he toiled for up to 20 hours per day on government business. In fact, the light was left on in his study for most of the night to back up this claim and to disguise the fact that the dictator usually retired to bed rather early.

The newspapers also suggested that the *Duce* was infallible. 'Mussolini is always right' became a popular phrase, an idea the dictator encouraged with such utterances as 'often I would like to be wrong, but so far it has never happened and events have always turned out just as I foresaw'. To maintain this impression, Mussolini was quick to claim the credit for any successes and still quicker to blame others for any mistakes.

The *Duce* was keen to be portrayed as a vigorous, athletic and courageous man – a model for all Italian males. Magazines and newspapers printed pictures of his horse-riding, enjoying winter sports, driving cars at high speed and flying aeroplanes. An image of youthfulness was maintained by the suppression of any references to his age or to the fact that he needed to wear glasses.

Not content with this, the dictator insisted that he must also be seen as a man of culture. Consequently, it was made known that he had read and digested all 35 volumes of the Italian encyclopaedia and had read nearly all the classics of European literature, including the complete works of William Shakespeare. Fascist propagandists also claimed that Mussolini was an accomplished musician.

SOURCE B

A 1927 photograph of Mussolini playing the violin. Propaganda photographs of the supposed myriad talents of the *Duce* were distributed to newspapers and magazines both in Italy and abroad.

The photo in Source B was designed to suggest a different aspect of Mussolini's character: what might this be and why might fascism want to promote this?

Mussolini's expectation that everyone would be taken in by this image and these exaggerated claims revealed his own vanity and also his low opinion of the public. Indeed, he declared that the public 'are stupid, dirty, do not work hard enough and are content with their little cinema shows'. Mussolini believed that the masses were not really interested in debate or discussion but preferred to be told what to do. They would enjoy the belief that they were ruled by a near superman and would feel proud that Italy was apparently so admired by the rest of the world. Spectacles, parades and constant propaganda would keep their interest and secure their allegiance. As Mussolini put it, 'one must always know how to strike the imagination of the public: that is the real secret of how to govern'.

It is uncertain how many people were impressed by the '**cult of the *Duce***'. Many, perhaps most, must have been extremely sceptical, but the cult did help to convince large numbers of Italians that there was no conceivable alternative to the Fascist regime. The sheer volume of propaganda stressing Mussolini's power and genius deterred potential opposition. To this extent, the cult of personality certainly achieved its aim.

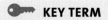 **KEY TERM**

Cult of the *Duce*
The promotion of Mussolini as the 'supreme leader' (*Duce*), the man who had saved Italy from socialism, and who was leading the country back to greatness; a man whose creation, fascism, was admired around the world.

Mussolini and government

▶ *What were the roles of the King, ministers and parliament?*
▶ *How did Mussolini attempt to win the support of key groups in the Italian state: civil service, armed forces, judges and local government?*

Mussolini was determined to ensure that all real power rested in his hands – he alone would devise policy and he alone would make all major decisions. The King would be an irrelevance, and cabinet, parliament and the institutions of state would be his loyal servants.

Role of the King

King Victor Emmanuel was easily dealt with. The monarchy had traditionally distanced itself from domestic policy and concerned itself principally with foreign affairs. Mussolini realised that he completely overawed Victor Emmanuel, and took advantage of this to deter the monarchy from any political involvement. The dictator still followed protocol by visiting the King twice a week, but Victor Emmanuel was never asked for his advice and was only told what Mussolini wanted him to hear.

Role of government ministers

Mussolini was not prepared to share power with his ministers. There would be no cabinet-style government with ministers jointly discussing and deciding government policy. There was to be no government 'team'. Instead, the role of ministers was simply to follow the *Duce*'s instructions unquestioningly. In fact, Mussolini himself held the most important ministries – foreign affairs, interior and the three armed services – for the greater part of his time as dictator.

Role of parliament

The *Duce* had even less regard for parliament. By 1926 it had lost its ability to discuss policy, to debate and amend proposed legislation, and to criticise the government. Its reputation and political significance were to sink still further in subsequent years. With opposition parties banned, the chamber was dominated by sycophantic Fascist deputies who did not even bother to vote formally on Mussolini's legislation: they simply shouted their assent. Free elections ceased to exist. The electorate was reduced to exclude most of the working classes, who had previously supported the Socialists. In addition, all candidates had to be approved by the Fascists, and the results were shamelessly rigged to show over 98 per cent approval for the regime. Eventually, in January 1939, parliament abolished itself altogether, to be replaced by the equally meaningless Chamber of Fasces and Corporations.

Gaining the support of the civil service

If the cabinet and parliament were to be Mussolini's servants then so, too, were the other institutions of the Italian state: the **civil service**, local government, the judiciary and the armed services. However, Mussolini was keen to achieve his goals without provoking the head-on clash with these institutions that the radicals in the Fascist Party desired. A wholesale sacking of personnel in the civil service, judiciary and army officer corps and their replacement by Fascist Party appointees would almost certainly have caused a crisis. Mussolini wanted to avoid any such crisis and was anxious to restrict the power of the party and to keep it under his complete command. The dictator recognised that the conservatives, who were prominent in state institutions, were largely sympathetic towards him, if distrustful of the party radicals. He set out to capitalise on this sympathy by using his powers of **patronage** to reward loyalty and by introducing policies that conservatives could support. However, at the same time, Mussolini made it clear that if his wishes were not supported and obeyed, he would be ruthless in seeking out and destroying opposition.

Mussolini's approach meant that there was no Fascist revolution in government. Indeed, the Fascist Party complained that party membership was dangerously low in the institutions of state. In 1927, for instance, it was estimated that only about fifteen per cent of the civil service was Fascist. Nevertheless, the civil service loyally carried out the instructions of its political master, the *Duce*. During the 1930s, Fascist Party membership did increase among civil servants, but this seems to have been largely the result of a recognition that promotion depended on being a card-carrying supporter of the regime.

Gaining support in the armed forces

The dictator adopted a similar policy in his dealings with the armed services. Mussolini emphasised that he and the military shared a common interest in expanding the armed forces and in pursuing an aggressive foreign policy. Further support was gained by promoting senior generals to the prestigious post of field marshal. Ambitious officers soon came to realise that a pro-Fascist attitude, and preferably party membership, would enormously enhance their prospects of promotion. The army did, admittedly, resent the pretensions of the Fascist militia to be a significant military force, but it was still willing to give its loyalty to the *Duce*.

Controlling the judges

Only with the judiciary did Mussolini conduct a purge of what he considered to be undesirable elements. Dozens of judges were sacked for being insufficiently sympathetic towards fascism or for being too independent of the government. The dictator wanted to ensure that the judiciary could be relied on to follow his government's instructions. The Italian legal system consequently lost all claim to impartiality. Imprisonment without trial became commonplace and, where

KEY TERMS

Civil service Civil servants advise government ministers on policy and ensure that government policies are carried out.

Patronage The use of appointments and promotions to reward support.

cases did come to court, Mussolini occasionally intervened to dictate verdicts and sentences.

Controlling local government

This determination to control all the institutions of state also extended to local government. Local self-government was abolished and elected mayors and town councils were replaced by officials appointed from Rome.

Mussolini's methods ensured that he extended his power throughout the Italian state, building up support based on self-interest and avoiding unnecessary conflict. His tactics in pursuit of his goal of complete personal power varied between aggression and conciliation, according to the nature of the institution in question.

Gaining support from powerful groups in Italian society

Mussolini adopted a broadly conciliatory approach when dealing with those interest groups whose support he needed to consolidate his regime: the Church and industry.

The *Duce* had wooed the Vatican even before he became prime minister, disavowing his earlier anticlericalism (see page 38) and emphasising that the Church had nothing to fear from fascism. Mussolini also pointed out that fascism and Catholicism faced common enemies in socialism and liberalism. Relations steadily warmed and in 1929 the Lateran Agreements were signed (see page 101), finally healing the breach between the Catholic Church and the Italian state. Mussolini could now rely on official Catholic support for his regime.

Mussolini also adopted conciliatory tactics, at least to begin with, when dealing with Italian industrialists. In the Vidoni Palace Pact of 1925 all Socialist and Catholic trade unions were banned and, in the following year, strikes were outlawed. A fuller discussion of fascism's policy towards industry is to be found on pages 84–9, but these early concessions were instrumental in securing industrialists' loyalty to the regime.

 # Mussolini and the Fascist Party

▶ *How did Mussolini cement his control over the Fascist Party?*

▶ *How did Mussolini ensure that there were no credible rivals to his leadership?*

Once he was in power, Mussolini had to decide what should be the role of his National Fascist Party (PNF). Should the PNF play a key role in the Fascist state or should Mussolini simply use government departments to bring about change? Should the PNF be a mass party or a disciplined elite? The *Duce* seems to have found it difficult to decide on these questions and his opinion varied over the years. However, his mind was clear and his policy unchanging on the question of the relationship between the leader and the party: the PNF would serve the *Duce* and not the other way around.

From the time of the Fascist breakthrough into Italian politics in 1920–1, Mussolini had stressed the need for discipline and central control. However, his struggle to assert his leadership had not been easy. Local Fascist leaders (*Ras*) acknowledged Mussolini as the *Duce* of fascism, but they were reluctant to accept central direction. In fact, their violent actions during 1921 and 1922 at times embarrassed a leader who was trying to reassure conservatives that his movement was a dynamic yet responsible political force. The 'March on Rome' (page 40) was at least in part a concession to pressure from the radical *squadristi*.

Mussolini as prime minister

Once he had been appointed prime minister, Mussolini moved to extend his control over his party. The creation of the militia provided paid employment for Fascist *squadristi* and helped to ensure their continued loyalty. The establishment of the Grand Council of Fascism (page 53) as the supreme policy-making body for the movement strengthened the leader's position still further since he appointed all of its members. As he rewarded loyalty, so he punished opposition: during 1923 local parties were purged of active or potential dissidents. Despite these efforts, Mussolini's control over the party was still not absolute, as the *Ras* (page 34) demonstrated when, during the Matteotti crisis of 1924, they demanded that he establish a dictatorship.

If the *Ras* and their *squadristi* hoped that the creation of a dictatorship would enhance party power, they were to be disappointed. Mussolini set up a personal dictatorship. With control over the institutions of state, his power was secure and he was no longer vulnerable to pressure from within the PNF. The *Duce* illustrated his mastery of the party at the final party congress, held in June 1925. Mussolini demanded that the party should end internal arguments and obey the orders of its leader. Dissenting voices were shouted down. Although it was scheduled to last three days, the convention lasted only a few hours.

By the end of 1928 the *Duce* had organised a further purge of Fascists suspected of disloyalty and had established the principle that all party posts should be appointments made from party headquarters in Rome, a headquarters that he controlled. The PNF had become totally subservient to its leader. The Grand Council of Fascism was under the complete control of the *Duce* and, as the years went by, he called it less and less frequently.

Divisions within the Fascist Party

That Mussolini had managed to achieve absolute dominance over fascism was testament to his political skills, but it also showed that without Mussolini there was nothing to hold the party together. The PNF was not a united, coherent movement but rather a broad, uneasy coalition of groups with differing views and priorities. *Squadristi* demanded the continuance of violent raids, ex-Socialists wanted the reorganisation of industry, Nationalists desired the revision of the First World War peace settlement, and conservatives hoped for the restoration of law and order and normality. Only Mussolini could provide unity. The disparate, disorganised factions came to recognise this and looked to win his interest and support. The dictator's concerns and enthusiasms would change over the years, and he was sympathetic first to one faction then to another; initially conciliatory to the conservatives to secure the support of interest groups such as industry, then enthusiastic for a reorganisation of industry into a corporate state (page 85). In the late 1930s he reverted to radical ideas of revolutionising Italian social habits. Of course, the real significance of this was that the *Duce* and not the party would be responsible for determining the course of Fascist policy.

Preventing the emergence of rivals

Given the Fascist Party's subservience to its *Duce*, it was not surprising that the men who occupied senior posts within the party were notable less for their ability than for their obedience and powers of flattery. The most senior post, that of party secretary, was held by a succession of utterly loyal Fascists of very modest ability. Under such men as Achille Starace, party secretary from 1931 to 1939, the PNF opened its doors to all those who saw party membership simply as a way to secure a safe job in the Fascist administration. By the mid-1930s workers and peasants, who had once made up almost 30 per cent of party membership, had become a tiny minority. The PNF now consisted overwhelmingly of white-collar state employees.

Mussolini's promotion of second-rate officials showed his susceptibility to flattery, but it also revealed his continuing concern to prevent the emergence of potential rivals. Men of drive and apparent ability found themselves moved far from the centre of power. For example, the young squad leader Italo Balbo (see page 73), who achieved fame in 1931 when he completed a trans-Atlantic flight, was soon sent to occupy a post of luxurious idleness in Libya. Another young *squadrista*, Dino Grandi, apparently had some ambition to succeed the *Duce* but found himself despatched to London as Italian ambassador, a post of honour but of little power. No serious rival to the *Duce* ever emerged. Indeed, even men who had made their name as radical *squadristi*, such as Roberto Farinacci (page 34), enthusiastically joined in the cult of the *Duce*. They realised that Mussolini was prepared to allow them to keep much of their power in the provinces providing they remained utterly loyal and obedient to him. They were also well aware that without Mussolini as dictator their own power would collapse.

Italo Balbo

1896	Born in Ferrara and politically active at a young age
1915–18	War service. Awarded medals for bravery and reached rank of captain
1919–20	University student and bank worker
1921	Leader of Fascist squads in Ferrara, in central Italy. In September he led a march of 3000 Fascists against Socialists in Ravenna
1922	Led Fascist squads in a rampage across the province of the Romagna, noting in his diary: 'It was a night of terror. Our passage was signed by plumes of smoke and fire'
	Demanded that Mussolini march on Rome to seize power
1923	Implicated in murder of anti-Fascist Catholic priest
1924	Appointed commander of Fascist militia
1926	Appointed secretary of state for air and expanded Italian air force
1930	Led flight of twelve flying boats in one of first trans-Atlantic crossings from Italy to Brazil
1933	Appointed governor-general of Libya
1940	Killed when his plane was shot down by Italian anti-aircraft fire over Libya

Balbo was in many ways a typical *Ras*, a local Fascist leader. An ex-serviceman with a taste for violence and a hatred of socialism, he built up his power base in the area around Ferrara in central Italy. He was one of a number of prominent Fascists who pressurised Mussolini into action in October 1922, demanding that he seize power by force if necessary.

With the Fascist dictatorship established from 1926, Balbo used his ministerial post to build up the prestige of fascism abroad through his highly publicised trans-Atlantic flights. Balbo's own high profile may have caused Mussolini to see him as a potential rival: it has been suggested that his appointment as the governor of Libya was Mussolini's ploy to get Balbo out of Italy and out of the public eye. Indeed, Balbo's widow believed that his death in 1940 was no accident, rather an assassination on Mussolini's orders.

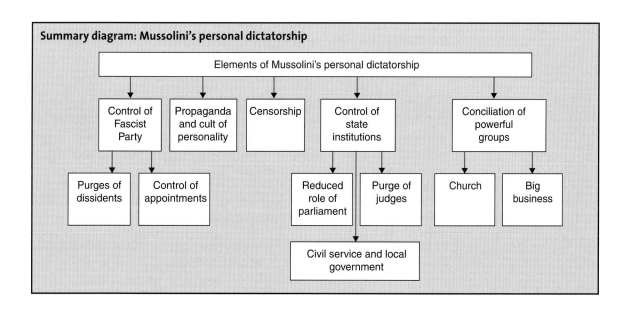

Summary diagram: Mussolini's personal dictatorship

Elements of Mussolini's personal dictatorship

- Control of Fascist Party
  - Purges of dissidents
  - Control of appointments
- Propaganda and cult of personality
- Censorship
- Control of state institutions
  - Reduced role of parliament
  - Purge of judges
  - Civil service and local government
- Conciliation of powerful groups
  - Church
  - Big business

Relations between party and state

▶ *Why were there rivalries between the party and government institutions and how did these rivalries increase Mussolini's power?*

▶ *How efficient was Fascist government?*

Although the party lost most of the dynamism it had once possessed and became a bloated bureaucracy offering secure, undemanding jobs to Fascist supporters, it still had a role in Mussolini's state. The *Duce* hoped that the party would help to transform ordinary Italians into obedient, disciplined Fascists and, in pursuit of this, he gave it a significant role, particularly in the areas of education, leisure and propaganda.

The PNF therefore represented a rival authority to that of the institutions of the state, and there were tensions and arguments between party organisations and government departments. For example, should the Fascist youth movement, the ONB, be controlled by the party or by the government's Ministry of Education? A similar argument took place over the question of who should run the organisation for adult leisure activities, the *Dopolavoro* ('After work'). There was rivalry between the government economics ministry and the Fascist bureaucracy controlling the new Fascist corporations.

In the armed forces there was rivalry between the Fascist militia and the regular army, the latter resenting the claim that blackshirt officers were equal in status to army officers. The army and militia also argued over the distribution of weapons between them. Such rivalry was not confined to national politics. It was particularly common in the provinces, where local party secretaries competed for power with provincial prefects who, according to the Ministry of the Interior in Rome, had responsibility for local government.

In these disputes over jurisdiction both sides looked to Mussolini to solve the disputes. This gave the *Duce* great power. For example, in 1927 he transferred control over the *Dopolavoro* organisation from the Ministry of National Economy to the party. In contrast, in 1929 he took the youth organisation, the ONB, out of the hands of the party organisation and handed control to the Ministry of National Education.

Effectiveness of Fascist government

Disputes between party organisations and government departments made government slow and inefficient. With so many matters awaiting the *Duce*'s personal decision, delays were unavoidable, despite his spurious claims to be working up to 20 hours each day. The dictator's determination that he should personally occupy the most important ministries of state only worsened the situation. When decisions were taken they were often made without proper thought or consultation, as when the *Duce* selected the air force's new fighter plane after only a most cursory glance at the relevant information. Mussolini's tenure of so many ministries also meant that he found it impossible to ensure that his decisions were actually being carried out as he had intended. Fascist government, then, was not nearly as streamlined and efficient as the *Duce* and his foreign admirers liked to suggest. Mussolini might have supreme personal power, but below him there was all too often confusion, delay and incompetence.

Summary diagram: Tensions between the Fascist Party and government institutions

Causes of tension
- Role of party not clearly defined by Mussolini
- Party responsibilities subject to change by Mussolini
- Ambitions of Fascist *Ras* to increase their power

Examples of tension
- Arguments between party and Ministry of Education over control of Fascist youth movement, the ONB
- Arguments between party and Ministry of National Economy over control of adult leisure organisation, *Dopolavoro*
- Arguments between Fascist militia and regular army over allocation of new weapons
- Arguments between local party secretaries and prefects, appointed by Ministry of Interior, over control of local government

---

6 Popular support and opposition

▶ *Why was there little effective opposition to fascism?*

▶ *To what extent did propaganda generate support for Mussolini?*

Mussolini's control over the Fascist Party and the great institutions of state made open opposition both difficult and dangerous. As the death of Matteotti proved (page 56), the *Duce* had no compunction about using violence and even murder to silence his critics. By 1926 it is probable that Fascist squads had murdered around 2000 opponents. The ban on political activity outside the Fascist Party, together with the imposition of press censorship, denied opponents a platform for their views. Dissidents were spied on by the dictator's secret police, the **OVRA**, who had thousands of informers. Suspects might be severely beaten up or brought before the OVRA court. This court had tried around 4500 defendants by 1943, and ordered the executions of 31.

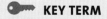 **KEY TERM**

OVRA Fascist secret police.

Anti-Fascist opposition

Faced with such an array of repressive measures, it was not surprising that opposition within Italy was disorganised and ineffective. Only a small number of sizeable networks of anti-Fascists existed within the country. There were the Communists who tried to maintain an underground party organisation within Italy. They published their own newspaper, *L'Unità*, and distributed anti-Fascist propaganda leaflets. It is estimated that they could count on no more than 7000 active supporters, who were consistently harried by the regime. The prominent Marxist writer and founder of *L'Unità*, Antonio Gramsci, was sentenced to twenty years' imprisonment in 1927. His health destroyed, he died in 1937.

A second group was named Justice and Liberty. It was founded by Carlo Roselli, who had escaped from a Fascist prison in 1929 and settled in Paris. He hoped to create an alliance between Socialists and Liberals opposed to the regime. From Paris, Justice and Liberty kept the international press informed about the repression and injustice within Italy, and smuggled leaflets to its supporters inside the country. In turn, these supporters tried to spread anti-Fascist propaganda in Italian cities. Like the Communists, Justice and Liberty had only a few thousand supporters. Despite the movement's small scale it still attracted the full attention of the Fascist state: Roselli was murdered in 1937 by Fascists acting on instructions from the government in Rome.

A significant reason for the limited impact of opposition groups was that they squabbled among themselves and failed to form a common anti-Fascist front. For example, Italian exiles led by the Socialist Pietro Nenni formed the *Concentrazione Antifascista* in Paris in 1927. They produced a weekly newspaper called *La Libertá*. However, internal disputes and the refusal of Communist anti-Fascists to co-operate led to its dissolution in 1934.

Encouraging co-operation with fascism

The lack of significant opposition within Italy was certainly a reflection of the strength of the regime's repressive machinery, but it was also proof that the dictator knew how to manipulate his subjects. Those Liberals and *Popolari* who had grown disillusioned with fascism were usually left alone, providing they did not dare to criticise the regime openly. From time to time, a few individuals would be assaulted by the OVRA or the militia simply to remind others that conformity was the safest option.

Journalists and intellectuals who might have been expected vigorously to oppose a system that so enthusiastically suppressed individual freedoms were encouraged to join that system. Loyal journalists received extra pay in the form of government grants. Given the easy rewards and the apparent impossibility of publishing critical material, most writers settled for the role of party hack or else avoided political journalism altogether. Mussolini offered similar inducements to academics and intellectuals. For example, Marconi, the inventor of radio, was awarded the title of marquis, while D'Annunzio, of Fiume fame (page 26), received a generous pension and a palatial villa for his services to fascism. The *Duce* used his newly created Fascist Academy to offer plum jobs and fat salaries to leading professors. Few could resist such temptations, particularly when they were well aware that any sign of dissent would lead to their immediate dismissal.

Other professions were regulated by the regime. Teachers had to join a Fascist Teachers' Association in order to keep their jobs, while musicians were required to join a National Fascist Union of Musicians. A small number did resist – the famous conductor, Toscanini, went into exile in 1929 – but the great majority joined.

The regime also used these tactics of fear and self-interest to deter opposition from the general public. Party membership became increasingly necessary for those seeking work or promotion in the public sector. Dissent could mean dismissal and persistent offenders might even be sent to some poor remote southern hill-town to serve a sentence of internal exile.

Impact of propaganda on support for fascism

The regime was determined not only to deter opposition but also to build up popular support. Extreme propaganda was its principal weapon. This propaganda, of which the cult of the *Duce* was a very important part, stressed the genius of Mussolini, the impossibility of opposition and the supposed achievements of fascism.

Much was heard of Fascist successes in foreign policy, such as Yugoslavia's cession of Fiume to Italy (page 118). Italians were informed that foreigners were loud in their admiration for the *Duce* and his policies. They were promised that Italy under Fascist rule would regain the greatness it had known under ancient Rome and during the Renaissance. Mussolini hoped to capture the imagination of the public and to win their commitment to the transformation of Italians into an energetic, disciplined, obedient and warlike people. Parades, processions, the press and education were all used in an attempt to convey the message that the present was one of the great moments in Italian history and that Italians had a duty to participate in this adventure.

It is uncertain how many Italians were fully convinced by this incessant propaganda – probably relatively few – but it appears that the *Duce* was personally very popular. For most Italians, at least until the late 1930s, the dictator was producing stability at home and success abroad. His regime seemed to be providing moderate prosperity without intruding too far into private lives and without making excessive demands on the public, while foreign adventures, as in Ethiopia, excited patriotic interest. Given this record, there seemed to be little need for opposition and, in any case, Italians were well aware that opposition was likely to prove highly dangerous.

Concentration camps

It is significant that although the regime set up prison camps on remote, inhospitable islands such as Lipari and Lampedusa, off the Italian mainland, these were on a much smaller scale than the Nazis' concentration camps for political dissidents. While several hundred thousand opponents of the Nazis were imprisoned, Italian camps probably held fewer than 5000 prisoners. Conditions were tough, and there was torture. However, the brutality was not systematic and was far less than that experienced by the opponents of the Nazis in Germany. In addition to prison camps, a further 12,000 opponents of fascism were sentenced to *confino*, a period of detention or house arrest in isolated southern villages far from their home towns.

Mussolini might occasionally advocate vicious punishments for those who did actively oppose him but, in practice, Italian fascism preferred to cajole its subjects into outward conformity, rather than ruthlessly to root out potential dissenters.

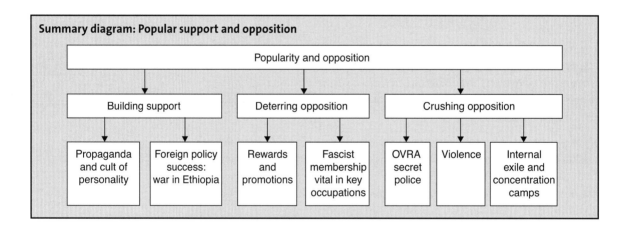

Summary diagram: Popular support and opposition

 Key debate

▶ *How popular was Mussolini's Fascist regime?*

Contemporary views on the popularity of the dictatorship were mixed. Many foreign journalists were impressed by the apparently spontaneous enthusiasm displayed at Fascist rallies and believed the *Duce* to be extremely popular. Italian anti-Fascist exiles, on the other hand, stressed the brutal, repressive aspects of the regime, and argued that only fear deterred widespread opposition.

Historians have generally agreed that repression was not the only reason for the absence of effective opposition to fascism, but there is still debate over the popularity of the regime. The prominent Italian historian Renzo De Felice, writing in the early 1970s, argued that Mussolini was genuinely popular, particularly in the years 1929–36 and culminating with the victory over Ethiopia (page 121), which was Mussolini's 'political masterpiece and greatest success'. The popular consensus in favour of Mussolini lasted until the ill-fated invasion of Greece in 1940 (page 142). This is a highly contentious claim but is supported by a recent British biographer of Mussolini (see Extract 1).

EXTRACT 1

From Nicholas Farrell, *Mussolini: A New Life*, Phoenix, 2004, pp. 215–16.

Renzo de Felice caused howls of protest in 1974 … a bomb was even thrown at his house. All he had claimed was that by the beginning of the 1930s the majority of Italians had accepted Fascism and that this acceptance could not be explained as resulting from fear …

The truth is that a critical mass of people in Italy did actively support Fascism and an even larger proportion, a clear majority, did actively support Mussolini … Writing in 1946, the American journalist Herbert Matthews said, 'The Duce truly did have in those years an enormous popular consensus'. Luigi Barzini wrote 'His success seemed incredible. He was more popular in Italy than anyone had ever been and probably will ever be'.

Farrell also cites the opinion of George Ward Price, the *Daily Mail*'s correspondent in Rome in 1937, that 'the overwhelming majority of Italians enthusiastically supported Mussolini' and highlights the fact that Mussolini during 1936–7 received over 30,000 supportive letters each month from ordinary Italians.

The prominent academic R.J.B. Bosworth, writing in 2006, is much more sceptical of the depth and sincerity of public support, pointing out that most of these letters were from Italians seeking a job or promotion or some other favour from the *Duce* (see Extract 2).

EXTRACT 2

From R.J.B. Bosworth, *Mussolini's Italy*, Penguin, 2006, pp. 5, 333, 571–2.

the dictatorship remained a nervous regime … unconvinced that it had swept away all opposition … When, in the middle of the 1930s, Fascism … had won the consent, however passive of its subjects, still Mussolini neurotically insisted on daily conversations with his Chief of police. The leader quizzed his official obsessively about the state of public opinion, asking if traces of anti-Fascism had surfaced.

The commitment of the Italian masses to Fascism … remained highly doubtful … Italians were more suspicious than believing. Italians had not become the fervent [followers] and warriors of a new political faith. Instead, they had found solace in the understanding that, in a dictatorship such as Benito Mussolini's, to endure was all.

Historian Donald Sassoon presents a third interpretation in Extract 3.

EXTRACT 3

From Donald Sassoon, *Mussolini and the Rise of Fascism*, HarperCollins, 2007, p. 142.

To [many Italians] Mussolini's Italy was no worse than what had preceded it. Life continued to be easy or difficult, but politics had little to do with it. What does it matter if one can longer vote, if no visible difference ensues? What does it matter if the press is muzzled, if one never reads a newspaper? At least now there was a leader telling them to be proud of being Italian, and promising a radiant future. Only when the regime led the country into a new war, and demanded sacrifices for which they had not been prepared, did the majority of Italians turn against Fascism.

? How far do the historians quoted in Extracts 1–3 agree or differ in their interpretation of public support for fascism?

Chapter summary

Mussolini was determined to sweep away parliamentary government and establish a personal dictatorship. He was not prepared to share power with other Fascist leaders and rejected pressure from those Fascist radicals who wanted to see the party take over every aspect of the Italian state. In fact, Mussolini was willing to allow the traditional elites – the armed forces, the civil service, the Church and industrialists – to retain some influence, providing they gave him their support and did not challenge his authority. Mussolini wielded enormous power but Fascist government was never efficient.

There was relatively little active opposition to fascism until Italy entered the Second World War in 1940, but there remains considerable debate on whether there was genuine enthusiasm for the regime or simply resigned, passive acceptance.

Refresher questions

Use these questions to remind yourself of the key material covered in this chapter.

1 What was meant by 'personal dictatorship'?

2 What was the purpose of the cult of personality?

3 How effective was the cult of personality?

4 What influence did the King, ministers and parliament have in the dictatorship?

5 How did Mussolini attempt to win the support of key groups in the Italian state?

6 How did Mussolini control the Fascist Party?

7 How efficient was Fascist government?

8 How much opposition was there to the Fascist regime?

9 How popular was Mussolini's regime?

Question practice

ESSAY QUESTIONS

1 'Mussolini was all-powerful in Italy in the years 1926–40.' Assess the validity of this view.

2 'Co-operation with the traditional Italian elites was a key feature of Mussolini's dictatorship.' Assess the validity of this view.

3 To what extent did the Fascist Party control the Italian state in 1925–40?

4 How significant was the cult of personality in generating support for Mussolini's regime in 1925–40?

5 'Opposition posed little threat to Mussolini's dictatorship in the years 1926–40.' How far do you agree?

6 Which of the following proved more effective in preventing opposition to the Fascist regime in the years 1926–40? i) The propaganda image of the *Duce*. ii) Fascist repression. Explain your answer with reference to both i) and ii).

7 How far did fascism command widespread popular support in the years 1925–40?

INTERPRETATION QUESTIONS

1 Read the interpretation and then answer the question that follows. 'The truth is that a critical mass of people in Italy did actively support fascism.' (From Nicholas Farrell, *Mussolini: A New Life*, Phoenix, 2004, pp. 215–16.) Evaluate the strengths and weaknesses of this interpretation, making reference to other interpretations that you have studied.

2 Read the interpretation and then answer the question that follows. 'The new system was a personal dictatorship under Mussolini.' (From S. Payne, *History of Fascism*, UCL Press, 1995, p. 116.) Evaluate the strengths and weaknesses of this interpretation, making reference to other interpretations that you have studied.

SOURCE ANALYSIS QUESTIONS

1 How far could the historian make use of Sources 1 and 2 (page 82) together to investigate the extent of popular support for Mussolini's regime? Explain your answer, using both sources, the information given about them and your own knowledge of the historical context.

2 With reference to Sources 1, 2 and 3 (page 82), and your understanding of the historical context, assess the value of these sources to a historian studying the extent of opposition to the Fascist regime.

SOURCE 1

From Winston Churchill on a visit to Italy in 1927, as quoted in *The Times* newspaper. Churchill was British chancellor of the exchequer at the time.

I could not help being charmed, like so many people have been, by Mussolini's gentle and simple bearing and by his calm and detached pose in spite of so many burdens and dangers. Anyone could see that he thought of nothing but the lasting good, as he understood it, of the Italian people … It was quite absurd to suggest that the Italian government does not stand upon a popular basis or that it is not upheld by the active and practical assent of the great masses. If I had been an Italian I should have been wholeheartedly with you … in your triumphal struggle against … Communism.

SOURCE 2

Ignazio Silone, an exiled Socialist writer, in his 1936 novel *Bread and Wine*. Quoted in J. Hite and C. Hinton, *Fascist Italy*, John Murray, 1998, p. 101.

It is well known that the police have their informers in every section of every big factory, in every bank, in every office. In every block of flats the porter is an informer for the police. This state of affairs spreads suspicion and distrust throughout all classes of the population. On this degradation of man into a frightened animal, who quivers with fear and hates his neighbour in his fear, and watches and betrays him, sells him and then lives in fear of discovery, the dictatorship is based. The real organisation on which the system is based is the secret manipulation of fear.

SOURCE 3

Adapted from Eric Lamet, *A Child in Confino*, Adams Media Corporation, 2010. Lamet and his mother were Jews sent by Mussolini's regime into internal exile (*confino*) in a remote village in southern Italy, during the early years of the Second World War.

The local official, Don Pepe, said to mother, 'I'm supposed to make certain you follow all the rules set by those imbeciles in Rome. They also want me to read all the mail you fine people receive every day. Can you imagine? I should read all the mail of so many people. Only idiots can think up such foolish regulations.' It was obvious that he relished poking fun at the Fascist government.

Mother said, 'How many prisoners are here?'

'About seventy', Don Pepe responded. He handed Mother the list of rules for prisoners and, from his expression of disgust, even I could tell he was not about to enforce any of them. 'But you will have to report to the local police twice daily', he added with a wink.

CHAPTER 6

Mussolini and the economy 1922–40

Mussolini claimed that his economic policy would transform the organisation of the Italian economy and prepare the nation for war. This chapter examines the extent to which the *Duce* achieved his aims, focusing principally on:

★ Mussolini's aims

★ The impact of Fascist policies on Italian industry

★ The impact of Fascist policies on Italian agriculture

The key debate on *page 93* of this chapter asks the question: How far did fascism improve the Italian economy?

Key dates

1925	Vidoni Palace Pact banned independent trade unions Start of the 'battle for grain'	1927	Revaluation of the lira damaged Italian economy
1926	Abolition of right to strike Ministry of Corporations set up; start of corporate state experiment	1929	Start of global economic depression
		1936	Mussolini increased drive for economic autarky

1 Mussolini's aims

▶ *In what ways was Mussolini trying to transform the Italian economy?*

Mussolini, like Hitler, was no economist. He had little knowledge of, or interest in, the workings of the economy and on coming to power had no coherent programme of reform. Mussolini was, however, determined to hang on to power and therefore, in his early years in office, he adopted economic policies that would make his position secure. As the 1920s progressed, Mussolini became more ambitious and increasingly attracted to the idea of an economic transformation of Italy. He proclaimed the world's first 'corporate state', supposedly a radically new way of organising and running a nation's economy, different from and superior to both the capitalist economies of Britain and the USA and the Communist economy of the USSR.

By the mid-1930s, Mussolini's priorities had begun to change again. His war in Ethiopia (see page 121) and his ever closer association with Nazi Germany (see page 125) convinced him that a new type of economic transformation was vital. Fascist Italy would need an economy capable of building and maintaining a modern war machine. In a major war, foreign imports of raw materials or food might be cut off, crippling the war effort. Italy, Mussolini declared, must strive for **autarky**: economic self-sufficiency. Mussolini's preoccupations first with the corporate state and then with autarky meant that the country's 'old problems' – industrial underdevelopment, rural poverty, the north–south divide and illiteracy – were largely ignored. They were only tackled with any determination if they were obstacles to the achievement of the *Duce*'s principal aims.

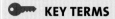

KEY TERMS

Autarky Economic self-sufficiency allowing a country to operate without importing food or other key materials from other countries.

Revaluation Changing the value of a currency compared to another country's currency. (The Fascist government tried to increase the value of the lira against other countries' currencies.)

 2 # The impact of Fascist policies on Italian industry

▶ *What were the consequences of the 'battle for the lira'?*
▶ *How far did the corporate state transform the Italian economy?*
▶ *How well prepared for war was Italian industry?*

Mussolini was lucky enough to come to power just as Italian industry was beginning a boom period. The economic climate throughout Europe was improving and many Italian companies were able to sell their products abroad with ease. Indeed, exports, particularly of cars, textiles and agricultural produce, doubled in the period 1922–5.

Policies 1922–7

Mussolini's government claimed the credit for increasing company profits and attempted to win over the support of industrialists by appointing an economics professor, Alberto de Stefani, as treasury minister. De Stefani's economic policy was traditional and reassuring to industrialists because it limited government spending, which helped to fight inflation. He also reduced state intervention in industry, for example, the telephone network was taken out of government control and handed back to private companies. Taxes levied on industries that had made huge profits from government contracts during the First World War were either reduced or abandoned. Industrialists were also pleased by the outlawing of Socialist and Catholic trade unions by the Vidoni Palace Pact of 1925 (see page 70).

'Battle for the lira'

After 1925, however, Mussolini began to take less notice of business interests. The dismissal of de Stefani and the **revaluation** of the Italian currency were two early but important examples of this. Revaluation was particularly significant. By 1926 the boom was coming to an end and the exchange rate of the lira was falling against other currencies. The exchange rate slipped to around 150 lire to the pound, a rate Mussolini that found unacceptable. Announcing his 'battle for the lira' he declared:

> The Fascist regime is ready to make the sacrifices needed, so that our lira, which is itself a symbol of our nation, our wealth, our efforts, our strength, our sacrifices, our tears, our blood, is and will be defended.

To emphasise his point that his strong, vibrant country should have a strong, vibrant currency he decided to try to set a new rate of exchange of 90 lire to the British pound in December 1927. This decision, restoring the value of the lira to its value in October 1922, the month of his appointment as prime minister, increased Mussolini's prestige both with the Italian public and with foreign bankers, who saw the policy as a way of restricting government spending. The *Duce* had achieved the propaganda victory he desired, but the effects on the Italian economy were far from beneficial. At a stroke, foreign buyers found Italian goods nearly twice as expensive, and it was not surprising that Italian export industries, particularly textiles, went into depression. Unemployment trebled in the years 1926–8. Even Fiat, the huge vehicle manufacturer based in Turin, was exporting fewer cars in the late 1930s than it had done in the early 1920s.

The revaluation of the lira should have helped the Italian consumer because imports of foods and other products from abroad should have become cheaper. However, the *Duce* prevented this by placing high **tariffs** on many foreign imports. The only winners in economic terms were those industries such as steel, armaments and shipbuilding that needed large supplies of cheap tariff-free imported raw materials. It was these heavy industries that would be promoted throughout Fascist rule. They made healthy profits from the protected domestic market while export industries were neglected.

Corporate state: the theory

At first, the workers benefited from the economic revival of the early 1920s. Unemployment fell and de Stefani's policies curbed inflation. Admittedly, the years 1925 and 1926 saw the banning of independent trade unions and the abolition of the right to strike, but Mussolini claimed to be about to transform the Italian economy. By 1926 he was committed to creating a **corporate state**, a supposedly revolutionary method of running an economy. Corporations would be set up for each sector of industry and within each corporation there would be employers and Fascist trade unions to represent the workers. Each corporation would organise production, pay and working conditions in its own industry. If employers and Fascist trade unions could not agree then they would go to a labour court, administered by the new Ministry of Corporations, where the dispute would be sorted out quickly and amicably.

 KEY TERMS

Tariffs Taxes placed on imports of foreign products.

Corporate state Mussolini's model for the economy whereby every industry would be part of a Fascist-led corporation that would sort out disputes between workers and management, and help to organise production, pay and conditions.

The Fascist regime claimed that this system would see employers and workers co-operating to maximise production for the good of the nation. Unlike Britain and France, there would be no bitter industrial disputes that led to strikes and class conflict. Unlike Communist Russia, there would still be a role for businessmen whose energy and entrepreneurship would help industries to prosper.

Corporate state: the reality

At first it did appear that the Fascist trade unions might provide a real say for workers in the running of their industries, but rivalries within the Fascist Party, and Mussolini's reluctance to alienate big business interests soon destroyed any such hopes. Rossoni, the head of the Fascist trade union movement, certainly envisaged a major role for his unions but he was opposed by the employers' organisation. *Confindustria* (see page 54) disliked all kinds of trade unions and was determined to ensure that businessmen kept control of their industries. In the middle was the Ministry of Corporations, headed by the Fascist Giuseppe Bottai. He distrusted Rossoni, saw little role for the unions, and wanted to see corporations dominated by a partnership of employers and technical experts from his own ministry. This, he hoped, would be the best way to maximise industrial production. All sides now looked to the *Duce* to clarify his vision of the corporate state.

In 1927 Mussolini came down on the side of Bottai and *Confindustria*: Bottai was charged with the task of writing a 'Labour Charter' setting out the rights of workers. When this charter was finally produced it posed no threat to the employers: private ownership of businesses was declared the most efficient method of running an economy and, as for workers' rights, employers might but were not obliged to provide annual paid holidays. Employers were also given the power to alter working hours and night shifts without any real consultation.

Rossoni's radical influence was reduced still further in 1928 when his single confederation of Fascist trade unions was split into six smaller federations and his followers in these federations were removed from their posts.

Three years after its creation in 1926, the Ministry of Corporations claimed success. The corporate state was ushering in a new economic era and had allegedly removed all class conflict in industry. By 1934 there were 22 corporations covering nearly every area of the economy and with the apparent ability to influence every aspect of industry. The reality, however, was quite different. Workers were unable to choose their own union representatives in their corporation, and instead had Fascist nominees foisted on them. These Fascist officials tended to side with the employers' representatives over the key issues of wages and working conditions. Only on issues such as sick pay for workers, and the belated introduction of paid national holidays in 1938, did the corporations further workers' interests. Industrialists, on the other hand, were allowed to keep their own non-Fascist employers' organisations, and largely ignored the very existence of these corporations. That regulations issued by corporations were only advisory meant that employers maintained their power and independence.

In truth, the 'corporative revolution' never materialised. Conflict between employer and employee was not solved, only suppressed, and the corporations never achieved the pivotal role in the state and the economy envisaged by the *Duce*. Although parliament itself was replaced by the Chamber of Fasces and Corporations in 1939, this meant nothing. Parliament had long since lost any power and the new Chamber was equally impotent.

Economic depression

The Wall Street Crash in the USA in 1929 caused a global economic **depression** that Italy did not escape. A large number of companies collapsed and car production fell by 50 per cent. From under half a million in 1928, unemployment had risen to 2 million by 1933.

The democratic governments of western Europe and the USA were reluctant to intervene to help the private sector out of its difficulties as their traditional economic philosophy of *laissez-faire* regarded such actions as reckless: raising the money to help struggling industries might plunge government into serious debt. The Italian Fascist state had no such worries. It introduced public works schemes, notably the building of motorways and hydroelectric power plants, which put the unemployed back to work. This was important because it significantly increased the amount of money in circulation which, in turn, stimulated demand and created more jobs. The state also did much to avoid the banking collapse which affected the USA and Germany in particular. Banks had lent money to industry, but many companies could no longer meet the repayments on their loans. The banks therefore found themselves without enough money to pay their investors. The Fascist government simply stepped in and bailed out the banks.

A result of this intervention was the creation of the Institute for Industrial Reconstruction (IRI) in January 1933. Many banks had major shareholdings in Italian companies and when these banks were bailed out of their financial troubles, IRI took control of these shares. The Italian state, in the guise of IRI, thus became the major shareholder and therefore the effective owner of many top Italian companies. IRI also took over from the banks the responsibility for providing loans for Italian industry. In addition, it attempted to promote the latest managerial techniques, with some success.

The government's measures may have cost the taxpayer a great deal of money, but they did enable Italy to weather the depression a little better than its democratic neighbours. Indeed, Mussolini was delighted to hear his admirers claim that President Roosevelt had copied the *Duce*'s example when drawing up his 'New Deal', the USA's attempt to combat unemployment and business failures.

 **KEY TERM**

Depression A period of economic stagnation that began in the USA and affected all European industrialised countries for most of the 1930s.

Preparing for war

Mussolini's economic policies had never been designed simply to increase the wealth of the country or the prosperity of the ordinary Italian, and this became very apparent by the mid-1930s. As the dictator became increasingly preoccupied with foreign affairs, living standards and the general welfare of the economy suffered. He believed that war, either in Europe or to further his African Empire, was almost inevitable and that Italy must be prepared. The armaments industries must be promoted, and Italy's economy must become self-sufficient. Italy should be an autarky, able to supply itself with all the food and material needed to fight a modern war.

The **economic sanctions** imposed by the **League of Nations** after Italy's invasion of Ethiopia in 1935 had banned trade with Italy in certain goods such as grain, steel and textiles. These sanctions seemed to prove Mussolini's point that there must be no reliance on imports.

Mussolini therefore encouraged heavy industries such as steel, chemicals and shipbuilding by placing large government contracts. State control was expanded to the point where 80 per cent of shipbuilding and 50 per cent of steel production was directed by the government. Economies of scale were looked for and the regime allowed major companies to merge into near-monopoly organisations. Fiat, for instance, controlled car manufacturing, while Pirelli dominated rubber, and Montecatini chemicals. Exports, as usual, took low priority.

The limits of autarky

Despite all the efforts, the Italian economy was still far from self-sufficient when the *Duce* joined the Second World War in 1940. Key materials such as oil, and coal and iron ore for the making of steel, still had to be imported in very large quantities. Italy was unable to match its enemies' levels of production and could not even replace its losses in shipping and aircraft. The drive for autarky in fact only succeeded in worsening Italy's financial difficulties. The government was spending huge sums on contracts related to the autarkic and closely related rearmament programme and also had to fund expensive military adventures in Ethiopia and Spain (see page 126). Ever aware of the need to maintain popularity, the regime did not want to bring in major tax increases and, consequently, government expenditure greatly exceeded its income by the late 1930s. The remedy for these massive government deficits was either swingeing cuts in military expenditure or very significant reductions in living standards. Typically, Mussolini refused to recognise the seriousness of the economic situation and the problem remained unsolved when Italy entered the Second World War.

KEY TERMS

Economic sanctions
The banning of trade with an aggressor nation in an attempt to force that country to change its policy.

League of Nations
International organisation of over 100 countries created after the First World War and designed to help to prevent wars and end disputes between countries.

Impact of industrial policy on living standards

According to the *Duce*, under the corporate state, conflict between workers and bosses would end, and workers would no longer be 'exploited' and would gain greater prosperity and increased respect within society. Open conflict between employers and workers did indeed decline, but only because free trade unions were banned and strikes ruled illegal. As for greater prosperity, many industrial workers actually suffered a serious decline in their standards of living.

As the economic revival petered out in the late 1920s, industry responded with wage cuts. In the early 1930s some of these wage cuts were offset by falling prices in the shops, but, from the mid-1930s, prices began to rise steeply as Mussolini's drive for autarky pushed up the cost of imported goods. Overall, it is estimated that during the period 1925–38 real wages for the Italian worker fell by over ten per cent. Falling consumption of meat, fruit and vegetables showed the impact of declining incomes. At the same time, unemployment began to rise, despite the public works programmes, and totalled some 2 million by 1933. This was a figure close to that of Britain, after allowing for the difference in populations.

The middle classes were far less likely to suffer from unemployment. The number of government employees virtually doubled to a million during the Fascist period and these people were not made redundant during the depression. Many state employees were in traditional jobs such as teaching, but the most explosive growth took place in the new Fascist organisations, principally the Ministry for Corporations, but also the *Dopolavoro* (see page 109), which organised leisure activities for workers. These middle-class office workers did suffer wage cuts during the 1930s but it was noticeable that these cuts were less than those for industrial workers.

That fascism failed to produce real rises in living standards for the mass of Italian workers did not unduly concern the *Duce*. Instead, by December 1930, Mussolini was saying: 'fortunately the Italian people were not accustomed to eat much and therefore feel the privation less than others'. And, by 1936, he was arguing: 'We must rid our minds of the idea that what we have called the days of prosperity may return. We are probably moving toward a period when humanity will exist on a lower standard of living.'

Mussolini had never really been committed to raising the standard of living of ordinary Italians and viewed economic hardship as by no means a bad thing for his people. Economic hardship would create harder, tougher Italians dismissive of a soft 'bourgeois' lifestyle!

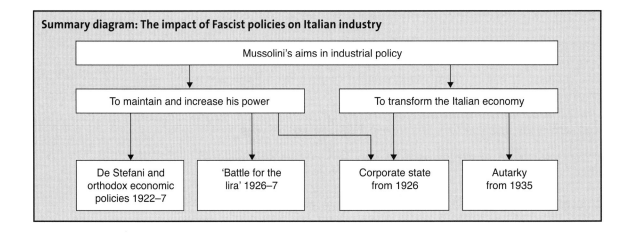

Summary diagram: The impact of Fascist policies on Italian industry

Mussolini's aims in industrial policy

To maintain and increase his power

To transform the Italian economy

De Stefani and orthodox economic policies 1922–7

'Battle for the lira' 1926–7

Corporate state from 1926

Autarky from 1935

③ The impact of Fascist policies on Italian agriculture

▶ *How successful were Mussolini's agricultural policies?*

▶ *How did agricultural workers fare under fascism?*

Mussolini did not concern himself with the underlying problems of Italian agriculture – the existence of a sizeable class of poor, land-hungry peasants and the use of backward, inefficient farming methods. Instead, as with industry, he occupied himself with projects that would either increase his personal power and prestige, or supposedly help Italy to become a self-sufficient state in case of war. The dictator's first major scheme was the '**battle for grain**'.

The 'battle for grain'

The 'battle for grain' began in 1925 and was an attempt to promote Fascist power and national self-sufficiency. Traditionally, Italy had needed to import large quantities of grain in order to feed its people. Mussolini saw this as a grave weakness, as in time of war supplies could be cut off and the country would face starvation. A campaign to increase grain production dramatically would solve this problem and would also illustrate to the world just how dynamic the new Fascist state was. Consequently, the government offered grants to enable farmers to buy tractors, fertiliser and other machinery necessary for wheat production. Free advice was made available on the latest, efficient farming techniques. Farmers were also guaranteed a high price for the grain they produced.

The incentives worked and the average harvest rose from 5.5 million tonnes per year in the early 1920s to over 7 million tonnes ten years later. Grain imports declined sharply, dropping by 75 per cent in the period 1925–35. The 'battle for

KEY TERM

Battle for grain Fascism's attempt to make Italy self-sufficient in the production of grain, and thus bread.

SOURCE A

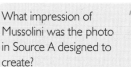

What impression of Mussolini was the photo in Source A designed to create?

Mussolini encouraging the harvesters in the 1930s.

grain' appeared to be a resounding success and Mussolini claimed the credit. He ensured that press photographers were on hand to record him visiting farms and helping out with the harvest. Not only was the *Duce* a genius for conceiving the 'battle for grain', he was also prepared to get his hands dirty in the fields – a true leader of his people. Appearances, however, were deceptive.

The 'battle for grain' certainly had dramatically increased production and helped farmers, but there had been a large price to be paid. First, much of the land in the central and southern regions that had been turned over to wheat was unsuitable for such a crop. The soil conditions and hotter, drier climate were better suited to the growing of citrus fruits or the production of wine and olive oil. The result was that these traditional agricultural exports declined.

Land reclamation

Fascism's second major initiative, and an equally highly publicised one, was land reclamation and improvement. Previous governments had made a start here, providing money to drain or irrigate farmland. Mussolini simply expanded these schemes. The Pontine marshes, only 50 kilometres from Rome, and thus easily reached by foreign journalists, were the showpiece. These malarial swamps were drained and a network of small farms was set up, owned by ex-servicemen. Overall, land reclamation was a success since it improved public health and provided thousands of jobs during the depression. The amount of land reclaimed was, however, very limited.

Impact of agricultural policy on living standards

Agricultural workers suffered even heavier wage cuts than industrial workers during the 1930s. In the past, a way out of this poverty had been emigration. In the first two decades of the century an average of 200,000 Italians, mainly southerners, had emigrated to the USA each year. From 1920, however, the USA decided to stop virtually all further immigration. With this escape route from rural poverty closed, more Italians left the countryside for the towns and cities to find work and a better standard of living. Up to half a million people left the land in the 1920s and 1930s, while between 1921 and 1941 the population of Rome doubled. And this was despite the fact that Mussolini tried to prevent all further migration.

Mussolini's resistance to migration into the cities was the result of his proclaimed love for the countryside and his desire to 'ruralise' Italy, creating a vigorous class of prosperous peasants devoted to fascism. However, his government did nothing to bring this about. In fact, his policies brought much more benefit to large landowners than to poor and landless peasants. Such peasants needed enough land to support their families: a law to break up big estates and to distribute them to the peasants had been introduced into parliament in 1922, but Mussolini quietly dropped the policy for fear of offending the great landowners, his political supporters.

The failure to break up the great landed estates only cemented the economic underdevelopment and poverty of the south. The gap between an industrialising north and a rural south had grown wider under the Liberal governments before the First World War, but with Fascist neglect it grew wider still. The fact that Mussolini visited the poverty-stricken island of Sicily only once after 1924 perhaps indicates a recognition of his own regime's failure towards the south. That Italy still lay eighteenth in a table of European states as regards the daily calorie intake of its people, with the lowest Italian figures recorded in the south, provided statistical proof of fascism's failure to tackle rural poverty.

SOURCE B

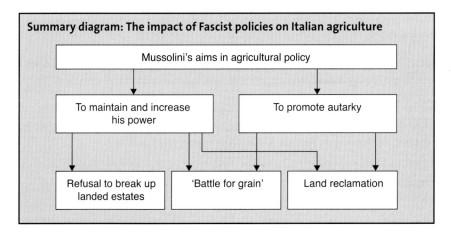

Study Source B. In what ways would this photograph promote the Fascist regime?

Mussolini cutting the first sod of the new city of Aprilla on the former Pontine marshes in 1936.

Summary diagram: The impact of Fascist policies on Italian agriculture

Mussolini's aims in agricultural policy

To maintain and increase his power

To promote autarky

Refusal to break up landed estates

'Battle for grain'

Land reclamation

④ Key debate

▶ *How far did fascism improve the Italian economy?*

During the 1920s and 1930s many foreign journalists were impressed by fascism's 'battle for grain', the land reclamation schemes, and the claims that the Italian economy was being modernised – summed up in the phrase **'Mussolini made the trains run on time'**. Newspapers such as Britain's *Financial Times* were intrigued by the idea of a corporate state. A number of modern historians still argue that fascism did much to improve the economy.

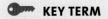 **KEY TERM**

'Mussolini made the trains run on time' This phrase was coined by foreign journalists to suggest that the Fascist regime had somehow improved the efficiency of Italian industries.

EXTRACT 1

From Nicholas Farrell, *Mussolini: A New Life*, Phoenix, 2004, pp. 190–1, 234–5.

What was undoubtedly a significant achievement of Fascism: a vast public works programme launched in 1928 whose crowning glory was the draining of the malaria infested Pontine Marshes … which made millions of hectares of unusable land farmable.

In addition, the fascists introduced electrification on 2100 km of Italy's railway network … Mussolini not only made the trains run in time but he made them run faster – halving the journey time between Rome and Sicily. And the programme included the construction of thousands of kilometres of roads and Europe's first motorway. The Fascists would later boast that in ten years they spent more on public works than the liberal regime in sixty years.

By 1938, total Italian production had increased by 154% since 1913, compared with 150% in Germany and 109% in France … The average real wage index shows that matters, though not good, were not that bad: 100 in 1913, 123 in 1922, 121 in 1928, and 125 in 1934.

Spencer DiScalia, writing in *Italy: From Revolution to Republic* (1995), also emphasises the positive effects of Fascist policies, arguing that they 'stimulated modern industries such as electricity, steel, engineering, chemicals … Italy's profile began to resemble that of modern European countries to a greater degree than in the past'.

Most modern historians do concede that some major industries such as vehicles and shipbuilding did expand and modernise, but are much more critical of Fascist economic policy.

EXTRACT 2

From E. Tannenbaum, *Fascism in Italy*, Allen Lane, 1973, p. 128.

Economically Fascism was a failure … the Corporative state did nothing to reduce class antagonisms or improve economic conditions … Italy became almost self sufficient in wheat production at the expense of the rest of her agriculture … Italy's performance [in the 1930s] was worse than that of any major country … The Fascist regime did more to hinder than to aid economic growth and modernisation … Even before the disastrous losses of the Second World War, growth in national income was retarded by restrictive cartels, discouragement of urban growth, the Battle of grain, the spread of autarky and promotion of war industry.

John Whittam in 1995 emphasises the negative impact of Fascist economic policies in the late 1930s in Extract 3.

EXTRACT 3

From John Whittam, *Fascist Italy*, Manchester University Press, 1995, p. 65.

Businessmen began to feel uneasy [with policies for autarky] … New taxes, price controls and import controls were regarded with dismay … Workers enjoyed some pay rises but they were still worse off than in the late 1920s, and their consumption of a whole range of foodstuffs had declined. The middle classes became more and more dependent on posts in the bureaucracy and in the dozens of party organisations which proliferated after 1925. One basic reason why over 2½ million men were PNF members by 1939 was because the party card was a passport to employment.

How far do the historians quoted in Extracts 1–3 agree or differ in their interpretation of the success of Fascist economic policies?

Where historians are united is in dismissing Fascist claims that the corporate state had transformed the economy and industrial relations. Alexander De Grand, a US professor of history writing in 2000, states that 'Fascism did not create its own unique economic system but rather grafted further statist [governmental] and bureaucratic tissue on the existing body of Italian capitalism.' Martin Blinkhorn, a British academic writing in 1984, adds that 'Corporativism in practice involved the thinly disguised exploitation and oppression of labour.'

Chapter summary

There were successes for Fascist economic policy, particularly in the improvements in rail and road transport, in land reclamation and in wheat production. Mussolini could also claim with some justification that his policies during the Depression had prevented banks and many companies from going bust. On the other hand, export industries suffered from the 'battle for the lira', the south remained neglected and impoverished, and the drive for autarky, spurred on by League of Nations sanctions in 1935–6, completely failed to make Italy ready for the Second World War.

Fascist economic policy created winners and losers. Industrialists and big landowners maintained their wealth and power while agricultural workers fared worst. Although industrial workers gained accident and sick pay, they lost their right to strike and suffered repeated wage cuts.

Perhaps Mussolini's greatest achievement as regards the economy was in generating propaganda opportunities for fascism both within Italy and abroad. The battles were promoted as examples of Fascist dynamism and energy, the building of the *autostrade* (motorways) illustrated how fascism was modernising Italy, and the corporate state was presented as a revolutionary solution to class conflict.

Refresher questions

Use these questions to remind yourself of the key material covered in this chapter.

1 What were Mussolini's aims in economic policy?

2 What was the Vidoni Palace Pact?

3 What was the 'battle for the lira'?

4 In what ways was the corporate state supposed to improve relations between workers and bosses?

5 What were the successes and failures of the corporate state?

6 How effective were Fascist policies in tackling the economic depression?

7 Why did Mussolini pursue the policy of autarky from 1935?

8 How successful was the 'battle for grain'?

9 What was the 'battle for the marshes'?

10 Who were the winners and losers in the Italian economy 1922–40?

 Question practice

ESSAY QUESTIONS

1 'Fascist economic policies failed to modernise the Italian economy in the years 1922–40.' Assess the validity of this view.

2 To what extent were Mussolini's economic policies a success in the years 1925–40?

3 How significant were Mussolini's economic policies in generating support for the regime in the years 1925–40?

4 'Fascist economic policies raised the standard of living of the ordinary Italian people.' How far do you agree?

5 Which of the following of Mussolini's economic policies proved more successful? i) Agrarian policies. ii) The corporate state. Explain your answer with reference to both i) and ii).

INTERPRETATION QUESTIONS

1 Read the interpretation and then answer the question that follows. 'The Fascist regime did more to hinder than to aid economic growth and modernisation.' (From E. Tannenbaum, *Fascism in Italy*, Allen Lane, 1973, p. 128.) Evaluate the strengths and limitations of this interpretation, making reference to other interpretations that you have studied.

2 Read the interpretation and then answer the question that follows. 'The battles for the lira and grain achieved more in propaganda terms than they did in reality.' (From N. Farrell, *Mussolini: A New Life*, Phoenix, 2004, p. 190.) Evaluate the strengths and limitations of this interpretation, making reference to other interpretations that you have studied.

SOURCE ANALYSIS QUESTIONS

1 Study Source 1. Why is Source 1 valuable to the historian for an enquiry into Mussolini's motives for creating the corporate state? Explain your answer using the source, the information given about it and your own knowledge of the historical context.

2 Study Source 2. How much weight do you give the evidence of Source 2 for an enquiry into why the Fascist regime created the corporate state? Explain your answer using the source, the information given about it and your own knowledge of the historical context.

3 How far could the historian make use of Sources 1 and 2 together to investigate Mussolini's motives for creating the corporate state? Explain your answer, using both sources, the information given about them and your own knowledge of the historical context.

4 With reference to Sources 1, 2 and 3 (page 98), and your understanding of the historical context, assess the value of these sources to a historian studying the achievements of the corporate state.

SOURCE I

From Benito Mussolini, *My Autobiography*, Charles Scribner's Sons, 1928, pp. 272, 275, 276, 278, 281. Here, Mussolini explains his motives for creating the corporate state.

Amid the innovations and experiments of the new Fascist civilization, there is one which is of interest to the whole world; it is the corporative organization of the state. …

It was necessary to emerge from the base [selfish] … habit of class competition and to put aside hates and enmities [anger]. After the war, especially following the subversive propaganda [of socialism], ill-will had reached perilous proportions. Agitations and strikes usually were accompanied by fights, with dead and wounded men as a result. …

The fact is that five years of harmonious work have transformed the economic life and, in consequence, the political and moral life of Italy. Let me add that the discipline that I have imposed is not a forced discipline … and does not obey the selfish interests of classes. Our discipline has one vision and one end – the welfare and good name of the Italian nation. …

Instead of the old [trade unions] we substituted Fascist corporations … We have abolished all … [the] old troubles and disorders and doubts that poisoned our national soul. We have given a rhythm, law and protection to Work; we have found in the co-operation of classes the [basis] for our future power. We do not waste time in brawls and strikes, which, … imperil our strength and the solidity of our economy.

SOURCE 2

Adapted from a lecture given by the exiled leader of the Italian Communist Party, Palmiro Togliatti, in Moscow, 1935.

The Fascist Party claims that Corporations were created to improve the living standards of the Italian people. This is a falsehood! Corporations were organised by the Fascist regime in Italy only after all democratic liberties had been denied. Corporations were only organised after the workers had been deprived of all representation, when all political parties had been destroyed, and when trade union freedom and freedom of the press had been crushed. Corporations were only created when every other possibility of expression for the Italian worker had been eliminated. Even if Corporations had some importance, they would not be able to do anything unless approved of by the Fascist Party.

SOURCE 3

Adapted from G. Seldes, *Sawdust Caesar*, Harper Press, 1936. George Seldes was an American journalist who was expelled from Italy in 1925 for writing an article which implicated Mussolini in the murder of Matteotti, the Socialist leader.

Although in turn the Battle for the Lira, the Battle for Grain, the Battle for Births, and many other triumphs have been announced by Mussolini as the 'outstanding event' of his reign, the Duce has also stated his greatest gift to civilisation, the accomplishment for which he will be remembered forever, is the Corporate State. Mussolini said that: 'the Corporate State's ultimate goal is the well-being of the Italian people'. The facts are, however, that Italy has one of the lowest standards of living in the civilized world, that this sorry state of affairs has been reached during the Fascist regime, and that it is one of the chief results of the Fascist economic programme.

CHAPTER 7

Life in Fascist Italy 1922–40

This chapter addresses the key question of how far Mussolini changed the lives of ordinary Italians and whether he transformed them into a nation of dedicated Fascists. His efforts to do so are studied under the following headings in this chapter:

★ Mussolini's aims

★ Fascism and the Catholic Church

★ Fascism and anti-Semitism

★ Fascism and women

★ Fascism and youth

★ Fascism and social life

★ How far did Mussolini achieve his aims in domestic policy?

Key dates

1923	Pope withdrew support for Catholic *Popolari* Party	1929	Lateran Agreements ended major dispute between Italian state and the Catholic Church
1925	Fascist leisure organisation, *Dopolavoro*, set up		Teachers forced to take an oath of loyalty
1926	ONB youth organisation created	1931	Fascist Teachers' Association set up
1927	Launch of the 'battle for births', designed to increase the Italian population	1938	Anti-Jewish racial laws introduced

1 Mussolini's aims

▶ *What was Mussolini's vision for Italian society?*

Mussolini's primary aim was to adopt policies that would help to secure his position as all-powerful *Duce* of Italy, but as the 1920s progressed he also revealed a desire to transform Italian society and even the Italian character. By the 1930s he expressed contempt for what he described as the 'bourgeois mentality' of many Italians, a mentality that stressed the importance of family, religion, local loyalties and a comfortable standard of living. Mussolini intended his new Italians to place fascism and the nation above these traditional loyalties.

They would be tough, disciplined, physically and psychologically conditioned for war, and obedient to their *Duce*. Fascist policies designed to create these new Italians would, however, begin to jeopardise Mussolini's support among both the public and powerful groups, such as the Church.

2 Fascism and the Catholic Church

▶ *Why did Mussolini want to improve relations with the Catholic Church?*

▶ *Why did the Lateran Agreements not end all conflict between fascism and the Church?*

Mussolini wanted to see fascism penetrate every aspect of Italian society, but he was neither systematic in his ideas nor prepared to force through policies that might make him unpopular. His realisation that fascism must compromise in order to secure support was particularly evident in his dealings with the Church.

Mussolini never lost the anti-religious attitudes of his youth, but he was aware that the Catholic Church occupied an important place in the lives of millions of Italians. He recognised that an accommodation with the Catholic Church could bring him great public support and increase the prestige of his regime abroad.

SOURCE A

Mussolini speaking to the Italian parliament in 1921, quoted in Bernardo Quaranta di San Severino, translator and editor, *Mussolini as Revealed in His Political Speeches (November 1914–August 1923)*, J.M. Dent & Sons, 1923, pp. 202–3.

I maintain that the Imperial and Latin tradition of Rome is represented to-day by Catholicism. … I advance this hypothesis, that if the Vatican should definitely renounce its temporal [earthly] ambitions [of political power and] furnish [Italy] with the necessary material help for the schools, churches, hospitals, etc., that a temporal power has at its disposal. Because the increase of Catholicism in the world, the addition of four hundred millions of men who from all quarters of the globe look towards Rome, is a source of pride and of special interest to us Italians.

> **?** What were Mussolini's motives in making the speech in Source A?

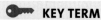 **KEY TERM**

Lateran Agreements
These comprised a treaty and a deal, known as a concordat, which officially ended the dispute about the role and status of the Catholic Church in the Italian state.

By the time he became prime minister in 1922, Mussolini was posing as an alternative to anti-Catholic Liberals and 'godless' Communists and Socialists. Restoring Catholic education in state schools and increasing government payments to priests secured the confidence of the Pope who, in 1923, withdrew his support for the *Popolari*, the Catholic political party. These moves neutralised, at least temporarily, the Church as a potential source of opposition. However, it did not mean that fascism had the active support of the Vatican – this would only come with the **Lateran Agreements** of 1929.

Lateran Agreements

The treaty and concordat (papal agreement) that comprised the Lateran Agreements officially ended the conflict between the Church and Italy that had existed since the foundation of the Italian kingdom some 60 years earlier. The Pope had resented the Italian state's seizure of his own territories of Rome and the Papal States, in central Italy. In the 1929 treaty, the Pope agreed to recognise the Italian state and its possession of Rome and the old Papal States. In return, the state recognised the Pope's control over the **Vatican City**, part of Rome but independent from the Italian state. The Pope also received financial compensation of £30 million for surrendering his claim to Rome.

The concordat established Catholicism as the state religion of Italy and outlined what this would mean in practice:

- The Pope could appoint all bishops, but the government could veto any politically suspect candidates.
- The state would pay the salaries of the clergy.
- Clergy could not belong to political parties.
- Religious education, of a Catholic nature, would be compulsory in state schools.
- There would be no divorce without the consent of the Church.
- Couples wishing to marry would no longer have to attend a civil ceremony in a register office – a Church service would now give full legal recognition to the marriage.

The Lateran Agreements signalled that Mussolini had given up any hope of removing the influence of Catholicism from Italian society. Nevertheless, he was very happy with the deal. Clerics could not become a focus of opposition and, more importantly, the Church would throw its support behind Mussolini as *Duce*.

While the Lateran Agreements were hailed as a great achievement, not all Italians were impressed.

KEY TERM

Vatican City The area of Rome, comprising St Peter's, the papal apartments and the offices of the papal bureaucracy, which was ruled directly by the Pope and was completely independent from the Italian state.

SOURCE B

An exiled intellectual, G.A. Borgese, writing in 1931, quoted in J. Hite and C. Hinton, *Fascist Italy*, John Murray, 1998, p. 177.

There was no reason why Pope and Duce *should not come together: no reason except in Christ; but Christianism was by no means the most decisive factor in Pope Ratti's mind. He was sure that he loved Italy; it is sure that he hated democracy and Socialism … the ruthless anti-Christianity of Fascism was nothing to him.*

The Church became [a collaborator with] atheistic tyranny, and tyranny rewarded it by making it supreme in … the family. Marriage and divorce became a monopoly of the Vatican, and the priest lent his hand to the [Fascist] in … the purpose of national violence and international anarchy. Over her new black shirt Italy donned her old black gown [clothes worn by Catholic clergy].

Why does Borgese in Source B dislike the agreement between fascism and the Catholic Church?

Tensions between fascism and the Catholic Church

Although the Lateran Agreements were hailed as a triumph by both Mussolini and the Pope, the 'love affair' between Catholicism and fascism was not a smooth one and it cooled as Mussolini tried to shape society into a more Fascist mould.

The first open dispute between Church and Mussolini's regime came in 1931 when the government attempted to suppress the Church-sponsored Catholic Action. This body provided a rival to fascism's own youth and leisure organisations and had 250,000 members. A compromise was reached banning Catholic Action youth groups from any political activities, but the Church remained determined to preserve its influence over the young. The Church made it clear that the Fascists must not attempt to suppress Catholic schools or interfere with the Catholic University of Milan and the Federation of Catholic University Students. The Church even had the confidence to declare the creed of the Fascist Balilla (see page 108) blasphemous. This resistance to fascism's totalitarian claims to control every aspect of life was also shown by Radio Vatican's broadcasting of alternative news and information.

In the mid- and late 1930s senior clergy did support Italian involvement in the wars in Ethiopia and Spain as they saw them as 'Christian Crusades', spreading and defending the faith, but from 1938 tensions between the regime and the Church surfaced again over the issue of anti-Semitism. As the regime brought in a raft of anti-Jewish laws (see page 103), Pope Pius XI voiced his disquiet. By 1939 the alliance between Catholicism and fascism was over, and the Pope openly regretted the Church's earlier eagerness to embrace the *Duce*.

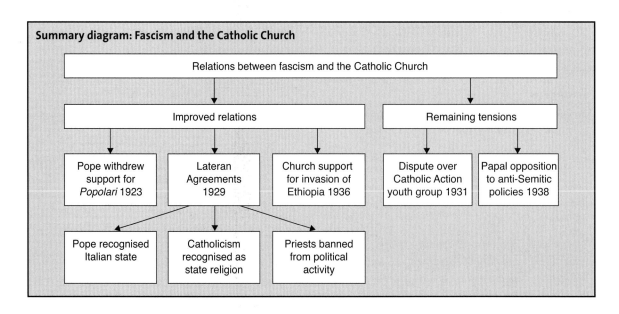

Summary diagram: Fascism and the Catholic Church

Fascism and anti-Semitism

▶ *Why did Mussolini pursue anti-Semitic policies?*

▶ *How extensive was the persecution of the Jews?*

Although the *Duce* became an admirer of the Nazi dictatorship in Germany he never shared Hitler's obsessive hatred of the Jews and had even had a Jewish mistress, Margherita Sarfatti. In 1932 Mussolini stated that Italian Jews 'have always behaved well as citizens and fought courageously as soldiers'. Nor was anti-Semitism prominent among leading Fascists: Italo Balbo had close ties to the Jewish community. Foreign Secretary Ciano wrote in his diary in 1937 'Nor do I believe that we should unleash in Italy an anti-Semitic campaign. The Jews are few, and, but for some exceptions, good.' The regime even allowed 3000 German Jews to enter the country as refugees from Nazi persecution. Why then did active persecution of Jews begin in 1938?

One factor was the relative ease with which Italy conquered Ethiopia in 1935–6 (see pages 121–5) and which seemed to confirm the Fascist view that Italians were a tough, warlike, even superior race. As the regime's new African subjects were condemned to a segregated, second-class status, a number of Fascists began to argue that there was also an inferior race within Italy, namely the Jews. Such views were encouraged by fascism's increasingly close relations with Nazi Germany (see pages 125–31). As Nazi racial ideas circulated in Italy, Mussolini found himself persuaded that there was a Jewish influence behind resistance to fascism both in Italy and across Europe. The *Duce* began to see an apparent significance in the fact that several members of the Italian anti-Fascist group 'Justice and Liberty' (see page 76) were Jewish. French opposition to Italian involvement in the Spanish Civil War could apparently be explained by the fact that their prime minister, Leon Blum, was Jewish.

The first clear example of the influence of Nazism appeared in July 1938 when the regime gave official blessing to the claims of Italian anti-Semites by publishing a tract entitled the 'Manifesto of Racial Scientists'. This declared that 'the Jews do not belong to the Italian race'.

Anti-Semitic policies

In August 1938 foreign-born Jews were banned from state schools, and in the following month the ban was extended to Italian-born Jews. Jews were banned from teaching in state schools and separate schools were to be set up for Jewish students. In October Jews were excluded from membership of the National Fascist Party and professional and cultural organisations, and prevented from owning large companies or large landed estates. From November 1938 they were even forbidden to marry non-Jews. Jews were also to be excluded from posts in the military and banking.

Italian Jews also suffered severely under these anti-Semitic laws, losing much of their liberty and their standard of living. They lived under the constant fear that fascism might adopt the murderous policies of their Nazi allies. Indeed, Mussolini was well aware of Nazi atrocities against Jews in eastern Europe by 1942 yet voiced no objection to them. However, at least until 1943, the regime did not collaborate with Nazi plans to exterminate all Jews in Europe. In fact, implementation of Italy's anti-Jewish laws was inconsistent.

The anti-Semitic laws contained exemptions for those Italian Jews who had served in the First World War or who had served the Fascist regime in some capacity. Farinacci, for example, kept his Jewish secretary. In addition, many government and Fascist officials made little effort to enforce the laws, either because they shared the Church's view that persecution was wrong, or because they had personal or family connections with Jewish Italians. Mussolini's own sons protected their Jewish friends from harassment.

If persecution was not as systematic as in Nazi Germany, there was nevertheless a hard core of racist Fascists who advocated the full-scale adoption of Nazi genocidal policies. The same Farinacci who had kept his Jewish secretary said in 1942, 'The Jews want to destroy us; we will destroy them.' When the original Fascist regime collapsed in July 1943 and was replaced by the Italian Social Republic (see pages 146–8) Mussolini allowed these racist Fascists to escalate the persecution of Jews. A decree of November 1943 ordered the confiscation of Jewish property and the rounding up of all Jews. Over 7500 Italian Jews were sent to Nazi death camps in eastern Europe. Only 600 survived.

 # Fascism and women

> ▶ *What was fascism's policy regarding the role of women?*
> ▶ *How successful was the 'battle for births'?*

One sphere of life where Fascist policy and Catholic belief coincided was the role of the sexes. Catholicism held that birth control and abortion were unnatural and offensive to God, and advocated that a woman's role should be that of wife and mother. Fascism shared this traditional attitude towards the place of women and was happy to ban contraception and to encourage women to have children. Schools emphasised traditional gender roles and the regime tried to discourage girls from entering higher education. However, the *Duce*'s concern was not simply to confine women to a domestic role; he wanted to raise the population dramatically and so provide soldiers for his armies and colonists for the new Italian Empire.

'Battle for births'

The 'battle for births', launched in 1927, was designed to increase the population from 40 million to 60 million by 1950. Mussolini specified twelve children per family as the ideal. To achieve this, a series of 'carrot and stick' measures was introduced. Marriage loans were offered to encourage couples to have more children. Part of the loan repayment was cancelled as each new child was born. A further financial inducement was that a married man with at least six children was exempt from all taxation. In addition, health care for mothers and children from poorer families was improved via infant welfare clinics. Propaganda suggested that all good Italians had a duty to produce children for the *Duce*. Indeed, Mussolini gave prizes to the most prolific mothers.

For those still reluctant to become parents, penalties were introduced. Bachelors were taxed increasingly, to the point where the government raised some 230 million lire in 1939, and, by the late 1930s, jobs and promotions in the civil service were open only to those who were married with children.

Pressure was exerted on women to stay at home: private companies promoted married men, and the state railway company sacked all women who had been appointed since 1915, with the exception of war widows. In 1933 a quota system was introduced into the public sector, limiting women to ten per cent of the workforce. In 1938 this was extended to large- and medium-sized private firms. Of course, the quota system was not applied to traditionally female, low-paid occupations such as cleaners or waitresses! Such discrimination revealed Fascist prejudices and was designed to help to win the 'battle for births'. But it also served to mask the unemployment problem as fewer women were employed.

Despite all the measures, and to Mussolini's mystification, the 'battle for births' was lost. The rate of marriage remained unchanged, while the birth rate declined until 1936 and rose only slightly thereafter. Indeed, the 1936 figure of 102 live births per 1000 women of child-bearing age compared very unfavourably with the 147 per 1000 in 1911.

As for the target population of 60 million by 1950, all the *Duce*'s efforts could only produce 47.5 million Italians by this date. During the Second World War Mussolini reflected bitterly that Italians' lack of patriotic effort in this field had lost him the equivalent of fifteen army divisions.

Even in the workplace, Fascist policies towards women had only limited success. Despite all the pressure to exclude them from paid employment, women still made up 33 per cent of the industrial workforce in 1936, a fall of only three per cent since 1921. Poorer women still needed to work to feed their families, while many middle-class women valued the independence which limiting family size afforded them.

Fascism and youth

▶ *How did Mussolini attempt to ensure that Fascist ideas were adopted by the young?*

Mussolini's dream of millions of aggressive, athletic, disciplined Fascists spreading Italian power overseas led to his interest in the education and training of the young. He was also fully aware that loyal youth could help to preserve the regime both at the time and in the future.

Schools

If Mussolini was to influence the youth of Italy he needed to ensure that schools promoted fascism. However, the 1923 school reforms designed by the prominent philosopher Giovanni Gentile reflected Mussolini's continued dependence on conservative support in his coalition government. These reforms focused on more rigorous examinations in the most prestigious secondary schools attended by only a minority of better-off Italian children. Radical Fascists were dismayed and it took another two years before the *Duce* produced a distinctively Fascist education policy. Influencing the teachers was a first step.

The regime took measures to compel the loyalty of teachers: teachers of suspect political views could be dismissed from 1925, and from 1929 all teachers were required to take an oath of loyalty to the regime. In 1931 a Fascist Teachers' Association was set up to regulate the profession, and membership was compulsory by 1937.

In schools the cult of personality was heavily promoted. Teachers were ordered to stress Mussolini's genius and were supplied with sycophantic biographies for use in the classroom. The *Duce*'s portrait had to be hung alongside that of the King. Italian youth was to have absolute, unquestioning faith, as the compulsory textbook for eight-year-olds explained:

> *The eyes of the* Duce *are on every one of you. A child who, even while not refusing to obey, asks 'Why?' is like a bayonet made of milk. You must obey because you must. What is the duty of a child? Obedience! The second? Obedience! The third? Obedience!*

Mussolini had, apparently, been sent by providence to restore Italian greatness and students must learn to take pride in the Italian nation. Accordingly, history and Italian literature became priorities in schools. Existing books that were insufficiently patriotic were banned. In 1926 this amounted to 101 out of 317 history texts in schools and, by 1936, a single official text was compulsory. Students were to be left in no doubt that Italy had been the cradle of European civilisation and that Italians had always been at the forefront of events. After all, Marco Polo had been Italian, as had Michelangelo and Christopher Columbus. According to the Fascists it had been Italian victories in the First World War that had saved Britain, France and the USA from defeat! Above all, under the guidance of the *Duce*, Italy would be restored to its rightful place in the world, as the creed of the Fascist youth organisation made clear (see Source C).

SOURCE C

Creed of the Fascist youth movement, quoted in J. Hite and C. Sinton, *Fascist Italy*, John Murray, 1998, p. 153.

I believe in Rome the Eternal, the mother of my country, and in Italy her eldest daughter, who was born in her virginal bosom by the grace of God; who suffered through the barbarian invasions, was crucified and buried, who descended to the grave and was raised from the dead in the nineteenth century, who ascended into heaven in her glory in 1918 and 1922. I believe in the genius of Mussolini, in our Holy Father Fascism, in the communion of its martyrs, in the conversion of Italians, and in the resurrection of the Empire.

Study Source C. What messages was fascism trying to promote? **?**

Young people were to identify themselves with Mussolini, fascism and Italy and to see the three as inseparable. To build a new Italy, young people had to work together and see themselves as a group. Mussolini outlined this in 1932:

Here in Italy we educate them in accordance with the ideal of the nation, whereas in Russia children are brought up in accordance with the ideals of a class. Still, the ultimate aim is identical. Both in Italy and in Russia the individual is subordinate to the state.

SOURCE D

What impression of Fascist youth is this photograph, Source D, designed to create? **?**

A typical propaganda stunt to reinforce the cult of personality: Italian children form the name of their *Duce*.

Fascist youth movement

Fascism was not just concerned with what happened at school, but also determined to influence young people in their leisure time. The *Opera Nazionale Balilla* (ONB) was set up in 1926 to organise youth movements and, by the early 1930s, membership had become compulsory at state schools for all children from the age of eight. By 1937 over 7 million had joined the ONB. Its aims, organisation and activities are explained in Source E by Fascist propagandist Missiroli.

SOURCE E

According to Source E, what activities in the ONB were designed to transform young Italians 'body and soul'?

The aims, organisation and activities of the ONB, as explained by Mario Missiroli, a Fascist propagandist, quoted in M. Missiroli, *What Italy Owes to Mussolini*, Novissima, 1937, p. 79.

It is a moral entity having as its objectives the assistance and moral and physical education of the youth of the country carried out by means of a continuous activity inside and outside the schools and intended to transform the Italian nation 'body and soul'. The Opera performs its functions through the Balilla *and* Avanguardisti *institutions. Children from 8 to 14 years old belong to the* Balilla *and the* Avanguardisti *include boys from 14 to 18 years of age. In respect of girls, the* Piccole Italiane *correspond to the* Balilla, *and the* Giovani Italiane *to the* Avanguardisti.

SOURCE F

According to Source F, what does the photograph suggest were the principal aims of Fascist policy towards the young?

Members of the *Balilla* Fascist youth greet Mussolini in Rome, 12 January 1939.

ONB activities focused largely on military training and Fascist ideology, but also included sport and fitness training. There were regular parades and annual summer camps. Girls were also involved in some sport and ideological training, but activities such as sewing, singing and childcare indicated the traditional role fascism expected of women.

At university level there was the youth organisation GUF (*Gruppi Universitari Fascisti*), which promoted Fascist ideas, and further sporting and military training. A popular development was the Littoriali Games, which enabled university students to compete against each other, initially in sports but then, from 1934, in cultural activities such as music and art. This was part of the regime's drive to generate support and create a new Fascist elite.

6 Fascism and social life

▶ *What was the purpose of the* Dopolavoro?

Dopolavoro

Despite all these efforts, Mussolini was not content to wait for youth to grow up and transform the Italian character. He sought to influence adult Italians there and then. Ordinary Italians had been tamed at work, through the banning of trade unions and by other Fascist controls, and the regime tried to maintain this control outside the workplace. The *Dopolavoro* was set up in 1925 to provide leisure activities that would influence workers towards a Fascist view of life and compensate for the now defunct trade-union-sponsored clubs.

The *Dopolavoro* organisation expanded quickly and by the mid-1930s controlled the following:

- all football clubs
- 1350 theatres
- 2000 drama societies
- 3000 brass bands
- 8000 libraries.

Virtually every town and village, even in the south, had its *Dopolavoro* clubhouse and membership had risen from 300,000 in 1926 to 2.4 million in 1935, representing twenty per cent of the industrial workforce and seven per cent of the peasantry. Membership peaked in 1939 at 4 million.

Coercing people into membership was rarely necessary as working-class Italians were quick to take advantage of subsidised sports, entertainments, excursions and holidays. The *Dopolavoro*'s popularity was also due to the fact that only lip service was paid to Fascist ideas of physical and military training. The emphasis was not on indoctrination, but on having a good time. The relative absence of propaganda can be illustrated by the programme of the theatre company *Carro di Tespi*. Of the seven plays performed in Rome in 1938, five were comedies or farces, and only two were serious plays, neither of which had any direct relevance to Fascist ideology.

Increasing Fascist interference in social life

If the *Dopolavoro* was a popular initiative, other Fascist policies affecting ordinary people only lost support for the regime. The late 1930s saw the attempted introduction of a range of initiatives which Mussolini believed would shake Italians out of their smug 'bourgeois mentality' and make them take a more vigorous, Fascist approach to life. His attempted **fascistisation** of Italian society, however, proved counter-productive, appearing to most Italians as petty, interfering and ridiculous. For example, the Fascist salute, a replacement for the handshake, was officially made compulsory in 1937, while in the following year Italians were told to stop using '*lei*', the polite form of address, and instead say '*voi*', a word apparently more completely 'Italian' in derivation. Attempts were made to change the calendar so that Year 1 would be 1922, the year of the Fascist seizure of power.

Even fashion was subject to the whims of the *Duce*. Fascism condemned women for wearing make-up and even tried to ban them from wearing trousers. Such rules were unenforceable and simply irritated Italians.

KEY TERM

Fascistisation Mussolini's attempts to make ordinary Italians adopt Fascist ideas and a Fascist approach to life.

 7 # How far did Mussolini achieve his aims in domestic policy?

▶ *How successful were Fascist attempts to alter the behaviour of ordinary Italians?*

The *Duce*'s principal aim was to maintain and increase his power, and his domestic policies did bring him substantial public support. Mussolini was constantly portrayed as an infallible genius, a man, even a superman, destined to lead Italy back to greatness. The *Duce*, so it was said, had a brilliant, original mind, but also appreciated the thoughts and needs of ordinary Italians, a claim emphasised by press photos of him helping out in the harvest (page 91) and laying the foundations of some new building or *autostrada*. Fascist initiatives were apparently always great successes, while Fascist failures such as the 'battle for births' were quietly forgotten.

Italians were not wholly taken in by this incessant stream of propaganda, but they were not averse to the *Duce*'s claims that Italy possessed the greatest civilisation. They enjoyed Italian successes, such as victories in the 1934 and 1938 football world cup and Primo Carnera's winning of the world heavyweight boxing championship. The *Duce*, of course, claimed the credit. However, much of Mussolini's enhanced support derived from the apparent results of foreign policy. In fact, his concordat with the Catholic Church was perhaps his only real achievement of any note in the domestic sphere and even that was beginning to sour by the late 1930s.

Mussolini had hoped to transform the Italian character and Italian society into a Fascist mould, but he was disappointed. The race of athletic, aggressive, obedient, Fascists never materialised. Fascism did not penetrate the psyche of most Italians, changing traditional habits and attitudes. There was outward conformity but little inner conviction. Although Fascist propaganda claimed that it was transforming Italy, the reality was rather different. Fascism might claim, for example, to be creating a Fascist youth via control of the school curriculum and the power of the ONB, but it is uncertain how many true converts there were. A substantial proportion left school at the age of eleven and so avoided the full programme of indoctrination, while in private and Catholic schools the state curriculum and ONB membership were never enforced. Even those who experienced a full Fascist education and progressed to university may not have been convinced: in 1931 the head of Fascist organisation for university students admitted that 'the masses in the universities are not yet what the *Duce* wants … those furthest from us are students of law, literature and philosophy …'.

Parents and the older generation were still more resistant to change, as they showed by their 'unpatriotic' reaction to the 'battle for births', and by their irritation at being told to adopt the new Fascist salute, the new form of address and the instructions on what to wear. Police reports based on informers suggested that Fascist policies might be welcomed if they afforded some apparent advantage, such as *Dopolavoro* cheap holidays, but were resisted if they seemed to threaten entrenched customs and habits. Thus, in the late 1930s, as fascism tried to intrude further into everyday life, popular support for the regime began to decline. Furthermore, the Fascist government had neither the means nor the self-confidence to force through unpopular policies.

Mussolini had brought stability of a sort to Italy. He remained in power for 21 years, being personally popular among many Italians for the greater part of this time, but he had not brought about a revolution.

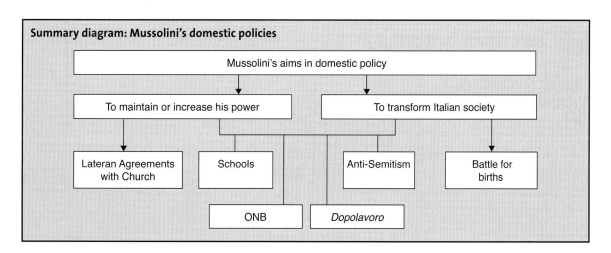

Summary diagram: Mussolini's domestic policies

Mussolini's aims in domestic policy

To maintain or increase his power → To transform Italian society

Lateran Agreements with Church | Schools | Anti-Semitism | Battle for births

ONB | *Dopolavoro*

Chapter summary

Mussolini set out to change Italians into Fascists through indoctrinating the young, influencing the social habits of adults and encouraging anti-Semitism. Seven million young Italians were enrolled in the ONB and some did become enthusiastic Fascists, but by no means all. Adults were more resistant to Fascist social policies. They might have enjoyed *Dopolavoro* activities but the *Duce* was not going to dictate how many children they had.

Consequently, the 'battle for births' was a failure and women resisted attempts to exclude them from employment. Fascist attempts to change social behaviour, in the field of fashion for example, simply caused irritation and resentment.

Mussolini's greatest success was the Lateran Agreements, which generated support from both the Catholic Church and ordinary Italians. By the late 1930s, however, relations with the Church were beginning to sour and public support for the regime was draining away.

 ## Refresher questions

Use these questions to remind yourself of the key material covered in this chapter.

1 What was Mussolini's vision for Italian society?

2 How did Mussolini improve relations with the Catholic Church in the years 1922–9?

3 Why were there tensions between the Church and fascism in the 1930s?

4 In what ways and why did Mussolini persecute Italian Jews?

5 What was the 'battle for births'?

6 To what extent did fascism exclude women from the workforce?

7 In what ways was education changed to encourage support for fascism?

8 What was the ONB?

9 Why was the *Dopolavoro* popular?

10 Why did fascism try to interfere in Italians' social lives?

 ## Question practice

ESSAY QUESTIONS

1 To what extent had Mussolini's regime brought about a 'Fascist social revolution' by 1945?

2 To what extent did relations between the Fascist regime and the Catholic Church improve in the years 1922–39?

3 How significant were the Lateran Accords in generating support for Mussolini's regime?

4 'Mussolini's social policies were a failure in the years 1922–40.' How far do you agree?

5 Which of the following Fascist policies was more successful? i) Policies towards women. ii) Policies towards youth. Explain your answer with reference to both i) and ii).

INTERPRETATION QUESTION

1   Read the interpretation and then answer the question that follows. 'The ONB and the wearing of uniforms did have some success in imparting a sense of [Fascist] unity and national solidarity to the youth of Italy.' (From John Whittam, *Fascist Italy*, Manchester University Press, 1995, p. 69.) Evaluate the strengths and weaknesses of this interpretation, making reference to other interpretations that you have studied.

SOURCE ANALYSIS QUESTIONS

1   Why is Source 1 valuable to the historian for an enquiry into relations between the Catholic Church and fascism 1929–39? Explain your answer using the source, the information given about it and your own knowledge of the historical context.

2   How much weight do you give the evidence of Source 2 (page 114) for an enquiry into tensions between the Church and the Fascist regime 1929–39? Explain your answer using the source, the information given about it and your own knowledge of the historical context.

3   How far could the historian make use of Sources 1 and 2 (page 114) together to investigate Church–State relations in Fascist Italy in the years 1929–39? Explain your answer, using both sources, the information given about them and your own knowledge of the historical context.

4   With reference to Sources 1, 2 and 3 (page 114), and your understanding of the historical context, assess the value of these sources to a historian studying Church–State relations in Fascist Italy in the years 1929–39.

SOURCE 1

From the 1939 revised edition of Mussolini's memoirs, Benito Mussolini, *My Autobiography*, Hutchinson & Co., 1939. Here, Mussolini reflects on the regime's 1929 concordat with the papacy.

The so-called Roman Question embittered the souls of many Italians since the foundation of the Kingdom of Italy. People found it difficult to love one's country and pray to God with a clear conscience because it was the King of Italy who had robbed the Pope of his territories in 1870. Mussolini ended all that. He signed a treaty with the Pope on February 11th 1929 in which the old problem was laid to rest forever. There was great rejoicing.

Mussolini came to power. A new conception of the State, a new rigid conception of the duties of citizens of the education of youth faced the Vatican's resistance. The clear-cut, uncompromising views of Mussolini made an agreement easier.

Peace of heart of the Italian people was the result of this agreement. An old problem was settled forever. Sons, educated to the love of new, forceful, active living, would not be in conflict with their fathers, who were attached to the traditions of the past. One could finally be both a good Italian, which is the same as being a Fascist, and a good Catholic. The Vatican itself found new dignity and new strength. The Lateran Treaty was, doubtlessly, one of the greatest achievements of the wise, realistic policies of Benito Mussolini.

SOURCE 2

From Pius XI's encyclical (a letter from the Pope to all Catholic bishops) *Non Abbiamo Bisogno* (*We Do Not Need*), written in 1931. Mussolini refused to allow it to be published in the Catholic press in Italy. Here, the Pope highlights the tension between the Church and fascism. Available at the Vatican website (http://vatican.va).

A conception of the State which makes the rising generations belong to it entirely, without any exception, from the tenderest years up to adult life, cannot be reconciled by a Catholic either with Catholic doctrine or with the natural rights of the family. It is not possible for a Catholic to accept the claim that the Church and the Pope must limit themselves to the external practices of religion … and that all of the rest of education belongs to the state …

How great is the importance of childhood and adolescence in this absolute universality and totality of the divine mandate to the Church, has been shown by the Divine Master Himself, the Creator and Redeemer of souls …

[The state must not] monopolize completely the young … for the exclusive advantage of a party and of a regime based on an ideology which clearly resolves itself into a true, a real pagan worship of the State.

SOURCE 3

A description of the Lateran Agreements in 1929, quoted in Patricia Knight, *Mussolini and Fascism*, Routledge, 2013, pp. 61–2.

Mussolini watched … Cardinals and Monsignors [high-ranking Catholic clergy] marching to the ballot box, attended by blaring brass bands and wildly cheering throngs. Never before have Princes of the Church shepherded their clergy and people to vote in a Parliamentary Election … Il Duce has restored a mite of earthly authority to Il Papa, and last week … cinema machines showed how mountainous is the Pontiff's gratitude to the Dictator … [Three Cardinals] proceeded directly from the celebration of High Mass to vote at the head of their clergy … [Pollsters] estimated that His Holiness's influence had flung into the scale of Fascismo *at least 1,000,000 extra votes … Last week's election statistics prove that those Italians who went to the polls are 98.28% pure endorsers of the* Duce.

CHAPTER 8

Mussolini's foreign policy 1922–40

Foreign policy was a key concern for Mussolini. He intended to make Italy a great power, an equal to Britain and France in Europe, and with a dominant position in the Mediterranean. He wanted to expand the Italian Empire in Africa and believed that success in foreign policy would strengthen the Fascist position at home. This chapter examines Mussolini's attempts to achieve all this, through the following headings:

★ Mussolini's aims

★ Diplomacy 1922–32

★ German–Italian relations 1933–5

★ War in Ethiopia 1935

★ Alliance with Germany 1936–9

★ Entry into the Second World War

★ How successful was Mussolini's foreign policy?

The key debate on *page 135* of this chapter asks the question: Why did Mussolini ally with Nazi Germany?

Key dates

1923	Corfu incident used by Mussolini to promote Italian power and prestige	1936	Sept.	Italian troops sent to Spain to aid 'Fascists' in civil war
1924	Pact of Rome – Yugoslavia ceded Fiume to Italy		Nov.	Rome–Berlin Axis formed – Mussolini drew closer to Nazi Germany
1925	Locarno Treaties – Mussolini posed as a major European statesman	1939	April	Italian invasion of Albania
			May	Pact of Steel with Germany committed Italy to the Nazi side in a future European conflict
1926	Treaty of Friendship increased Italian influence over Albania		Sept.	Germany's invasion of Poland started the Second World War
1933	Hitler came to power in Germany	1940	May	German invasion of France
1933–4	Conflict over Austria		June	Italy entered the Second World War on the Nazi side
1935	Italian invasion of Ethiopia			

Mussolini's aims

▶ *What did Mussolini mean by saying he wanted to make Italy 'great, respected and feared'?*

On coming to power in 1922, Mussolini did not have any clear foreign policy. It was apparent that he had completely rejected the **anti-imperialist**, anti-war beliefs of his youth, but it was uncertain how far he had adopted the views of his political allies, the Nationalists. He had loudly supported entry into the First World War and had condemned the peace settlement – the 'mutilated victory' (see page 26) – but it was unclear what revisions to the peace treaties he would seek.

There was no foreign policy 'master plan', but in his first few months in office the new prime minister did begin to develop a general aim: in his words, 'to make Italy great, respected and feared'. Italy would achieve Great Power status via military build-up, diplomatic intrigue and, if need be, war. Italy would one day be the dominant power in the Mediterranean, would develop and even expand its colonial empire in Africa, and would have the **Balkans** as its own **sphere of influence**. The *Duce* intended to be the architect of all this, and would have transformed the Italians into a more energetic and aggressive people in the process.

Until the 1930s Mussolini's plans lacked detail. Mussolini was not sure which colonies would expand. Nor did he know how he would achieve 'dominance' in the Mediterranean, or how much power he desired in the Balkans. Nevertheless, the *Duce*'s overall objectives remained the same, even if circumstances, particularly the general situation in Europe, would force him to adopt a variety of tactics in pursuing these objectives.

The *Duce* soon recognised that foreign affairs could provide him with the ideal stage; he would impress his fellow countrymen with spectacles where he would overshadow foreign statesmen, and defend and promote Italian interests with unending success. He would conduct foreign policy himself, avoiding the old, stuffy foreign office, and reap international prestige and internal support. Foreign affairs came to take up more and more of his time.

Mussolini appears to have convinced himself that he was beginning a new era in Italian foreign policy. In truth, desire for Great Power status, high military expenditure and colonial adventures had also been a feature of the Liberal regime. However, Mussolini exceeded his Liberal predecessors in his ambitions and pursued his goals more relentlessly and recklessly, particularly in the 1930s. He squandered vast sums on colonial conflicts, and led Italy into a disastrous world war, the results of which were the collapse of fascism, the onset of civil war and the death of the *Duce* himself.

2 Diplomacy 1922–32

▶ *What factors limited Fascist foreign policy in the 1920s?*

▶ *Why did Fascist policy become more ambitious and aggressive from the late 1920s?*

Italy in 1922 had a secure position in Europe but was unable to exert a great deal of influence, either diplomatically or militarily. The potential threat to its northern frontiers had been removed by the friendship with France and the dismemberment of the Austro-Hungarian Empire, and Italy had no powerful enemies. However, Britain and France were the dominant powers of Europe. They were the enforcers of the peace treaties signed at the end of the First World War, their colonies dominated Africa and their fleets controlled the Mediterranean. Furthermore, France was busy consolidating its political and economic influence in central and eastern Europe, including the Balkans. Any changes in the European *status quo* would require the consent of Britain and France, and smaller powers had few means of extracting concessions. A resurgent Italy would have to move carefully. Mussolini was to learn this lesson in his first real foray into European affairs.

Policy towards the Balkans

Greece and Corfu

In August 1923 an Italian general and four of his staff were assassinated in Greece. They had been working for the international boundary commission set up under the terms of the peace settlement and were advising on the precise location of the new Greek–Albanian border. On hearing of the assassinations, Mussolini blamed the Greek government and demanded a full apology together with 50 million lire in compensation. When the Greeks refused, he ordered the bombardment and occupation of the island of Corfu, off the Greek mainland (see the map on page 130). The dispute posed a challenge to the League of Nations, which had been established after the First World War to maintain international peace. In support of the League, Britain, backed by its Mediterranean fleet, demanded that Italy withdraw. The *Duce* had little choice but to agree and, although he did receive the 50 million lire compensation, he did not receive a full apology from the Greeks.

The episode was hailed in Italy as a great success for dynamic fascism, but it also showed that, although Mussolini might be able to bully smaller powers, he was unable to stand up to the 'great' powers. This realisation rankled with Mussolini but it made him aware of the necessity of good relations with Britain, at least in the short term. He was fortunate that Austen Chamberlain, Britain's foreign secretary for much of the 1920s, was an admirer of the fledgling Italian regime and was inclined to look tolerantly on the *Duce*'s actions.

Yugoslavia and Albania

Mussolini had more success in the Balkans in 1924 when, in the Pact of Rome, Italy received Fiume, an Italian-speaking town on the Yugoslavian coast. This town had long been a target of Italian territorial ambitions, and had been occupied, temporarily, by Italian Nationalists in 1919 (see pages 26–7). Mussolini's diplomatic success therefore brought him great prestige and popularity.

The *Duce*'s success over Fiume persuaded him that Yugoslavia could be pushed around. Mussolini resented French influence in Yugoslavia and was keen to demonstrate to this new state, which had been formed only in 1919, that Italy was the dominant power in the region. He wanted to make it clear that he could make life very difficult for Yugoslavia if it tried to resist Italian influence. An opportunity to illustrate this arose in 1924 when an Italian-sponsored local chieftain, Ahmed Zog, managed to take power in Albania on Yugoslavia's southern border. The Fascist government supplied Zog with money, encouraged Italian companies to invest in the Albanian economy and employed Italian officers as advisers to the Albanian army. By the time a Treaty of Friendship was signed in 1926 Albania was little more than an Italian **satellite state**.

Italy was clearly a potential military threat to Yugoslavia, a threat emphasised by Mussolini's funding of those ethnic minorities, notably the Croats, who wanted to break away from the Yugoslav state. Yugoslavia responded by doing its best not to antagonise Fascist Italy, but it also refused to be intimidated into subservience. Throughout the 1930s the *Duce* maintained his aggressive posture and eventually occupied much of Yugoslavia during the Second World War, after that country's defeat at the hands of Nazi Germany, Italy's ally (see map on page 130).

Relations with Britain and France

While the *Duce* was meddling in the Balkans, he was careful not to antagonise the two dominant European powers of the 1920s, Britain and France. Mussolini recognised that the main British and French interests lay in western Europe and here he was determined to play the part of a moderate statesman. Italy remained in the League of Nations, signed the Locarno Treaties, which confirmed the permanence of Germany's western borders, and entered into the Kellogg–Briand Pact of 1928, outlawing war.

Italy and Britain also came to an agreement over the location of the border between their north African colonial territories, Libya and Egypt. However, Mussolini had little interest in the details of such treaties and pacts, and rarely took the time to read them through thoroughly. But he did see the advantages of participating in these diplomatic spectacles. He enjoyed being taken seriously

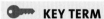

KEY TERM

Satellite state A country that is very heavily influenced or virtually controlled by another state.

as a European statesman, hoped that his apparent moderation would lead to concessions of some sort from Britain and France, and, perhaps above all, saw an opportunity to enhance his prestige and power at home. He organised dramatic entrances to international conferences, as when, in 1925, he raced across Lake Maggiore in a flotilla of speedboats to Locarno. Italian press coverage was always extensive, suggesting that the *Duce* was being treated as an equal by the leaders of the Great Powers and that Mussolini's presence and contributions had been crucial in reaching such momentous European agreements. This was gross exaggeration – at Locarno, for instance, he attended only one session of the conference and did not even bother to read the final draft of the treaties – but it created a powerful impression in Italy.

Increasing ambitions

Mussolini posed as a good neighbour for the eyes of Britain and France but, by the late 1920s, he was increasingly determined to revise the peace settlement and make Italy 'great, respected and feared'. However, in order to do this he needed friends and stronger armed forces.

Italy signed a friendship treaty in 1927 with Hungary, another **revisionist** state, and Mussolini funded right-wing groups in Germany in the hope that a pro-Fascist government might come to power there. He even went so far as to train German military pilots in Italy, a clear breach of the Treaty of Versailles. As for military power, the dictator told the Italian parliament in 1927 that he would create an air force 'large enough to blot out the sun'. And when he signed the Kellogg–Briand Pact of 1928 outlawing war, he immediately dismissed it in a speech to that same parliament. By the early 1930s the Fascist regime was clearly ready to do more than meddle in Balkan affairs; it was now prepared to challenge the European *status quo* directly in pursuit of a 'greater' Italy. The 1930s were to see Italy becoming increasingly aggressive not only in the Balkans but in western Europe and Africa too. What had prompted this development?

It can be argued that the regime adopted a more aggressive policy in an attempt to distract public attention away from problems at home. Mussolini certainly recognised that foreign successes would bolster his regime and, perhaps, felt that he needed new, dramatic successes now that domestic policies, such as the corporate state (see pages 85–7), were producing disappointing results, but his aims had always been expansionist and aggressive, even if the power of Britain and France had caused him to disguise this. Fascist foreign policy became increasingly belligerent, partly as the result of frustration with the limited gains won by Italian diplomacy in the 1920s, but mainly due to the recognition that the rise to power of the Nazis had transformed the European situation and opened the way for Italian ambitions.

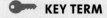

KEY TERM

Revisionist A state that wanted to change the peace treaties signed after the First World War.

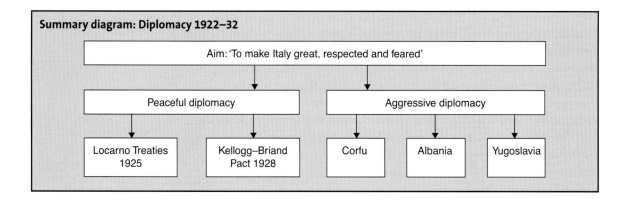

Summary diagram: Diplomacy 1922–32

Aim: 'To make Italy great, respected and feared'

Peaceful diplomacy | Aggressive diplomacy

Locarno Treaties 1925 | Kellogg–Briand Pact 1928 | Corfu | Albania | Yugoslavia

③ German–Italian relations 1933–5

▶ *Why did the rise of Hitler's Germany encourage Mussolini to be more aggressive?*

Mussolini realised in the 1920s that a strong, resurgent Germany, seeking revision of Versailles, would frighten Britain and France and make them more amenable to Italian demands. Indeed, neither wanted Italy as an enemy and it would, therefore, be able to play off the two camps against each other to Italy's own advantage. Mussolini had probably funded the Nazis, along with a number of other right-wing groups, in the Germany of the late 1920s. On the face of it, therefore, he should have been delighted about Hitler's accession to power in 1933. But, in fact, early relations between the two regimes were rather difficult.

Mussolini enjoyed claiming that 'his creation', fascism, was spreading through Europe, but he was a little apprehensive lest Germany be seen as the centre of fascism and he be overshadowed by the new *Führer*. A more concrete concern was that this new German regime might take over Austria, thus creating a powerful 'greater Germany' that would share an Alpine frontier with Italy. If this were to occur, Italy would have lost the security of its northern border guaranteed by victory over Austria-Hungary in 1918, and might even be pressured into handing back those German-speaking areas in north-eastern Italy gained at the peace conference in 1919.

The danger of an Austro-German union (***Anschluss***) was even more apparent to the Austrian government in Vienna. Any union of the two countries would not be a merger, it would effectively be the takeover of the weaker military power (Austria) by the stronger (Germany). Consequently, Dollfuss, the Austrian Chancellor, looked for outside support and he visited Rome three times during 1933. He was relieved to be told that he should suppress the Nazi Party in Austria and that Italy would protect Austria from any German aggression. In February 1934 Mussolini encouraged Dollfuss to set up a right-wing authoritarian regime which would be partly modelled on Italian fascism,

KEY TERM

Anschluss Literally meaning 'union', referring to the annexation of Austria by Germany, which had been prohibited by the Treaty of Versailles.

but which would be anti-Nazi. The Chancellor attempted to do this but was assassinated by Nazi sympathisers in July 1934. Mussolini was outraged and immediately despatched troops to the Austrian border to deter Germany from attempting an armed *Anschluss*. Relations between the two Fascist regimes had not got off to an auspicious start. Indeed, in 1933 Mussolini had described his fellow dictator as: 'an ideologue who talks more than he governs … a muddle-headed fellow; his brain is stuffed with philosophical and political tags that are utterly incoherent'. On hearing of Dollfuss's assassination the *Duce* went further and called Hitler a 'horrible sexual degenerate'.

Stresa Front 1935

Relations between Italy and Germany reached a low in March 1935 when Hitler revealed that he had developed an air force, the *Luftwaffe*, in breach of Versailles, and announced that he was introducing military conscription to create an army five times the size permitted by the peace treaty. In the face of this challenge, Mussolini agreed to meet the British and French in the Italian town of Stresa to organise a joint response to the emerging German threat. The result was a declaration that the three powers in the 'Stresa Front' would collaborate to prevent any further breaches in the treaties that might threaten peace.

Nevertheless, although Mussolini certainly feared and distrusted Nazi Germany, he realised that Britain and France had just as much, if not more, reason to fear Hitler. A rearmed and hostile Germany reminded the Western allies of the horrors of the First World War. The *Duce* was shrewd enough to make use of this. The 'Stresa Front' gave him added protection against an *Anschluss*, but it also indicated to him that the Western powers were anxious to avoid Germany's allying with other states to revise the peace settlement. Mussolini was convinced that the thought of a German–Italian friendship would horrify Britain and France. To avoid such a possibility they might be more sympathetic towards Italian ambitions and more tolerant towards Italian adventures overseas. Mussolini saw this an ideal opportunity to expand his colonial empire at minimal risk. His chosen area for expansion was to be Ethiopia, known then as Abyssinia.

War in Ethiopia 1935

▶ *What was the impact of the war on Mussolini's foreign policy?*
▶ *How far did the war increase domestic support for Mussolini?*

Mussolini's aims

The *Duce* believed that Italian colonies should be developed and expanded, not primarily for commercial motives, such as to secure markets or to extract raw materials, but because a growing empire would enhance Italy's claim to be a Great Power. Colonies were also part of Italy's historic destiny. After all, Italy was the descendant of the Roman Empire that had controlled huge areas of North Africa and had dominated the Mediterranean. The possession of new African territories would provide another benefit: large numbers of colonial troops to enhance Italy's military might. Furthermore, this offered the prospect of securing military glory on the cheap, impressing the Great Powers and propping up the regime's prestige at home. With the corporate state a disappointment, and the 'battles' for grain and births (see pages 90–2) losing momentum, Mussolini needed a new adventure to restore dwindling public confidence.

Ethiopia was an ideal target for Mussolini's ambitions (see map on page 130). It was a large country uncolonised by Europeans, but it lacked the means to fight a modern war. The neighbouring Italian colonies of Eritrea and Somaliland provided convenient avenues of attack, while the uncertain location of Ethiopia's borders with these colonies might provide 'incidents' between armed forces that could be used as a justification for war. A successful conquest would also avenge Italy's humiliating defeat by Ethiopia in 1896. This, of course, would bolster the *Duce*'s claim that he, and he alone, could restore Italy to international grandeur.

The pretext for war

The Fascist government had taken an interest in Ethiopia since the early 1920s. Italy had sponsored Ethiopia's membership of the League of Nations in 1923 and had even signed a Treaty of Friendship in 1928. Despite these acts of a supposed 'good neighbour', the Fascist regime was, by 1929, drawing up plans to **annex** the country. In fact, in that year, Italian soldiers began to occupy disputed border areas. It was in one of these areas that, in December 1934, the incident occurred that gave the *Duce* an excuse for war. At the oasis of Wal-Wal a skirmish took place between Italian and Ethiopian troops, in which 30 Italian soldiers were killed. Mussolini immediately demanded a full apology and hefty compensation. The Ethiopian government replied by requesting a League of Nations investigation. The League agreed and set up an inquiry.

Mussolini had no interest in waiting for the results of such an investigation, as he issued a secret order for the 'total conquest of Ethiopia', and built up his military forces in the area. A huge army, together with civilian support, totalling half a million men, was transported to Africa. The announcement of German military conscription and rearmament did cause the *Duce* to pause to consider whether he was leaving himself exposed in Europe, but the Stresa conference assured him that he had nothing to fear. In addition, his conviction that Britain and France were too preoccupied with Germany to oppose him seemed to be confirmed. Talks with their foreign ministers during the first half of 1935 showed that both countries were prepared to accede to Italian control of at least part of Ethiopia. Britain might well object to a full conquest, but its protests would be confined to disapproving notes sent by British diplomats.

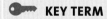 **KEY TERM**

Annex To take over or seize a country.

Military victory

In October 1935 Italian armies attacked Ethiopia. On the previous day the *Duce* had justified his invasion to the Italian public (see Source A).

SOURCE A

From a speech by Mussolini, 2 October 1935, quoted in S.C. Tucker and P.M. Roberts, editors, *Encyclopedia of World War II: A Political, Social, and Military History*, ABC-CLIO, 2004.

It is not only an army marching towards its goals, but as if 44,000,000 Italians were marching in unity behind this army because the blackest of injustices is being attempted against them, that of taking from them their place in the sun.

When, in 1915, Italy threw in her fate with that of the Allies [in the First World War], how many cries of admiration, how many promises! But after the common victory, which cost Italy 600,000 dead, 400,000 lost, 1,000,000 wounded, when peace was being discussed around the table only the crumbs of a rich colonial booty [in the peace treaties] were left for us to pick up.

Study Source A. What were Mussolini's motives in making this speech?

The Ethiopian forces were disorganised and armed with antiquated weapons. They were soon forced on to the defensive and suffered the full effects of modern war. The Italians used aerial bombing and poison gas in their campaigns. In April 1936 the Ethiopian army was heavily defeated at Lake Ashangi and, in the following month, the capital, Addis Ababa, was occupied. The Ethiopian Emperor, Haile Selassie, fled to Britain and organised opposition ceased. However, sporadic guerrilla attacks continued and the Italian forces began a ruthless campaign of suppression that Mussolini was keen to encourage, as can be seen in the telegrams sent to his commander in the field (see Source B).

SOURCE B

From telegrams by Mussolini, quoted in M. Knox, *Mussolini Unleashed*, Cambridge University Press, 1982, pp. 3–4.

5 June 1936 – All rebels made prisoner are to be shot.

Secret – 8 June 1936. To finish off rebels as … at Ancober use gas.

Secret – 8 July 1936. I repeat my authorization to initiate and systematically conduct policy of terror and extermination against rebels and populations in complicity with them. Without the law of ten eyes for one we cannot heal this wound in good time. Acknowledge.

21 February 1937 – Agreed that male population of Goggetti over 18 years of age is to be shot and village destroyed.

21 February 1937 – No persons arrested are to be released without my order. All civilians and clerics in any way suspect are to be shot without delay.

What do the telegrams in Source B tell us about the nature of Italian rule over Ethiopia?

SOURCE C

What does the cartoonist in Source C see as the significance of Mussolini's invasion of Ethiopia?

THE MAN WHO TOOK THE LID OFF.

'The man who took the lid off.' A David Low cartoon from the *Evening Standard* newspaper, 4 October 1935.

These brutal tactics did succeed in pacifying Ethiopia, but they did nothing to reconcile the people to Fascist rule.

Italian public opinion

As the war began, the mood of the public was uncertain. Some Italians, no doubt, had been taken in by the orchestrated press campaign stressing Italy's right to an East African empire and suggesting the presence of enormous quantities of valuable resources, such as precious metals, in Ethiopia. However, many remained unenthusiastic. It was the condemnation of the invasion by the League of Nations, however, that caused the public to rally round the regime in order to defend the honour of Italy. When the war was won quickly and with only around 1000 Italian casualties, Mussolini's popularity soared. The Fascist philosopher Giovanni Gentile claimed that 'Mussolini today has not just founded empire in Ethiopia. He has made something more. He has created a new Italy.' For Gentile and for many Italians, Italy was now indisputably a Great Power: it had proven military strength and a sizeable colonial empire, and demanded to be considered an equal to Britain and France.

Impact of the war on relations with Britain and France

Public opinion in Britain and France was outraged by the invasion and the Italian tactics such as the use of poison gas. There was widespread support for the League of Nations' imposition of economic sanctions: no arms were to be sold to Italy and member nations were to ban the import of Italian goods. However, these measures were little more than symbolic: there was no ban imposed on the strategic commodities of oil, coal and steel, and the Suez Canal (see the map on page 130) was not closed to Italian ships. Had Britain chosen to close this canal, Italy's vital supply route to its forces in East Africa would have been cut off.

The sanctions irritated Mussolini without hindering his war effort. He was convinced that Britain and France, the leading powers in the League, were timid and weak. His opinion was confirmed by the Western powers' reluctance to use the forces at their disposal and by their efforts to bring the conflict to an end by diplomatic means, culminating in the **Hoare–Laval Pact** of December 1935. This agreement between the foreign ministers of Britain and France would have handed over the greater part of Ethiopia to Italy, leaving the Emperor Haile Selassie with only a small, unviable independent state. A public outcry in Britain and France put paid to this agreement, but it appeared to the *Duce* that the governments of both countries were desperate to avoid having Fascist Italy as an enemy.

Mussolini despised such apparent weakness. He increasingly saw the Western democracies as cowardly. The 1933 Oxford University Union debate in which the supposed cream of British youth had argued that they were no longer prepared to 'fight for King and Country' had probably encouraged such a notion. Mussolini thought that Britain and France were decadent, interested only in money-making and a comfortable life. His fascism was, in contrast, dynamic and contemptuous of material comforts. He hoped it might even replace 'bourgeois democracy' as the dominant force in Europe.

Mussolini remained willing to negotiate with Britain and France if he could see some advantage, but relations never fully recovered.

> **KEY TERM**
>
> **Hoare–Laval Pact** An Anglo-French attempt to find a compromise peace, giving Mussolini most of Ethiopia.

5 Alliance with Germany 1936–9

▶ *Why did Mussolini ally with Nazi Germany?*

▶ *Why did Italy not join the Second World War in September 1939?*

Mussolini now looked towards Nazi Germany with more favour. Here was another vibrant Fascist regime, one which had played no part in the sanctions and which, like Italy, had grievances against Britain and France dating back to the 1919 peace conferences. Mussolini thought that Italian friendship, and the prospect of a military alliance, with Nazi Germany would terrify Britain and France and would allow him to prise concessions out of them. He was still not sure exactly what these concessions might be, but he could now see the possibility of realising his dream of Mediterranean domination.

Rome–Berlin Axis 1936

A reconciliation between the two Fascist regimes had begun as early as January 1936 when Hitler agreed not to carry out an *Anschluss* and, in return, Mussolini dropped his objection to Nazi interference in Austrian politics. Europe became aware of the warming of relations when Ciano, Italy's foreign minister, visited Berlin in October and in the following month Mussolini proclaimed the existence of the Rome–Berlin Axis. This public declaration of friendship was cemented by a secret understanding that Italy would direct its expansionist energies towards the Mediterranean while Germany looked towards eastern Europe and the Baltic, thus ensuring that they did not compete with one another. Hitler even went so far as to suggest that he was preparing his country to be at war in three years' time.

Hitler's talk of war did not frighten Mussolini. In fact, he revelled in such bellicose phrases and saw war as the 'supreme test' both of the individual and of the nation. Italy was rearming and, although he certainly had not committed himself to taking the country into a European war, he was prepared to risk such a conflict in pursuit of his foreign policy goals.

Intervention in the Spanish Civil War 1936

From 1936 the arrangement with Germany was the central facet of Italian foreign policy. German and Italian forces fought on the same side in the Spanish Civil War that had begun in July 1936. They supported the attempts of Spanish conservatives and Fascists to overthrow the elected Republican government. Mussolini had been reluctant to get involved, at first lending only transport planes to the rebels. However, when two of these planes crashed in French-controlled Morocco, Mussolini's involvement was heavily criticised in the French press. Angry at the French reaction and fearful that the left-of-centre French government would supply weapons to the anti-Fascist forces in Spain, Mussolini decided to intervene in the civil war. He expected that the war would be short and victorious, and would generate the same passion among the Italian public as the war in Ethiopia.

Despite the commitment of over 40,000 Italian troops, there was no quick victory and no public enthusiasm. Italian forces were withdrawn only in 1939 after Republican resistance finally collapsed. It had been the anti-Republican Spanish who had borne the brunt of the fighting, but the conflict had still cost 4000 Italian lives and the expenditure of over 8 billion lire. It had also done nothing to improve relations with Britain and France, both of whom remained neutral during the war.

Closer Italo-German relations 1937–8

In November 1937 the Rome–Berlin Axis was further strengthened when Italy joined Germany and Japan in the Anti-Comintern Pact. In practice, this was a declaration that the three countries would work together against Soviet Russia. However, the relationship between the two European Fascist states cooled somewhat in March 1938 when Hitler finally carried out the *Anschluss* without consulting the *Duce*. In response, Mussolini signed an agreement with Britain guaranteeing the *status quo* in the Mediterranean. But the two dictators were soon reconciled. The *Duce* had no interest in maintaining the *status quo* and, despite his annoyance at not being informed about the *Anschluss*, his admiration for German dynamism only increased.

In September 1938 Hitler's demands over the **Sudetenland** seemed likely to lead to a general European war. British Prime Minister Neville Chamberlain asked Mussolini to act as a mediator at the conference, which had been called at Munich, to seek a diplomatic solution to the crisis. Mussolini enjoyed the favourable publicity he received in the British and French press, but he was not even-handed as mediator. In fact, he secretly colluded with Hitler to find a compromise favourable to Nazi claims. The Sudetenland was handed over to Germany.

KEY TERM

Sudetenland An area of Czechoslovakia, bordering Germany and with a substantial German-speaking population. Hitler used this as a pretext to wage war against the western European powers.

SOURCE D

Mussolini and Hitler watch a parade in Munich 1937.

Study Source D. Why would the Fascist regime circulate this photograph within Italy and across Europe in 1937?

Territorial demands 1938–9

The *Duce* was hailed in Europe as an architect of peace. But, in his view, Munich had only confirmed the weakness of Britain and France, a weakness on which he was determined to capitalise. In November 1938 the Italian parliament was recalled and Mussolini instructed it to demand the annexation of Nice, Corsica and Tunis from France. He clearly planned to dominate the Mediterranean, in his eyes **Mare Nostrum**. He emphasised this when he spoke to the Grand Council of Fascism in November 1938 (see Source E).

KEY TERM

Mare Nostrum Literally 'our sea'.

SOURCE E

From a secret speech by Mussolini to the Grand Council of Fascism, November 1938, quoted in M. Knox, *Mussolini Unleashed*, Cambridge University Press, 1982, pp. 38–9.

I announce to you the immediate goals of Fascist dynamism … Albania will become Italian. I cannot tell you … how or when. But it will come to pass. Then, for the requirements of our security in this Mediterranean that still confines us, we need Tunis and Corsica. The [French] frontier must move to the [river] Var … All this is a program. I cannot lay down a fixed timetable. I merely indicate the route along which we shall march.

At last, Mussolini was beginning to clarify those vague expansionist ideas that he had held for well over a decade.

SOURCE F

Study Source F. To what extent is this evidence that Italy commanded the respect of the major European powers?

Mussolini taking centre stage at the Munich conference in 1938.

By 1939, with France rearming and French opinion outraged by Italian territorial claims, the *Duce* was very aware that if he was to realise his ambitions war was almost inevitable. However, he hoped and believed that he could win a war with France, particularly if he had a military alliance with Germany. As for Britain, he had seen Prime Minister Chamberlain's desperation to avoid war at the Munich conference and believed it would keep out of such a conflict. In February 1939 the dictator presented his most candid analysis of his foreign policy aims and made it clear that he was even prepared for confrontation with Britain, if need be. He again spoke to the Grand Council (see Source G).

SOURCE G

From a speech by Mussolini to the Grand Council of Fascism, quoted in M. Knox, *Mussolini Unleashed*, Cambridge University Press, 1982.

Italy … is bathed by a landlocked sea [the Mediterranean] that communicates with the oceans through the Suez Canal, … [which is] easily blocked … and through the straits of Gibraltar, dominated by the cannons of Great Britain …

Italy therefore does not have free connection with the oceans. Italy is therefore in truth a prisoner of the Mediterranean, and the more populous and prosperous Italy becomes, the more its imprisonment will gall [frustrate].

The bars of this prison are Corsica, Tunis, Malta, Cyprus … [all occupied by France or Britain]. The sentinels of this prison are Gibraltar and Suez [controlled by Britain]. From this situation … one can draw the following conclusions:

1. The task of Italian policy, which … does not have … territorial [ambitions in mainland Europe] … except for Albania, is to first of all break the bars of the prison.

2. Once the bars are broken, Italy's policy can have only one watchword – to march to the ocean. Which ocean? The Indian Ocean, joining Libya with Ethiopia through the Sudan, or the Atlantic, through French North Africa. In either case, we will find ourselves confronted with Anglo-French opposition.

> Study Sources E and G. Why would these ambitions be likely to lead to war with Britain and France?

That this was not mere bravado was shown by Mussolini's instructions that detailed plans be drawn up to invade and formally annex Albania, thus intimidating Yugoslavia and making the Adriatic virtually an 'Italian sea'.

While preparations were going ahead for this invasion, Mussolini received a second shock from his German friends. German troops marched into Czechoslovakia in March 1939. Again, as over the *Anschluss,* he was furious and again contemplated changing sides. Such thoughts of a major switch in policy lasted no longer than similar ideas a year earlier. Real fear of Germany was now added to grudging admiration for its successes. The Nazi state seemed intent on redrawing the map of Europe and Mussolini was convinced it had the military resources to achieve this, even against the combined armies of Britain and France. Surely it was better to be friends with such a dynamic regime and pick up some of the spoils of victory?

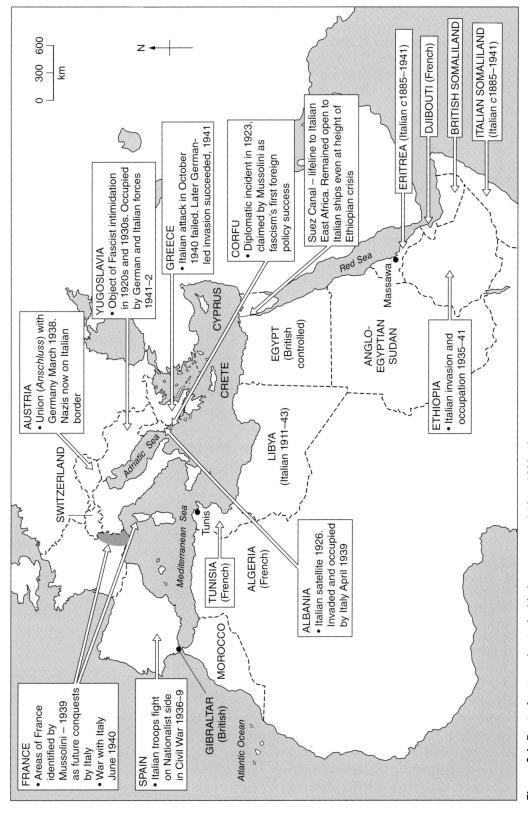

Figure 8.1 Fascist foreign policy in the Mediterranean and Africa 1922–43.

Invasion of Albania 1939

The Italian invasion of Albania finally took place in April 1939 and put the *Duce* back in the limelight. Fascist Italy was also realising its destiny by taking over a weaker, 'inferior' state. The Italian regime conveniently ignored the fact that Albania had been a satellite for over ten years. Victory was won without any major fighting.

Pact of Steel 1939

While Mussolini was delighted with his success, he was angry that his Albanian adventure had caused Britain and France to give guarantees of military assistance to Greece and Turkey should they, too, be attacked. To the *Duce* these guarantees were an aggressive move against legitimate Italian interests: he had long considered Greece as within Italy's sphere of influence and had been trying to emphasise this point in 1923 when he had bombarded Corfu.

These guarantees may have finally convinced Mussolini to conclude a military alliance with Germany but, in any case, such an alliance was the logical conclusion of Italian actions since the war in Ethiopia. The Pact of Steel was signed in May 1939. It committed each nation to join the other in war even if that other country had caused the war by an act of aggression. In short, if Germany were to provoke a war with Britain and France, Italy would be duty-bound to enter the war on Germany's side.

It is uncertain why Mussolini agreed to such terms. Indeed, it has been suggested that he took no notice of the precise wording of treaties, regarding them as simply pieces of paper that could be discarded whenever it suited him. Whether or not Mussolini understood the full consequences of the agreement when he signed it, his government soon realised its meaning and took fright. Foreign Secretary Ciano seems to have persuaded his *Duce* that Italy should make its position clear to its German ally. Consequently, at the end of May the Fascist government told the Germans that, although there was no doubt about Italy's willingness to go to war, any war should be postponed for at least three years to allow it to rearm fully. An angry Hitler ignored this appeal, and did not even bother to reply.

Non-belligerence

Despite his misgivings, Mussolini made no attempt to delay Hitler's preparations for the invasion of Poland. Only at the end of August, when the attack was imminent, did he repeat his assertion that Italy needed several more years of peace. Hitler again ignored this and demanded that Italy stand by the terms of the Pact of Steel. Mussolini realised that Italy was not yet in a position to fight, that such a war would be unpopular in Italy, and that the war would not be fought for Italian interests. He, therefore, attempted to wriggle out of his obligations by arguing that Italy would join the war only if it was supplied with enormous, and unrealistic, quantities of war materiel. When Germany and the Western democracies went to war over Poland in September, the *Duce* declared that his ally had been 'treacherous' and had thereby made the Pact defunct. It was then announced that Italy would be a 'non-belligerent'. The overwhelming majority of Italians were greatly relieved.

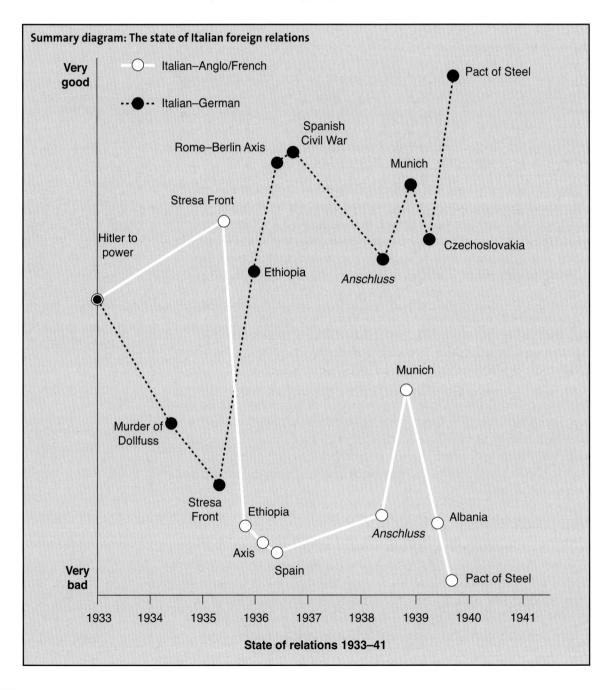

Summary diagram: The state of Italian foreign relations

6 Entry into the Second World War

▶ *Why did Italy join the Second World War in June 1940?*

Mussolini was embarrassed by Italy's neutrality. It made him look rather pathetic after all his bellicose talk. However, he realised that the risks of intervention, both for his country and consequently for his regime, were too great. Throughout the winter of 1939 the supposedly dynamic, decisive *Duce* could not make up his mind what policy to pursue. He still favoured Germany, but was also jealous of Nazi successes and, at one point, even considered acting as a mediator to bring the sides to the negotiating table.

On 10 May 1940 Hitler launched his ***Blitzkrieg*** against France and the Low Countries, catching the Allied forces by surprise and throwing them into disarray. The Netherlands surrendered within five days and within another week the German armies had reached the Channel coast. Belgium surrendered and, by the end of May, the British Expeditionary Force had left the Continent after a desperate evacuation from Dunkirk. German forces were sweeping through France and were meeting only disorganised opposition.

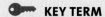 **KEY TERM**

Blitzkrieg 'Lightning war' tactics employed by the Nazis very successfully in the early years of the Second World War. Involved co-ordinated use of aircraft, tanks and infantry.

It appeared to Mussolini, and indeed to the watching world, that the Western allies were on the brink of total defeat. France would almost certainly collapse within days and Britain, left to fight the war alone, would probably follow within a few months or else seek a humiliating negotiated peace. The view from Rome was that if Italy remained neutral it would be faced with a Europe dominated by Germany, a Germany angry at Italy's refusal to honour its treaty obligations. Italy would have gained nothing, would lack Great Power status and would be under physical threat from its Nazi neighbour. On the other hand, if Italy now committed itself to the Axis cause, Germany would be a friend and not a potential enemy. Italy and Germany would share Europe, with the Italians possibly having a free hand in the Mediterranean. In June 1940 Mussolini, therefore, decided to seize what he thought was the opportunity to redeem his lost honour and to win military glory. He declared war on Britain and France.

7 How successful was Mussolini's foreign policy?

From a Fascist perspective, Mussolini could certainly claim some successes by 1940: the empire in Africa had been expanded, Albania had been seized, a pro-Fascist regime had taken control in Spain, and Britain and France had accorded Italy some respect as a Great Power. Foreign policy, particularly the war in Ethiopia, had also generated greater domestic support for the regime.

On the other hand, Mussolini's foreign policy goals had been far too ambitious. It was wholly unrealistic to imagine an Italy simultaneously dominating the Mediterranean militarily, expanding its colonial empire, and exercising economic and even political control over the Balkans. To have achieved even one of these aims Italy would have required far-sighted leadership, efficient and modernised armed forces, a committed populace and, above all, an advanced industrialised economy geared for war. The Fascist state possessed none of these assets.

The events of the 1920s and early 1930s had proved that Italy was not strong enough to prise major concessions from Britain and France by diplomatic means. Italy had established political control over Albania, appeared to be Austria's protector against a German-imposed *Anschluss* and had played a highly publicised part in international conferences, but this was far from being 'great, respected and feared'.

Hitler's impact

Certainly, Hitler's rise to power did make Britain and France more tolerant towards Italian ambitions, but Mussolini was unable to adopt the role of the 'balancing power', able to exact concessions from both sides. The Western democracies would have preferred Mussolini as an ally or, more probably, as a moderating influence on the Nazi dictator, but Fascist Italy's aggressive behaviour in Ethiopia and the Spanish Civil War seemed to indicate that the *Duce* had little interest in keeping the peace. The Western powers continued to deal with Mussolini, hoping that he might restrain his Nazi friend, but by the end of 1938 they had learned to expect very little from him. It was clear to them that he was temperamentally disposed towards Germany and that whatever his territorial demands were, they were impossible to concede.

As for Germany, Hitler preferred Italy as an ally but did not take it seriously as a military power. Italian neutrality or hostility would not have deflected the *Führer* from his foreign policy goals. Indeed, both the *Anschluss* and the seizure of Czechoslovakia showed an insensitivity towards Italian interests, and when Germany went to war against Britain and France in September 1939, the Nazis were neither altogether surprised nor overly concerned by Mussolini's 'non-belligerence'.

Diplomatic methods had not succeeded in realising the *Duce*'s ambitions and the events of 1940–3 were to prove that war could not lead to the permanent expansion of the Fascist state. In fact, it would cause its destruction. Admittedly, in June 1940 Italy did appear to be in an advantageous position, with France on the brink of defeat and Britain severely weakened. However, Italy's armed forces and economy were ill prepared for a major war, as the next chapter will explain.

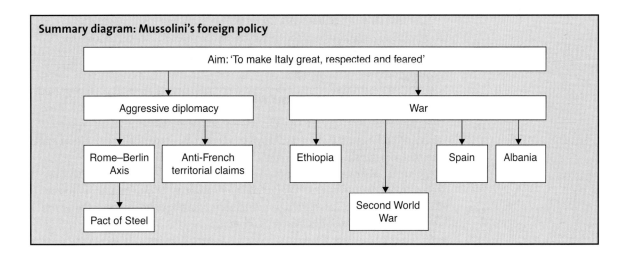

Summary diagram: Mussolini's foreign policy

Aim: 'To make Italy great, respected and feared'

Aggressive diplomacy — Rome–Berlin Axis — Anti-French territorial claims — Pact of Steel

War — Ethiopia — Second World War — Spain — Albania

8 # Key debate

▶ *Why did Mussolini ally with Nazi Germany?*

A number of historians have seen an inevitability in Mussolini's alliance with Nazi Germany. MacGregor Knox, for example, has argued that fascism's brutality in Ethiopia, its adoption of Nazi racial ideas and its aggressive territorial demands are evidence of a shared ideology which culminated in an 'Italo-German revolutionary alliance against the west'. This alliance brought about the war which both dictators desired.

In contrast, Renzo de Felice, a very prominent Italian historian writing in the 1970s, argues strongly that the foreign policies of the two states had little in common, and that had Britain and France acted differently, then Mussolini would not have allied with Nazi Germany. A biographer of Mussolini, Nicholas Farrell, has sympathy with this view (see Extract 1).

EXTRACT I

From N. Farrell, *Mussolini: A New Life*, Phoenix, 2004, pp. xviii and 242.

Mussolini's fatal error was his alliance with Hitler, whom he despised, but this alliance was far from inevitable … Mussolini's policy towards Germany was driven by fear of Germany, not a feeling that Fascism and Nazism should march together … Nevertheless, Mussolini was adamant that Italy had to be a nation prepared and armed for war – not for the purposes of attack or invasion but for the purposes of defence and bargaining … Mussolini had no territorial ambitions in western Europe at all and only minor ones in the Mediterranean, such as Albania. Unlike Hitler, Mussolini did not want to invade his neighbours. The Pact of Steel resulted more from Mussolini's fear of Hitler than from any wild desire for world domination.

Other historians, while agreeing that it is important not to overstate the ideological affinity between the dictators, have emphasised other motives behind the alliance.

EXTRACT 2

From P. Bell, *Origins of the Second World War*, Longman, 1986, p. 67.

Ideology was called in at a late date to consolidate an alliance which began with political and economic matters: German support for Italy during the Abyssinian conflict; the supply of German coal on which Italy became increasingly dependent; and cooperation in the Spanish Civil War. Above all, the objectives which Mussolini set for his foreign policy, amounting to Italian domination in the Mediterranean, could only be attained in opposition to France and Britain, and therefore only in alliance with Germany.

EXTRACT 3

From R. Overy and A. Wheatcroft, *The Road to War*, Macmillan, 1989, p. 169.

During 1936, as a direct result of Ethiopia and Spain, Italy moved out of the Western camp and closer to Hitler's Germany … What they had in common was the fact that they were have-nots in contrast with the powers [Britain and France] that were satiated [satisfied] with the peace treaties [at the end of the First World War] … Mussolini could never reconcile himself fully to the fact that although he was the senior Fascist in Europe, Hitler had greater national power behind him. The fact that they were both Fascist powers gave the relationship a gloss of ideological brotherhood and dictatorial solidarity, but co-operation between them was always more cautious. Italy was useful to Hitler as a Fascist outpost in the Mediterranean keeping Britain and France away from Central Europe. Germany was useful to Mussolini as a source of economic assistance for rearmament, and as a power to divert the attention of Britain and France for Italian adventures in the Mediterranean. Each saw the other as an instrument in his own power game; manipulation rather than friendship bound them together.

? How far do the historians quoted in Extracts 1–3 agree or differ in their interpretations of Mussolini's motives in allying with Nazi Germany?

Chapter summary

Mussolini's foreign policy was relatively successful in the 1920s. Gaining Fiume from Yugoslavia and bullying Greece over Corfu won him support at home and thus helped to secure his dictatorship. The Locarno Agreements and the Kellogg–Briand Pact increased the *Duce*'s international prestige.

The invasion of Ethiopia in 1935 was a turning point. Although it generated great public support within Italy, relations with Britain and France were severely damaged, and Mussolini was drawn ever closer to Nazi Germany. Victory convinced the *Duce* that an aggressive foreign policy would energise fascism at home and win territorial concessions from Britain and France. He did conquer Albania and gained domestic and international prestige from his role at the Munich conference. However, the war in Spain and the alliance with Germany only alienated the Italian public, while the Pact of Steel increasingly drew Italy into a general European war. Mussolini finally joined the Second World War in June 1940, hoping for a cheap and easy victory, a miscalculation that was to prove fatal to the Fascist regime.

 Refresher questions

Use these questions to remind yourself of the key material covered in the chapter.

1. What were Mussolini's aims in foreign policy?
2. In what ways did Mussolini exert increasing influence over the Balkans in the 1920s?
3. Why did Fascist foreign policy become more aggressive from the late 1920s?
4. Why were relations between Fascist Italy and Nazi Germany poor in the years 1933–5?
5. What was the impact of the war in Ethiopia on Mussolini's foreign policy?
6. What was the Rome–Berlin Axis?
7. Why did relations between Fascist Italy and Nazi Germany improve in the years 1936–8?
8. What were Mussolini's territorial demands by 1938–9?
9. What was the Pact of Steel?
10. Why did Mussolini not enter the Second World War when it began in September 1939?
11. Why did Mussolini enter Second World War in June 1940?
12. How successful was Mussolini's foreign policy?

Question practice

ESSAY QUESTIONS

1 'Mussolini's foreign policy failed to make Italy "great, respected, and feared".' Assess the validity of this view.

2 To what extent was Mussolini's foreign policy a success in the years 1935–9?

3 How significant was fear of Germany in Mussolini's decision to ally with the Nazi regime in the years 1936–40?

4 Assess the consequences for Italy of the war in Abyssinia (Ethiopia).

5 How far did Mussolini's foreign policy achieve its aims in the years 1922–40?

SOURCE ANALYSIS QUESTIONS

1 Why is Source 1 valuable to the historian for an enquiry into the extent of public support for Italy's war in Abyssinia in the years 1935–6? Explain your answer using the source, the information given about it and your own knowledge of the historical context.

2 How much weight do you give the evidence of Source 2 for an enquiry into the extent of public support for Italy's war in Abyssinia in the years 1935–6? Explain your answer using the source, the information given about it and your own knowledge of the historical context.

3 How far could the historian make use of Sources 1 and 2 together to investigate the extent of public support for Italy's war in Abyssinia in the years 1935–6? Explain your answer, using both sources, the information given about them and your own knowledge of the historical context

4 With reference to Sources 1, 2 and 3, and your understanding of the historical context, assess the value of these sources to a historian studying the response of the Italian people to the war in Abyssinia.

SOURCE 1

Ward Price of the _Daily Mail_ describing Mussolini's announcement of war against Abyssinia, 3 October 1935. At this time, Ward Price was a supporter of the British Union of Fascists and wrote articles sympathetic to the Nazi regime in Germany. Quoted in N. Farrell, _Mussolini: A New Life_, Phoenix, 2004.

From a window in one of the thick walls of the old palace, I looked down on the scene in the Piazza Venezia. It was a vast mosaic of pink faces under the soft evening light, gazing eagerly upward at the closed window of Mussolini's room. The square can hold 200,000 people but in the surrounding streets at least as many more were packed in solid masses. Every window and roof was crowded to capacity. Slowly, while the nation waited in suspense a honey-coloured moon rose in the green evening sky. Then at 7.30 a sudden roar like a huge volcanic eruption broke from the crowd. Mussolini, in the grey uniform and round black cap of the Fascist militia, had stepped out onto the floodlit balcony.

SOURCE 2

Adapted from Carlo Levi's book *Christ Stopped at Eboli* (republished by Penguin Books, 2000), in which he describes how peasants reacted to Mussolini's declaration of war on Abyssinia in 1935. Levi was an anti-Fascist writer who was arrested and sent into exile in a remote region of southern Italy in 1935. The book was published after his release from prison in 1943.

The peasants were not interested in war. They considered war to be just another unavoidable misfortune, like a tax on goats. 3 October, the day of the official opening of the war was a miserable sort of day. About twenty or twenty-five peasants roped in by the police and the Fascist scouts stood woodenly in the square to listen to the historical pronouncements that came over the radio. The war, so light-heartedly set in motion in Rome, was greeted in Caglioni with stony indifference. Don Luigi spoke from the balcony of the town hall. He enthused about the eternal grandeur of Rome. He said the world hated us for our greatness but that the enemies of Rome would soon bite the dust, because Rome was everlasting and invincible. Huddled against the wall below, the peasants listened in silence, shielding their eyes from the sun and looking … as dark and gloomy as bats.

SOURCE 3

Luigi Barzini, an Italian journalist, describing the effect of victory in the Abyssinian War, 1936. Barzini worked for the *Corriere della Sera*, a long-established newspaper which had been closely linked to the Liberal regime. He was arrested in 1940 for criticising the Fascist regime. Quoted in J. Hite and C. Sinton, *Fascist Italy*, John Murray, 1998, p. 219.

Mussolini's pictures were cut out of newspapers and magazines and pasted on the walls of the poor peasant cottages, at the side of the Madonna and Saint Joseph. Schoolgirls fell in love with him as with a film star. His more memorable words were written large on village houses for all to read. One of his collaborators exclaimed, after listening to him announce from the balcony that Abyssinia had been conquered and that Rome had again become the capital of an Empire, 'Is he like a god?' 'No', said another, 'He is God'.

CHAPTER 9

The Second World War and the fall of Mussolini

The Second World War was to bring about the destruction of the Fascist state and the death of Mussolini. The war revealed the inefficiency and incompetence of the regime, and exposed the fragility of public support for the *Duce*. This chapter examines these themes under the following headings:

★ Italy in the Second World War

★ The fall of Mussolini

★ Armistice and civil war

★ Death of Mussolini

★ Aftermath: Italy in 1945

Key dates

1940	**June**	Italy entered the Second World War
	Sept.	Italian invasion of Egypt
	Oct.	Italian invasion of Greece
1941	**April**	Defeat of Italian forces in East Africa
1942	**Oct.**	Retreat of Axis forces from Egypt
1943	**Jan.**	Libya abandoned by Italian forces
	July	Allied invasion of Sicily
	July 25	Dismissal and arrest of Mussolini
	Sept. 8	Italy signed armistice with Allies

1943	**Sept. 12**	Mussolini freed from prison by Germans
	Sept. 15	Mussolini proclaimed new Fascist state: Italian Social Republic
1943–5		Civil war in German-occupied northern Italy
1945	**April 28**	Execution of Mussolini by Italian anti-Fascists
	June	First post-war government set up
	Nov.	Christian Democrats began dominance of post-war Italian governments

1 Italy in the Second World War

▶ *Why did Fascist Italy suffer military defeats 1940–3?*

Military unpreparedness

Despite all Mussolini's talk of war in the years leading up to 1940, there had been no concerted effort on the part of the *Duce* or his military leaders to prepare Italy for a sustained conflict. Mussolini joined the war only when he thought Britain and France were on the verge of utter defeat. He expected the fighting to be over by September 1940 and commented to a Fascist subordinate that Italy needed 'a few thousand dead to be able to attend the peace conference as a belligerent'. As the war dragged on beyond 1940 and Britain refused to sue for peace, the extent of Italian lack of preparedness became painfully apparent.

Large sums had been spent on rearmament. In the period 1935–8 Italy spent 11.8 per cent of national income on armed forces, compared to 12.9 per cent in Germany, 6.9 per cent in France and 5.5 per cent in Britain, but much of this money had been squandered on purchasing inadequate weaponry and on providing luxurious living quarters for officers. The air force, for example, possessed only 1000 effective planes with which to 'blot out the sun' and these were also of inferior quality – the main fighter aircraft, the Fiat CR42 biplane, was slow and under-armed, and was grounded in large numbers during the North African campaigns for want of sand filters for the engines.

SOURCE A

Study Source A. What clues are there to suggest the Italian air force was not as powerful as Mussolini claimed?

The much-vaunted Fascist air force, *c.*1936. In reality, many of these aircraft were outdated.

The army was also outdated. Mussolini claimed that he had 'eight million bayonets' ready for service, but in June 1940 fewer than 800,000 men were ready to fight and these were largely equipped with rifles and artillery dating back to the First World War. Above all, the Italian army was lacking in tanks. The Second World War was to be a mechanised war but, in 1940, Italy possessed only about 1500 armoured cars and light tanks.

Inadequate leadership

Italian soldiers were not only poorly equipped, they were also poorly trained and badly led. The generals, of whom there were over 600, were steeped in the defensive traditions of the First World War and were sceptical of armoured warfare and air support. As for the navy, probably the best equipped of the three services, its admirals were reluctant to risk their new battleships against the British Mediterranean fleet, and adopted a defensive strategy throughout the war. It was largely Mussolini's fault that the military leadership was incompetent. He concentrated power in his own hands, making all the key strategic decisions on which countries to attack, and promoted officers more for their obedience and powers of flattery than for their military expertise.

Economic weakness

Despite the pre-war policy of encouraging autarky, the Italian economy was far from self-sufficient in 1940. To make matters worse, the regime had given little thought to the problem of large-scale armaments production during wartime. Strategic materials, notably coal and iron ore, had to be imported from Germany and German-occupied territories. As the war began to go badly for the Axis, the Germans became increasingly reluctant to divert such scarce resources to their ineffectual Italian allies. This led to a fall of twenty per cent in Italian steel production between 1940 and 1942 with the result that losses, particularly in tanks and aircraft, could not be replaced. Food production also fell. The wheat harvest dropped by 1.5 million tonnes as a result of many peasant farmers being drafted into the army.

Military defeats

In September 1940 Mussolini launched his campaign to expand the Italian Empire in North Africa (see the map on page 130). Italian forces in Libya attacked British positions in Egypt. Not content with this, the *Duce* opened a new front in the Balkans in the following month when the Italian army in Albania invaded Greece. The Italian army, however, did not have the resources to fight two campaigns simultaneously and both offensives rapidly ground to a halt. By the end of the year the Fascist armies had been pushed back into Libya and Albania, respectively. The navy fared no better, losing half its battle fleet to a British air attack on the port of Taranto in November.

Hopes of military glory on the cheap were now fading. Britain still controlled Egypt and most of the Mediterranean, and had thwarted German plans to invade across the English Channel. The *Duce*, nevertheless, remained confident of ultimate victory. His Nazi ally, however, lacked faith in Italian arms. In February 1941 Mussolini was persuaded, reluctantly, to accept the German General Rommel as Axis commander in North Africa. In April German armies finally ended the stalemate in the Balkans, sweeping through Yugoslavia and defeating Greece in little more than a week.

The Axis powers appeared to be winning, but it was becoming increasingly clear that Italy was not just a junior partner to Germany but also a subservient one. Italy relied on Germany for raw materials, particularly coal, and found that the crucial political and military decisions were taken by the Germans, usually without any consultation. Mussolini resented this dependency but could do little about it. The loss of Ethiopia and the neighbouring colony of Italian Somaliland to British troops in April 1941 was final proof of Italy's military failure. The *Duce* managed to send 200,000 soldiers to the Russian front, but these men were too poorly trained and equipped to be of real value. If Italy was to gain anything at all from the war it would be through German success, not its own, while German defeat would bring down Italian fascism with it.

In 1942 there were some modest Axis successes in Russia and North Africa, but by the end of the year the Germans were on the brink of catastrophic defeat at Stalingrad and Rommel's forces in North Africa were in full retreat. Libya was abandoned to the British in January 1943 and by May the whole Axis army in North Africa had surrendered. Two months later the Anglo-American forces landed in Sicily. The invasion of the Italian mainland itself was imminent.

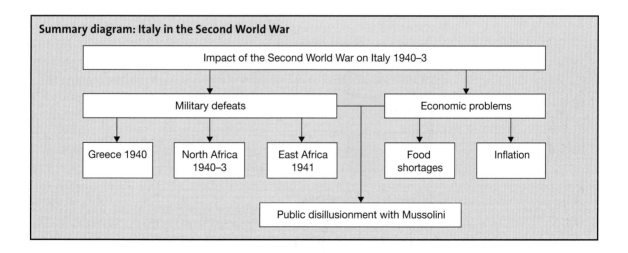

Summary diagram: Italy in the Second World War

The fall of Mussolini

▶ *Why did Mussolini fall from power?*

Public disillusionment

Public opinion had been divided over the decision to enter the war in June 1940. There had been many doubters, but a significant number of Italians had hoped for a quick and profitable victory. Defeats in Greece and Egypt had soon destroyed such optimism. Those Italians who had believed the Fascist propaganda about an army of 8 million bayonets and an air force that could 'blot out the sun' became particularly disillusioned when they witnessed the organisational chaos, the antiquated weaponry and the lack of battle training. Soldiers home on leave recounted how the attack on Greece had begun at the start of the rainy season and how, once winter set in, the army provided only totally inadequate winter clothing. Veterans of the North African campaign described the desperate shortage of armoured vehicles.

Italian civilians, in any case, did not need to be told about fascism's lack of preparedness for a prolonged war: they could see the evidence all around them. Food became short as grain imports fell – the result of British naval blockade in the Mediterranean – and, since the government refused to introduce rationing, prices rose dramatically. Coffee, petrol and soap became virtually unobtainable, except for those rich enough to afford the inflated prices on the flourishing black market. Eventually, in 1941, rationing was introduced, but by then stocks had run very low. Supplies were scarce and badly organised, and ordinary Italians were faced with a bread ration of only 150 grams per person per day – the lowest of any combatant country except the USSR.

By the end of 1940 the Italian public was heartily sick of the war. People's faith in the *Duce*'s infallibility had been shattered. There was no longer any interest in the possible spoils of war, particularly as it was becoming increasingly apparent that further fighting would only increase German control over the country. The years 1941 and 1942 only increased the disillusionment of the Italian public, as defeat followed defeat, shortages worsened and working hours lengthened. Opposition groups, from Communist to Catholic, began to emerge. These groups were still small and disorganised but, in early 1943, shortages and anti-war sentiment led to a wave of strikes in Italian industry.

Dismissal of Mussolini

The regime was well aware of the deep unpopularity of the war and the growing contempt for the *Duce*. By late 1942 major industrialists and even prominent Fascists, notably Dino Grandi and Galeazzo Ciano, the dictator's own son-in-law, were inclined to make peace. Their realisation that Mussolini would not contemplate this, and that the Allies would not negotiate with him anyway, led them to the belief that the *Duce* must go. He could be a sacrifice or a scapegoat, peace could be arranged, and the Fascists might keep at least some of their power. Such views were echoed by conservatives at the court of King Victor Emmanuel, and among the leading generals, who feared a collapse of social order and perhaps even a Communist revolution.

The Allied conquest of Sicily in July 1943 was the final straw. The mainland was in danger of invasion and utter defeat appeared inevitable. A group of senior Fascists led by Roberto Farinacci (page 34), the ex-squad leader, and De Bono, a Fascist general in the Ethiopian campaign, persuaded Mussolini to call a meeting of the Grand Council of Fascism to discuss the military situation. The Grand Council, which had not sat since 1939, met on the night of 24–25 July 1943 and voted nineteen to seven to ask the King to restore all those powers to parliament, ministers and the Grand Council that Mussolini had taken away. In effect, they were seeking a way to get rid of the *Duce*, make peace, and save, if not the regime, then at least themselves.

The members of the Grand Council had expected a spirited defence, and even physical violence, from Mussolini and they were surprised to see the dictator subdued, perhaps ill. He could not bring himself to protest. But by the morning of 25 July the *Duce* had recovered himself and he visited the King, intending to name new ministers, punish those who had voted against him and continue the war. However, the King, encouraged by the events of the previous night and spurred on by the army high command, told Mussolini that he was now the 'most hated man in Italy'. He declared that the war was lost and that Marshal Badoglio would take over as prime minister with a brief to make peace. The *Duce* was then arrested.

With the dismissal of Mussolini, the Fascist regime collapsed. There were no public protests, only public relief. Fascists, far from attempting to restore the *Duce* by calling supporters into the streets, meekly accepted the change in government. Leading Fascists tried to ingratiate themselves with the new prime minister. Even the Fascist mouthpiece, *Il Popolo d'Italia*, simply replaced Mussolini's photograph on the front page with that of Marshal Badoglio. It had been a bloodless coup.

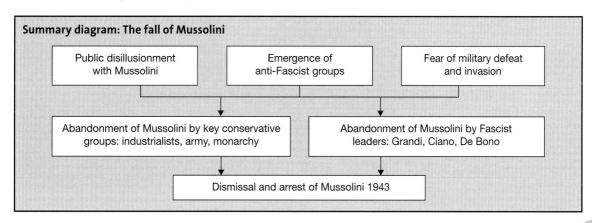

Summary diagram: The fall of Mussolini

③ Armistice and civil war

▶ *What were the consequences of the fall of Mussolini's regime?*

During what is sometimes known as the 45 days, the time between Mussolini's dismissal and his escape from captivity, events moved fast. Demonstrations in favour of peace took place across Italy, the German army took control of Rome, and Marshal Badoglio's government held peace talks in secret with the Allies.

An armistice with Britain and the USA was signed on 8 September 1943, but it was Italy's misfortune that this did not bring peace. Nazi Germany could not afford to let this 'backdoor' to Europe fall into Allied hands, and promptly occupied northern and central Italy. Hitler, informed that the fallen *Duce* was being imprisoned in a ski resort in the Apennine mountains, ordered his rescue. In a daring mission, German troops landed by glider, seized Mussolini from his Italian captors and crammed him into a small two-seater plane. Transferred first to a German airbase in Italy, Mussolini was flown on to Germany to meet Hitler. Greeting the *Führer*, Mussolini is reputed to have declared, 'I am here to receive my orders'.

On 15 September 1943 Mussolini announced the creation of a new German-sponsored Fascist state, the **Italian Social Republic**. This is often known as the Salò Republic, named after the town on Lake Garda in northern Italy where many of its offices were based.

KEY TERM

Italian Social Republic
Mussolini's Fascist regime in northern Italy 1943–5.

SOURCE B

? Study Source B. Why would Nazi Germany circulate this photograph within Italy and across Europe?

Mussolini being escorted on to a German plane after his rescue from prison by German troops in September 1943.

This new Fascist regime, heavily reliant on German arms, controlled only a relatively small area of northern Italy. It lacked any real public support and was rejected by those conservative groups, notably industrialists and the Church, who had largely embraced the pre-war Fascist state. Mussolini's supporters were mainly those Fascists, such as Farinacci, who had resented the *Duce's* compromises with the traditional Italian elites – the industrialists, the army generals, the Church – and who hoped to revive the 'pure' fascism of violent *squadrismo* and contempt for Italian conservatives. Many of these men, Farinacci included, were attracted by Nazi ideology, particularly anti-Semitism. Other supporters were simply opportunists looking for wealth and some share of power.

Although the new Fascist republic lacked a capital city, any coherent structure of government and an army, it did spawn a brutal militia, numbering close to 50,000 men. The militia supported German forces in northern Italy and helped in rounding up 7500 Italian Jews who were then despatched to Nazi death camps. Many of these militia groups owed more allegiance to local Fascist leaders than to the *Duce*. Often acting as little more than gangsters, they murdered and terrorised suspected opponents, and extorted money from local businesses. Mussolini indulged his own taste for violence by wreaking vengeance on those Grand Council members who had voted against him: Ciano and De Bono were shot in 1944.

Anti-Fascist groups

In response to the new Fascist state and its brutality, resistance grew among a range of anti-Fascist groups. The Communist Party raised 30,000 fighters or **partisans**, while another 20,000 were Catholics, former supporters of the *Popolari* or members of Catholic Action youth groups. The Action Party, representing left-of-centre middle-class anti-Fascists, provided a further 25,000 men. These partisans fought against the Fascist militia, attacked German army patrols and carried out acts of sabotage. The Germans and their Fascist allies responded with vicious reprisals. In the most notorious case, 335 civilian hostages were murdered in the Ardeatine Caves, near Rome, in revenge for a partisan attack which had left 28 Germans dead.

The anti-Fascist partisans did try to work together by forming the Committee for National Liberation in January 1944, but mistrust between the Communists and other groups limited any real military co-operation. In total, the partisans killed about 5000 German soldiers, probably suffering 10,000 dead themselves. Their efforts did tie down significant numbers of German troops who would otherwise have been fighting British and US forces in Italy, but they were never strong enough to defeat the Germans or overthrow Mussolini's Fascist regime. It was the Allied forces, slowly pushing into northern Italy in late 1944 and early 1945, who expelled the Germans and finally liberated Italy from fascism.

 **KEY TERM**

Partisans Armed anti-Fascist groups.

Summary diagram: Armistice and civil war

Second World War in Italy 1943–5	Civil war in Italy 1943–5
• Armistice ended fighting between Italian and Anglo-American forces • German forces occupied northern and central Italy • Anglo-American armies slowly fought their way northwards through Italy, facing determined German resistance	• Fascist Italian Social Republic set up in northern Italy • Emergence of anti-Fascist groups – Catholic, Socialist, Communist • Fighting between Fascist militia, supported by German forces, and anti-Fascist partisans

---

 # Death of Mussolini

▶ *Which political group executed Mussolini?*

By the beginning of 1945 the Nazi forces in Italy were in full retreat towards the Austrian border. Mussolini, surrounded by a dwindling band of supporters, tried to flee. On 25 April he joined a group of German soldiers heading for Austria and disguised himself in a German uniform. At Dongo on Lake Garda, the group was stopped by Italian Communist partisans. The *Duce* was recognised. He and his mistress, Clara Petacci, were executed by the partisans on 28 April, their bodies taken to Milan and put on public display, strung up by the heels from the roof of a petrol station in Piazzale Loreto. It was a humiliating and ignominious end for a *Duce* once hailed as a 'Titan', a 'Genius' and even the 'Sun god' by his Fascist admirers.

 # Aftermath: Italy in 1945

▶ *Why did the Christian Democrats become the dominant political party after the Second World War?*

As the war ended there were revenge killings and executions, notably of the former party secretaries, Starace and Farinacci, but there was no bloodbath. In June 1945 the various anti-Fascist groups set up the first free government of Italy since 1922. This was a coalition government under the leadership of Ferruccio Parri, a resistance hero, and included his own Action Party, together with Socialists, Communists and Christian Democrats. However, Parri's party proved too small to dominate the coalition and, in November 1945, he was replaced as coalition prime minister by Alcide De Gasperi of the Christian Democrats.

SOURCE C

Study Source C. Why would the partisans display the body of Mussolini so publicly? ?

The bodies of Mussolini and Clara Petacci on public display in Milan's Piazzale Loreto in 1945.

Elections for a Constituent Assembly which would draw up a new constitution for Italy were called for June 1946. For the first time Italian women would be allowed to vote. In these elections the Christian Democrats won 35 per cent of the vote, with the Socialists and Communists taking 21 per cent and 19 per cent, respectively. The remains of the old Liberal Party could secure only seven per cent of the votes cast. The Christian Democrats, successors of the Catholic *Popolari* and drawing support from the middle classes and business, had displaced the Liberals as the party of the centre-right. In fact, the Christian Democrats would dominate the new democratic Italy for the next 40 years.

A new constitution was drawn up, establishing an Italian democracy, and confirming the relationship between Church and State set out in Mussolini's Lateran Accords of 1929. However, there was to be no place for the monarchy. A referendum on the future of the monarchy had been held at the same time as the elections for the Constituent Assembly and 54 per cent of Italians had voted for a republic. The members of the royal family – the House of Savoy (which had never been much loved) – left the country immediately.

In the post-war peace settlement Italy lost its empire in Africa, had to hand back Fiume to Yugoslavia, and was required to pay $360 million to Yugoslavia, Albania, Greece and Ethiopia as reparations for damage done. The USA and UK, however, partly in recognition of the anti-Fascist resistance and partly due to their fear that communism might grow in Italy, did not demand any reparations for themselves. Indeed, during 1948 the USA provided $2 billion in aid to get the Italian economy back on its feet. The USA was determined that Italy would remain a democracy and become one of European allies in the emerging Cold War with Communist Russia.

Chapter summary

Mussolini's decision to declare war on Britain and France was to prove fatal to his regime. Italian armed forces and the economy were hopelessly ill prepared for a prolonged war. As defeat followed defeat public and elite support for the *Duce* drained away. By July 1943 the public was desperate for peace. Fearing invasion and perhaps even a popular revolt, army generals, the King, industrialists and even leading Fascists looked for a way to end the war and to maintain at least some of their own power. Mussolini had to be removed.

Although the new government of Marshal Badoglio signed an armistice with the Allies, it failed to prevent the Nazis from seizing Mussolini and installing him as ruler of the Italian Social Republic. Italy became a battlefield between Allied and German forces, and northern Italy descended into a bitter civil war. It took until 1945 for British and US forces to push the Nazis out of Italy and to put an end to the Fascist regime. By the end of 1946 the public had voted to end the monarchy and Italy had become a democracy.

 Refresher questions

Use these questions to remind yourself of the key material covered in the chapter.

1 Why did Italy perform so badly in the Second World War?

2 Which countries did Italy invade in the Second World War?

3 Why had Mussolini lost public support by 1943?

4 Why did the Grand Council of Fascism vote to remove Mussolini's powers?

5 Which powerful groups in the Italian state were included in the dismissed of Mussolini as prime minister?

6 What was the Italian Social Republic?

7 Why was there a civil war 1943–5?

8 How did Italy become a democracy after the Second World War?

Question practice

ESSAY QUESTIONS

1 'Italian anti-Fascist resistance caused the final failure of fascism in the years 1943–5.' Assess the validity of this view.

2 To what extent was the Second World War the main reason for the collapse of Mussolini's Fascist regime?

3 How significant was public dissent in the collapse of Mussolini's regime in July 1943?

4 Assess the impact of the Second World War on Italy up until 1943.

5 How far do you agree that Mussolini's poor leadership was responsible for Italian defeats in the Second World War between 1940 and 1943?

SOURCE ANALYSIS QUESTIONS

1 Why is Source 1 valuable to the historian investigating the reasons why leading Fascists turned against Mussolini in July 1943? Explain your answer using the source, the information given about it and your own knowledge of the historical context.

2 How much weight do you give the evidence of Source 2 (page 152) for an enquiry into the King's motives in dismissing Mussolini as prime minister in July 1943? Explain your answer using the source, the information given about it and your own knowledge of the historical context.

3 How far could the historian make use of Sources 1 and 2 (page 152) together to investigate the reasons why Mussolini fell from power in July 1943? Explain your answer, using both sources, the information given about them and your own knowledge of the historical context.

4 With reference to Sources 1, 2 and 3 (page 152), and your understanding of the historical context, assess the value of these sources to a historian studying the collapse of the Fascist regime in July 1943.

SOURCE I

From Federzoni's summary of the speech made by Dino Grandi to the Grand Council of Fascism on 25 July 1943. Federzoni supported Grandi's attempt to remove Mussolini from power. Quoted in J. Whittam, *Fascist Italy*, Manchester University Press, 1995, p. 166.

The Head of government, Grandi observed, has spoken of the unpardonable errors committed by military leaders and by the armed forces that he personally commands. But Mussolini, Head of government and the minister in charge of all the armed services, has had seventeen years to create, organise, prepare and to select the officer corps, the troops and the equipment … Military preparedness was therefore the major task for the man who had the honour of guiding the destiny of the nation.

The Grand Council must decide that the regime of dictatorship is over because it has compromised the vital interests of the nation, has brought Italy to the brink of military defeat and has damaged the revolution and fascism itself. The Grand Council must decide to restore all the authority and responsibility of state institutions which the dictatorship has absorbed and return to the Crown, the Grand Council, the Parliament and the corporations all the tasks assigned to them by our constitutional laws.

SOURCE 2

From the conversation between the King and Mussolini on 25 July 1943, recalled by a bodyguard who was standing outside the door. Quoted in J. Hite and C. Hinton, *Fascist Italy*, John Murray, 1998, p. 248.

I heard the King say 'My dear Duce, it's no longer any good. Italy is on its knees. The army's morale is at rock bottom, and the soldiers do not want to fight any more. The vote of the Grand Council is dreadful. At this moment you are the most hated man in Italy. Only one friend has remained with you – myself. I have demonstrated my friendship many times, defending you from every attack, but this time I must ask you to leave me free to place the government in other hands'. Mussolini said 'Then everything is finished?' The King answered: 'I am sorry, I am very sorry. There is no other solution.'

SOURCE 3

From the diary of Bottai, made just before the meeting of the Grand Council. Bottai supported Grandi's attempt to remove Mussolini from power. Quoted in N. Farrell, *Mussolini: A New Life*, Phoenix, 2004, p. 392.

Our duty has placed us at a crossroads, between country and party, between Italy and regime, between King and Duce.

It is no longer a question of betraying or not betraying, but of having the courage to confess the betrayal done by him, consummated by him day by day, from the first disappointment to this moral collapse. Not one idea, one agreement, one institution, one law to which he has remained faithful. Everything was broken, distorted, corrupted by him … [he was] conceited and cunning … [he has] a contempt for men and their ideals.

Our resolution [in the Grand Council] means we place ourselves at stake: it is a game without alternatives, that will end in … sacrifice.

AQA A level History

Essay guidance

At both AS and A level for AQA Component 2: Depth Study: Italy 1900–45, you will need to answer an essay question in the exam. Each essay question is marked out of 25:

- for the AS exam, Section B: answer **one** essay question from a choice of two
- for the A level exam, Section B: answer **two** essay questions from a choice of three.

There are several question stems which all have the same basic requirement: to analyse and reach a conclusion, based on the evidence that you provide.

The AS questions often give a quotation and then ask whether you agree or disagree with this view. Almost inevitably, your answer will be a mixture of both. It is the same task as for A level – just phrased differently in the question. Detailed essays are more likely to do well than vague or generalised essays, especially in the Depth Studies of Paper 2.

The AQA mark scheme is essentially the same for AS and the full A level (see the AQA website, www.aqa.org.uk). Both emphasise the need to analyse and evaluate the key features related to the periods studied. The key feature of the highest level is sustained analysis: analysis that unites the whole of the essay.

Writing an essay: general skills

- *Focus and structure.* Be sure what the question is asking and plan what the paragraphs should be about.
- *Focused introduction to the essay.* Be sure that the introductory sentence relates directly to the focus of the question and that each paragraph highlights the structure of the answer.
- *Use detail.* Make sure that you show detailed knowledge, but only as part of an explanation

being made in relation to the question. No knowledge should be standalone; it should be used in context.

- *Explanatory analysis and evaluation.* Consider what words and phrases to use in an answer to strengthen the explanation.
- *Argument and counter-argument.* Think how arguments can be balanced so as to give contrasting views.
- *Resolution.* Think how best to 'resolve' contradictory arguments.
- *Relative significance and evaluation.* Think how best to reach a judgement when trying to assess the relative importance of various factors, and their possible interrelationship.

Planning an essay

Practice question 1

'Italian democracy collapsed in 1922 because the conservative elites feared socialism more than they feared fascism.' Explain why you agree or disagree with this view.

This question requires you to analyse why Italian democracy collapsed in 1922. You must discuss the following:

- How the fear of socialism among the conservative elites helped to cause the collapse of Italian democracy in 1922 (your primary focus).
- The other factors that allowed this to happen (your secondary focus).

A clear structure makes for a much more effective essay and is crucial for achieving the highest marks. You need three or four paragraphs to structure this question effectively. In each paragraph you will deal with one factor. One of these *must* be the factor in the question.

A very basic plan for this question might look like this:

- Paragraph 1: How the fear of socialism among the conservative elites (meaning leading members of the Liberal Party such as Salandra, plus the King, the Catholic Church, rich industrialists and landowners, and generals in the army) made Mussolini appear an acceptable choice for prime minister, despite Fascist violence.
- Paragraph 2: How the divisions and weaknesses of the Liberals helped Italian democracy to collapse.
- Paragraph 3: How Mussolini's political skills helped to destroy Italian democracy by 1922.

It is a good idea to cover the factor named in the question first, so that you don't run out of time and forget to do it. Then cover the others in what you think is their order of importance, or in the order that appears logical in terms of the sequence of paragraphs.

The introduction

Maintaining focus is vital. One way to do this from the beginning of your essay is to use the words in the question to help write your argument. The first sentence of question 1, for example, could look like this:

Italian democracy collapsed in 1922 partly because the conservative elites were terrified of a socialist revolution and saw Mussolini as the man to prevent this, but there were other factors as well to explain this collapse.

This opening sentence provides a clear focus on the demands of the question.

Focus throughout the essay

Structuring your essay well will help with keeping the focus of your essay on the question. To maintain a focus on the wording in question 1, you could begin your first main paragraph with 'weakness'.

[Weakness and? Otherwise 'weakness' isn't here] Fear of socialism among the conservative elites was one very important factor in causing the collapse of Italian democracy.

- This sentence begins with a clear point that refers to the primary focus of the question (collapse of Italian democracy) while linking it to a factor (fear of socialism among the conservative elites).
- You could then have a paragraph for each of your other factors.
- It will be important to make sure that each paragraph focuses on analysis and includes relevant details that are used as part of the argument.
- You may wish to number your factors. This helps to make your structure clear and helps you to maintain focus.

Deploying detail

As well as focus and structure, your essay will be judged on the extent to which it includes accurate detail. There are several different kinds of evidence you could use that might be described as detailed. These include correct dates, names of relevant people, statistics and events. For example, for sample question 1 you could use terms such as land seizures and the March on Rome. You can also make your essays more detailed by using the correct technical vocabulary.

Analysis and explanation

'Analysis' covers a variety of high-level skills including explanation and evaluation; in essence, it means breaking down something complex into smaller parts. A clear structure which breaks down a complex question into a series of paragraphs is the first step towards writing an analytical essay. The purpose of explanation is to provide evidence for why something happened, or why something is true or false. An explanatory statement requires two parts: a *claim* and a *justification*. For example, for question 1, you might want to argue that one important reason was the conservatives' fear of the land seizures by peasants who supported the Socialists. Once you have made your point, and supported it with relevant detail, you can then explain how this answers the question. For example, you could conclude your paragraph like this:

So the land seizures by the Socialists were important[1] because the conservative elites feared losing their land and property[2], and began to look favourably on the Fascist squads who attacked the Socialists in the countryside[3].

1 The first part of this sentence is the claim while the second part justifies the claim.
2 'Because' is a very important word to use when writing an explanation, as it shows the relationship between the claim and the justification.
3 The justification.

Evaluation

Evaluation means considering the importance of two or more different factors, weighing them against each other, and reaching a judgement. This is a good skill to use at the end of an essay because the conclusion should reach a judgement which answers the question. For example, your conclusion to question 1 might read:

Clearly[1], fear of socialism meant that the conservative elites, principally the King, industrialists and landowners, were looking to support a government which would crush what they saw as the Socialist threat. However[2], they had lost faith in the weak and divided Liberal governments which had failed to deal with Socialist strikes and land seizures, and they turned instead to Mussolini. Therefore[3], the fear of socialism enabled Mussolini to present himself to the conservative elites as a dynamic alternative to Italian democracy.

1–3 Words like 'clearly', 'however' and 'therefore' are helpful to contrast the importance of the different factors.

Complex essay writing: argument and counter-argument

Essays that develop a good argument are more likely to reach the highest levels. This is because argumentative essays are much more likely to develop sustained analysis. As you know, your essays are judged on the extent to which they analyse.

After setting up an argument in your introduction, you should develop it throughout the essay. One way of doing this is to adopt an argument–counter-argument structure. A counter-argument is one that disagrees with the main argument of the essay. This is a good way of evaluating the importance of the different factors that you discuss. Essays of this type will develop an argument in one paragraph and then set out an opposing argument in another paragraph. Sometimes this will include juxtaposing the differing views of historians on a topic.

Good essays will analyse the key issues. They will probably have a clear piece of analysis at the end of each paragraph. While this analysis might be good, it will generally relate only to the issue discussed in that paragraph.

Excellent essays will be analytical throughout. As well as the analysis of each factor discussed above, there will be an overall analysis. This will run throughout the essay and can be achieved through developing a clear, relevant and coherent argument.

A good way of achieving sustained analysis is to consider which factor is most important. Here is an example of an introduction that sets out an argument for question 1:

Fear of socialism among the conservative elites escalated in the years 1919-22 as support for the party among the industrial working class and poor peasantry grew[1]. However, this was not the only reason for the collapse of Italian democracy in 1922. The divisions and rivalries among the Liberals meant that governments in the period were short lived and unable to agree on how to respond to Socialist strikes and land seizures[2]. But the most important reason why Italian democracy collapsed and Mussolini was appointed prime minister was that he took advantage of the fear of socialism and of the weakness of the Liberals[3].

1 The introduction begins with a claim.
2 The introduction continues with another reason.
3 Concludes with outline of argument of the most important reason.

- This introduction focuses on the question and sets out the key factors that the essay will develop.
- It introduces an argument about which factor was most significant.
- However, it also sets out an argument that can then be developed throughout each paragraph, and is rounded off with an overall judgement in the conclusion.

Complex essay writing: resolution and relative significance

Having written an essay that explains argument and counter-arguments, you should then resolve the tension between the argument and the counter-argument in your conclusion. It is important that the writing is precise and summarises the arguments made in the main body of the essay. You need to reach a supported overall judgement. One very appropriate way to do this is by evaluating the relative significance of different factors, in the light of valid criteria. Relative significance means how important one factor is compared to another.

The best essays will always make a judgement about which was most important based on valid criteria. These can be very simple, and will depend on the topic and the exact question.

The following criteria are often useful:

- Duration: which factor was important for the longest amount of time?
- Scope: which factor affected the most people?
- Effectiveness: which factor achieved most?
- Impact: which factor led to the most fundamental change?

As an example, you could compare the factors in terms of their duration and their impact. A conclusion that follows this advice should be capable of reaching a high level (if written, in full, with appropriate details) because it reaches an overall judgement that is supported through evaluating the relative significance of different factors in the light of valid criteria.

Having written an introduction and the main body of an essay for question 1, a concluding paragraph that aims to meet the exacting criteria for reaching a complex judgement could look like this:

Thus, the reasons for the collapse of Italian democracy in 1922 were complex, with several interrelated factors. The collapse of democracy and the rise of Mussolini to power were not inevitable. They were the result of particular circumstances. Fear of socialism and Liberal governments' inability to deal with this Socialist threat caused the conservative elites to become disillusioned with the Liberals. However, Mussolini's political skills were vital in convincing the conservative elites that he should become prime minister. Mussolini managed to persuade them that only he could crush the Socialists but also that he could be trusted to control the more radical, violent elements within fascism.

Sources guidance

Whether you are taking the AS exam or the full A level exam for AQA Component 2: Depth Study: Italy 1900–45, Section A presents you with sources and a question which involves evaluation of their utility or value.

AS exam	A level exam
Section A: answer question 1, based on two primary sources. (25 marks)	Section A: answer question 1, based on three primary sources. (30 marks)
Question focus: with reference to these sources and your understanding of the historical context, which of these two sources is more valuable in explaining … ?	Question focus: with reference to these sources and your understanding of the historical context, assess the value of these three sources to a historian studying …

Sources and sample questions

Study the sources. They are all concerned with the reasons for the growth of fascism in the years 1920–2.

SOURCE 1

From Tasca, a former Communist, writing in 1938 about the rise of fascism 1920–2, quoted in J. Whittam, *Fascist Italy*, Manchester University Press, 1995, p. 150.

Out of 280 villages in Emilia 223 were in Socialist hands. The landowners were powerless before the all-powerful workers' trade unions. In the countryside the prizes of public life were almost entirely denied to the whole middle class who were not members of the Socialist organisations. The country landowner who for years had been head of the village, was ousted [from his position]. On the land he had to reckon with the [Socialist] league which controlled employment, in the market with the Socialist co-operative which fixed prices … Profit, position, power were lost to him and his children. Hatred and bitterness were welling up, ready at any moment to overflow … The old ruling classes felt that they were being swept away to make room for the new social structure.

SOURCE 2

From an article in the Liberal newspaper *La Stampa* in May 1921 describing a Fascist crowd, quoted in J. Hite and C. Hinton, *Fascist Italy*, John Murray, 1998, p. 48.

[Ex-army officers] who have sought and not found employment; it is a mixture of hope and desperation; [there are] public sector employees scarcely able to eat; swarms of shopkeepers hit by the slump, who detest with a deadly hatred the trade union run shops; students and young graduates with no jobs … convinced that their misfortunes were due to the sinister plots of old politicians; adolescents aged 16–19 made bitter by bad luck which made the war finish too soon … because they wished to do great deeds; and bands of ex Socialists who had become war enthusiasts in 1915 …

SOURCE 3

From Italo Balbo, Fascist leader in Ferrara, writing in 1932, quoted in N. Farrell, *Mussolini: A New Life*, Phoenix, 2004, p. 101.

When I came back from the war, just like so many, I hated politics and politicians, who in my opinion had betrayed the hopes of the combatants, reducing Italy to a shameful peace and systematic humiliation of any Italians who supported the cult of heroes. Fight, combat, to come back to the country of Giolitti, who offered every ideal as an item for sale? No. Better to deny everything, to destroy everything, so as to rebuild everything from scratch. Many in those days turned to Socialism. It was the ready-made revolutionary programme and, apparently the most radical ... It is certain, in my opinion, that, without Mussolini, three-quarters of the Italian youth which had returned from the trenches would have become Bolsheviks ...

AS style question

With reference to Sources 1 and 2, and your understanding of the historical context, which of these two sources is more valuable in explaining why support grew for fascism in the years 1920–2?

AS mark scheme

See the AQA website (www.aqa.org.uk) for the full mark schemes. This summary of the AS mark scheme shows how it rewards analysis and evaluation of the source material within the historical context.

Level 1	Describing the source content or offering generic phrases.
Level 2	Some relevant but limited comments on the value of one source or some limited comment on both sources.
Level 3	Some relevant comments on the value of the sources and some explicit reference to the issue identified in the question.
Level 4	Relevant well-supported comments on the value and a supported conclusion, but with limited judgement.
Level 5	Very good understanding of the value in relation to the issue identified. Sources evaluated thoroughly and with a well-substantiated conclusion related to which is more valuable.

A level style question

With reference to Sources 1, 2 and 3, and your understanding of the historical context, assess the value of these sources to a historian studying the rise of fascism 1920–2.

A level mark scheme

This summary of the A level mark scheme shows how it is similar to the AS, but covers three sources. Also, the wording of the question means there is no explicit requirement to decide which of the three sources is the most valuable. Concentrate instead on a very thorough analysis of the content and evaluation of the provenance of each source, using contextual knowledge.

Level 1	Some limited comment on the value of at least one source.
Level 2	Some limited comments on the value of the sources or on content or provenance, or comments on all three sources but no reference to the value of the sources.
Level 3	Some understanding of all three sources in relation to both content and provenance, with some historical context; but analysis limited.
Level 4	Good understanding of all three sources in relation to content, provenance and historical context to give a balanced argument on their value for the purpose specified in the question.
Level 5	As Level 4, but with a substantiated judgement on all three sources.

Working towards an answer

It is important that knowledge is used to show an understanding of the relationship between the sources and the issue raised in the question. Answers should be concerned with:

- provenance
- arguments used (and you can agree/disagree)
- tone and emphasis of the sources.

The sources

The two or three sources used each time will be contemporary – probably of varying types (for example, diaries, newspaper accounts, government reports). The sources will all be on the same broad topic area. Each source will have value. Your task is to evaluate how much – in terms of its content and its provenance.

You will need to assess the *value of the content* by using your own knowledge. Is the information accurate? Is it giving only part of the evidence and ignoring other aspects? Is the tone of the writing significant?

You will need to evaluate the *provenance* of the source by considering who wrote it, and when, where and why. What was its purpose? Was it produced to express an opinion; to record facts; to influence the opinion of others? Even if it was intended to be accurate, the writer may have been biased – either deliberately or unconsciously. The writer, for example, might have only known part of the situation and reached a judgement solely based on that.

Here is a guide to analysing the provenance, content and tone for Sources 1, 2 and 3 (pages 157–8).

Analysing the sources

To answer the question effectively, you need to read the sources carefully and pull out the relevant points as well as add your own knowledge. You must remember to keep the focus on the question at all times.

Source 1 (page 157)

Provenance:

- The source is from a speech by Angelo Tasca, a former Communist. He will have a particular view on why support for fascism grew.
- It is written in 1938, while Mussolini was still firmly in power. It is trying to explain to anti-Fascists the basis of Fascist support.

Content and argument:

- The source argues that fascism emerged from the struggle between social classes in the countryside of central and northern Italy.
- The growth of socialism challenged the traditional power and wealth of landowners.
- Fear and hatred of socialism drove these landowners to support fascism.

Tone and emphasis:

- The tone tries to convey the outrage of the traditional ruling classes towards the growth of socialism, emphasising their emotional response: 'hatred and bitterness'.

Own knowledge:

- Use your own knowledge to agree/disagree with the source, for example: details about the emergence of Fascist squads in the countryside during 1920–1, their attacks on Socialist councils and trade unions, and the support they received from landowners.

Source 2 (page 157)

Provenance:

- The source is from a Liberal newspaper, which would have had a particular view on the rise of fascism.
- It is written in May 1921, when the Fascists were just emerging as a significant political party, with 35 MPs in the Italian parliament.

Content and argument:

- The source argues that those who suffered in the economic depression after the First World War became attracted to fascism.
- Fascist supporters were likely to be young and/or middle class.
- Young people saw fascism as an exciting adventure.

Tone and emphasis:

- The tone suggests that Fascist support came from the desperate and those disillusioned with the major political parties.

Own knowledge:

- Use your own knowledge to agree/disagree with the source, for example: many Fascist supporters were ex-army officers such as Italo Balbo, disillusioned with the 'mutilated victory'; shopkeepers feared competition from Socialist-run co-operative shops.

Source 3 (page 158)

Provenance:

- The source is from one of the earliest leaders of fascism.
- It is written during the Fascist dictatorship and is arguing that Italy after the First World War needed fascism.

Content and argument:

- The source argues that fascism drew support from those disillusioned with Liberal governments immediately following the First World War.
- Liberal government had betrayed the soldiers by agreeing to a 'mutilated victory'.
- Mussolini was vital in gaining supporters for fascism.

Tone and emphasis:

- The writer stresses the idealism of the supporters of fascism.

Own knowledge:

- Use your knowledge to agree/disagree with the source, for example: detailed knowledge about public reaction to the 'mutilated victory', the propaganda and political skills of Mussolini in channelling this disillusionment with Liberal Italy into support for the Fascist movement.

Answering AS questions

You have 45 minutes to answer the question. It is important that you spend at least one quarter of the time reading and planning your answer. Generally, when writing an answer, you need to check that you are remaining focused on the issue identified in the question and are relating this to the sources and your knowledge.

- You might decide to write a paragraph on each 'strand' (that is, provenance, content and tone), comparing the two sources, and then write a short concluding paragraph with an explained judgement on which source is more valuable.
- For writing about content, you may find it helpful to adopt a comparative approach, for example when the evidence in one source is contradicted or questioned by the evidence in another source.

At AS level you are asked to provide a judgement on which is more valuable. Make sure that this is based on clear arguments with strong evidence, and not on general assertions.

Planning and writing your answer

- Think how you can best plan an answer.
- Plan in terms of the headings above, perhaps combining 'provenance' with 'tone and emphasis', and compare the two sources.

As an example, here is a comparison of Sources 1 and 2 in terms of provenance, and tone and emphasis:

The two sources have different viewpoints. In terms of their provenance, Source 2 was written just as fascism was beginning to generate significant support and, as a Liberal newspaper, has only limited sympathy for Fascist supporters, who are portrayed as a disorganised mass of the disappointed and disillusioned. Source 1 is more studied in its analysis, focusing on events in the countryside which promoted the growth of fascism. However, the author shows the influence of his Communist past by heavily emphasising the importance of struggle between social classes.

- Then compare the *content and argument* of each source, by using your knowledge. For example:

Source 1 is arguing that the growth of socialism in the countryside of northern and central Italy challenged the traditional power and wealth of the landowners and the middle class. These groups reacted to this threat from the lower classes by supporting Fascist squads, who attacked Socialist councils and trade unions. Source 2, however, largely ignores the growth of socialism as well as events in the countryside. Instead, it sees Fascist support emerging from the lack of jobs and opportunity during the economic depression following the First World War. It highlights the disillusion of the young and middle class with Liberal politicians.

Which is more *valuable*? This can be judged in terms of which is likely to be more valuable in terms of where the source came from; or in terms of the accuracy of its content. However, remember the focus of the question – in this case, why support grew for fascism in 1920–2.

With these sources you could argue that Source 2 is the more valuable because it was written during the period 1920–2 and gives a real sense of the types of people who became early supporters of fascism and how their frustrations pushed them towards this radical movement. Source 1 is valuable in stressing how fear of socialism led to the emergence of Fascist squadrismo, but it perhaps overemphasises the importance of conflict between social classes.

Then check the following:

- Have you covered the 'provenance' and 'content' strands?
- Have you included sufficient knowledge to show understanding of the historical context?

Answering A level questions

The same general points for answering AS questions (see 'Answering AS questions') apply to A level questions, although of course here there are three sources and you need to assess the value of each of the three, rather than choose which is most valuable. Make sure that you remain focused on the question and that when you use your knowledge it is used to substantiate (add to) an argument relating to the content or provenance of the source.

If you are answering the A level question on page 158 with Sources 1, 2 and 3 (pages 157–8):

- Keep the different 'strands' explained above in your mind when working out how best to plan an answer.
- Follow the guidance about 'provenance' and 'content' (see the AS guidance).
- Here you are *not* asked to explain which is the most valuable of the three sources. You can deal with each of the three sources in turn if you wish.
- However, you can build in comparisons if it is helpful, but it is not essential. It will depend to some extent on the three sources.
- You need to include sufficient knowledge to show understanding of the historical context. This might encourage cross-referencing of the content of the three sources, mixed with your own knowledge.
- Each paragraph needs to show clarity of argument in terms of the issue identified by the question.

Edexcel A level History

Essay guidance

Edexcel's Paper 2, Unit 2G.1: The rise and fall of fascism in Italy 1911–1946 is assessed by an exam comprising two sections:

- Section A tests the depth of your historical knowledge through source analysis (see page 166 for guidance on this).
- Section B requires you to write one essay from a choice of two from your own knowledge.

The following advice relates to Paper 2, Section B. It is relevant to A level and AS level questions. Generally, the AS exam is similar to the A level exam. Both examine the same content and require similar skills; nonetheless, there are differences, which are discussed below.

Essay skills

In order to get a high grade in Section B of Paper 2 your essay must contain four essential qualities:

- focused analysis
- relevant detail
- supported judgement
- organisation, coherence and clarity.

This section focuses on the following aspects of exam technique:

- understanding the nature of the question
- planning an answer to the question set
- writing a focused introduction
- deploying relevant detail
- writing analytically
- reaching a supported judgement.

The nature of the question

Section B questions are designed to test the depth of your historical knowledge. Therefore, they can focus on relatively short periods, or single events, or indeed on the whole period from 1911 to 1946. Moreover, they can focus on different historical processes or 'concepts'. These include:

- cause
- consequence
- change/continuity
- similarity/difference
- significance.

These different question focuses require slightly different approaches:

Cause	1 To what extent was military defeat in the Second World War the main reason for the collapse of fascism?
Consequence	2 To what extent did Mussolini's economic policies, 1925–40, modernise the Italian economy?
Continuity and change	3 To what extent did Church–State relations improve in Fascist Italy in the years 1929–39?
Similarities and differences	4 'Mussolini's foreign policy from 1935 was radically different from his policy in the 1920s and early 1930s.' How far do you agree with this statement?
Significance	5 How significant were Mussolini's economic policies in generating support for the regime in the years 1925–40?

Some questions include a 'stated factor'. The most common type of stated factor question would ask how far one factor caused something. For example, question 1 in the table asks: 'To what extent was military defeat in the Second World War the main reason for the collapse of fascism?' In this type of question you would be expected to evaluate the importance of the Second World War – the 'stated factor' – compared to other factors.

AS and A level questions

AS level questions are generally similar to A level questions. However, the wording of AS questions will be slightly less complex than the wording of A level questions.

A level question	AS level question	Differences
To what extent did Mussolini's economic policies, 1925–40, modernise the Italian economy?	To what extent did Mussolini's economic policies, 1925–40, improve the Italian economy?	The A level question focuses on the complex notion of 'modernisation' whereas the AS question focuses on the relatively simple issue of 'change'.
'Mussolini's foreign policy from 1935 was radically different from his policy in the 1920s and early 1930s.' How far do you agree with this statement?	How far did Mussolini's foreign policy change in the period 1923–40?	The AS question asks how far Mussolini's foreign policy changed. The A level question asks you to make the more complex judgement: how far were his policies 'radically different'?

To achieve the highest level at A level, you will have to deal with the full complexity of the question. For example, if you were dealing with question 4, about Mussolini's changing foreign policy, you would have to deal with the question of how far his policies were 'radically different', not merely how far they changed.

Planning your answer

It is crucial that you understand the focus of the question. Therefore, read the question carefully before you start planning. Check the following:

- The chronological focus: which years should your essay deal with?

- The topic focus: what aspect of your course does the question deal with?
- The conceptual focus: is this a causes, consequences, change/continuity, similarity/difference or significance question?

For example, for question 3 you could point these out as follows:

To what extent did Church–State relations[1] improve in Fascist Italy[2] in the years 1929–39[3]?

1 Topic focus: relations between the Catholic Church and the Fascist regime.
2 Conceptual focus: continuity/change.
3 Chronological focus: 1929–39.

Your plan should reflect the task that you have been set. Section B asks you to write an analytical, coherent and well-structured essay from your own knowledge, which reaches a supported conclusion in around 40 minutes.

- To ensure that your essay is coherent and well structured, it should comprise a series of paragraphs, each focusing on a different point.
- Your paragraphs should come in a logical order. For example, you could write your paragraphs in order of importance, so you begin with the most important issues and end with the least important.
- In essays where there is a 'stated factor', it is a good idea to start with the stated factor before moving on to the other points.
- To make sure you keep to time, you should aim to write three or four paragraphs plus an introduction and a conclusion.

The opening paragraph

The opening paragraph should do four main things:

- answer the question directly
- set out your essential argument
- outline the factors or issues that you will discuss
- define key terms used in the question – where necessary.

Different questions require you to define different terms, for example:

A level question	Key terms
To what extent did Mussolini's economic policies, 1925–40, modernise the Italian economy?	Here it is worth defining 'modernise'.
'Mussolini's foreign policy from 1935 was radically different from his policy in the 1920s and early 1930s.' How far do you agree with this statement?	In this example, it is worth defining 'radically different'.

Here's an example introduction in answer to question 2 in the table on page 162: 'To what extent did Mussolini's economic policies, 1925–40, modernise the Italian economy?'

Mussolini's economic policies led to partial economic modernisation between 1925 and 1940[1]. Fascist policies improved roads and railways, promoted mechanisation of Italian agriculture, and sought to boost the production of heavy industry. On the other hand, transport, industry and agriculture in the south were neglected[2]. The extent of modernisation therefore varied: the north gained much more than the south; heavy industry developed more than consumer goods; and cereal production took precedence over citrus and livestock farming[3].

1 The essay starts with a clear answer to the question.
2 This sentence simultaneously defines modernisation and sets out the key areas the essay will consider.
3 Finally, the essential argument is stated.

The opening paragraph: advice

- Don't write more than a couple of sentences on general background knowledge. This is unlikely to focus explicitly on the question.
- After defining key terms, refer back to these definitions when justifying your conclusion.
- The introduction should reflect the rest of the essay. Don't make one argument in your introduction, then make a different argument in the essay.

Deploying relevant detail

Paper 2 tests the depth of your historical knowledge. Therefore, you will need to deploy historical detail. In the main body of your essay your paragraphs should begin with a clear point, be full of relevant detail and end with explanation or evaluation. A detailed answer might include statistics, proper names, dates and technical terms. For example, if you were writing a paragraph about the modernisation of the Italian economy under fascism, you might include statistics dealing with industrial expansion, such as how much steel and chemicals were produced.

Writing analytically

The quality of your analysis is one of the key factors that determines the mark you achieve. Writing analytically means clearly showing the relationships between the ideas in your essay. Analysis includes two key skills: explanation and evaluation.

Explanation

Explanation means giving reasons. An explanatory sentence has three parts:

- a claim: a statement that something is true or false
- a reason: a statement that justifies the claim
- a relationship: a word or phrase that shows the relationship between the claim and the reason.

Imagine you are answering question 1 in the table on page 162: 'To what extent was military defeat in the Second World War the main reason for the collapse of fascism?' Your paragraph on the Second World War should start with a clear point, which would be supported by a series of examples. Finally, you would round off the paragraph with some explanation:

Therefore, military defeat in the Second World War was one reason for the collapse of fascism[1] because it destroyed public support for the regime and[2] led to prominent Fascists, the King and his army generals plotting to remove Mussolini in 1943[3].

1 Claim.   2 Relationship.   3 Reason.

Make sure of the following:

- The reason you give genuinely justifies the claim you have made.
- Your explanation is focused on the question.

Reaching a supported judgement

Finally, your essay should reach a supported judgement. The obvious place to do this is in the conclusion of your essay. Even so, the judgement should reflect the findings of your essay. The conclusion should present:

- a clear judgement that answers the question
- an evaluation of the evidence that supports the judgement.

Finally, the evaluation should reflect valid criteria.

Evaluation and criteria

Evaluation means weighing up to reach a judgement. Therefore, evaluation requires you to:

- summarise both sides of the issue
- reach a conclusion that reflects the proper weight of both sides.

So, for question 2 in the table on page 162: 'To what extent did Mussolini's economic policies, 1925–40, modernise the Italian economy?', the conclusion might look like like the following:

In conclusion, Mussolini's economic policies led to partial economic modernisation[1]. Clearly, the Italian economy was significantly modernised as industrialisation grew. Overall industrial output grew by close to 50 per cent during the years 1925-40. Railways were made more efficient and a number of motorways were built[2]. However, modern machinery and fertilisers were still lacking in agriculture, particularly in the south, and living standards of ordinary Italians fell during the 1930s[3]. Therefore, Mussolini's economic policies did help modernise the Italian economy, but by 1940 Italian infrastructure, and industrial and agricultural production, still lagged far behind the modern European economies of Britain, France, and Germany[4].

1 The conclusion starts with a clear judgement that answers the question.
2 This sentence considers the ways in which modernisation was achieved, presenting a summary of the evidence.
3 The conclusion also considers evidence of the limits of modernisation.
4 The essay ends with a final judgement that is supported by the evidence of the essay.

The judgement is supported in part by evaluating the evidence, and in part by linking it to valid criteria. In this case, the criterion is the definition of modernisation set out in the introduction. Significantly, this criterion is specific to this essay, and different essays will require you to think of different criteria to help you make your judgement.

Sources guidance

Edexcel's Paper 2, Unit 2G.1: The rise and fall of fascism in Italy 1911–1946 is assessed by an exam comprising two sections:

- Section A tests the depth of your historical knowledge through source analysis.
- Section B requires you to write one essay from a choice of two from your own knowledge (see page 162 for guidance on this).

The following advice relates to Paper 2, Section A. It is relevant to A level and AS level questions. Generally, the AS exam is similar to the A level exam. Both examine the same content and require similar skills; nonetheless, there are differences, which are discussed below.

The questions in Paper 2, Section A, are structured differently in the A level and AS exams.

AS exam	Full A level exam
Section A: contains one compulsory question divided into two parts.	Section A: contains a single compulsory question worth 20 marks. The question asks you to evaluate the usefulness of two sources for a specific historical enquiry.
Part a) is worth 8 marks. It focuses on the value of a single source for a specific enquiry.	
Part b) is worth 12 marks. It asks you to weigh the value of a single source for a specific enquiry.	
Together the two sources will comprise about 350 words.	Together the two sources will comprise about 400 words.
Questions will start with the following stems:	Questions will start with the following stem:
a) Why is Source 1 valuable to the historian for an enquiry about … ?	1 How far could the historian make use of Sources 1 and 2 together to investigate … ?
b) How much weight do you give the evidence of Source 2 for an enquiry into … ?	

Edexcel style questions

AS style question

Study Sources 1 and 2 before you answer this question.

a) Why is Source 1 valuable to the historian investigating the reasons why leading Fascists turned against Mussolini in July 1943?

Explain your answer using the source, the information given about it and your own knowledge of the historical context.

b) How much weight do you give the evidence of Source 2 for an enquiry into King Victor Emmanuel III's motives for dismissing Mussolini as prime minister in July 1943?

Explain your answer using the source, the information given about it and your own knowledge of the historical context.

A level style question

Study Sources 1 and 2 before you answer this question.

How far could the historian make use of Sources 1 and 2 together to investigate the reasons why Mussolini fell from power in July 1943?

Explain your answer using both sources, the information given about them and your own knowledge of the historical context.

Sources 1 and 2

SOURCE 1

From Federzoni's summary of the speech made by Dino Grandi to the Grand Council of Fascism on 25 July 1943. Federzoni supported Grandi's attempt to remove Mussolini from power. Quoted in J. Whittam, *Fascist Italy*, Manchester University Press, 1995, p. 166.

The Head of Government, Grandi observed, has spoken of the unpardonable errors committed by military leaders and by the armed forces that he personally commands. But Mussolini, Head of Government and the minister in charge of all the armed services, has had seventeen years to create, organise, prepare and to select the officer corps, the troops and the equipment … Military preparedness was therefore the major task for the man who had the honour of guiding the destiny of the nation.

The Grand Council must decide that the regime of dictatorship is over because it has compromised the vital interests of the nation, has brought Italy to the brink of military defeat and has damaged the revolution and fascism itself. The Grand Council must decide to restore all the authority and responsibility of state institutions which the dictatorship has absorbed and return to the Crown, the Grand Council, the Parliament and the corporations all the tasks assigned to them by our constitutional laws.

SOURCE 2

From the conversation between the King and Mussolini on 25 July 1943, recalled by a bodyguard who was standing outside the door. Quoted in J. Hite and C. Hinton, *Fascist Italy*, John Murray, 1998, p. 248.

I heard the King say 'My dear Duce, it's no longer any good. Italy is on its knees. The army's morale is at rock bottom, and the soldiers do not want to fight any more. The vote of the Grand Council is dreadful. At this moment you are the most hated man in Italy … I have demonstrated my friendship

many times, defending you from every attack, but this time I must ask you to leave me free to place the government in other hands'. Mussolini said 'Then everything is finished?' The King answered: 'I am sorry, I am very sorry. There is no other solution.'

Understanding the questions

- To answer the question successfully you must understand how the question works.
- The question is written precisely in order to make sure that you understand the task. Each part of the question has a specific meaning.
- You must use the source, the information given about the source and your own knowledge of the historical context when answering the question.

Understanding the AS question

a) Why is Source 1 valuable to the historian[1] investigating the reasons why leading Fascists turned against Mussolini in July 1943[2]?

1 You must focus on the reasons why the source could be helpful to a historian. Indeed, you can get maximum marks without considering the source's limitations.

2 The final part of the question focuses on a specific topic that a historian might investigate. In this case: 'why leading Fascists turned against Mussolini in July 1943'.

b) How much weight do you give the evidence of Source 2[1] for an enquiry into[2] King Victor Emmanuel III's motives in dismissing Mussolini as prime minister in July 1943[3]?

1 This question focuses on evaluating the extent to which the source contains evidence. Therefore, you must consider the ways in which the source is valuable and the limitations of the source.
2 This is the essence of the task: you must focus on what a historian could legitimately conclude from studying this source.
3 This is the specific topic that you are considering the Source for: 'King Victor Emmanuel III's motives in dismissing Mussolini as prime minister in July 1943'.

Understanding the A level question

How far[1] could the historian make use of Sources 1 and 2[2] together[3] to investigate the reasons why Mussolini fell from power in July 1943[4]?

Explain your answer using both sources, the information given about them and your own knowledge of the historical context[5].

1 You must evaluate the extent of something, rather than giving a simple 'yes' or 'no' answer.
2 This is the essence of the task: you must focus on what a historian could legitimately conclude from studying these sources.
3 You must examine the sources as a pair and make a judgement about both sources, rather than simply making separate judgements about each source.
4 The final part of the question focuses on a specific topic that a historian might investigate. In this case: 'why Mussolini fell from power in July 1943'.
5 This instruction lists the resources you should use: the sources, the information given about the sources and your own knowledge of the historical context that you have learnt during the course.

Source skills

Generally, Section A of Paper 2 tests your ability to evaluate source material. More specifically, the sources presented in Section A will be taken from the period that you have studied: 1911–46, or be written by people who witnessed these events. Your job is to analyse the sources by reading them in the context of the values and assumptions of the society and the period that produced them.

Examiners will mark your work by focusing on the extent to which you are able to:

- Interpret and analyse source material:
  - At a basic level, this means you can understand the sources and select, copy, paraphrase and summarise the source or sources to help answer the question.
  - At a higher level, your interpretation of the sources includes the ability to explain, analyse and make inferences based on the sources.
  - At the highest levels, you will be expected to analyse the source in a sophisticated way. This includes the ability to distinguish between information, opinions and arguments contained in the sources.
- Deploy knowledge of historical context in relation to the sources:
  - At a basic level, this means the ability to link the sources to your knowledge of the context in which the source was written, using this knowledge to expand or support the information contained in the sources.
  - At a higher level, you will be able to use your contextual knowledge to make inferences, and to expand, support or challenge the details mentioned in the sources.
  - At the highest levels, you will be able to examine the value and limits of the material contained in the sources by interpreting the sources in the context of the values and assumptions of the society that produced them.
- Evaluate the usefulness and weight of the source material:
  - At a basic level, evaluation of the source will be based on simplistic criteria about reliability and bias.
  - At a higher level, evaluation of the source will be based on the nature and purpose of the source.
  - At the highest levels, evaluation of the source will be based on a valid criterion that is justified in the course of the essay. You will also be able to distinguish between the value of different aspects of the sources.

Make sure your source evaluation is sophisticated. Avoid crude statements about bias, and avoid simplistic assumptions such as that a source written immediately after an event is reliable, whereas a source written years later is unreliable.

Try to see things through the eyes of the writer:

- How does the writer understand the world?
- What assumptions does the writer have?
- Who is the writer trying to influence?
- What views is the writer trying to challenge?

Basic skill: comprehension

The most basic source skill is comprehension: understanding what the sources mean. There are a variety of techniques that you can use to aid comprehension. For example, you could read the sources included in this book and in past papers:

- Read the sources out loud.
- Look up any words that you don't understand and make a glossary.
- Make flash cards containing brief biographies of the writers of the sources.

You can demonstrate comprehension by copying, paraphrasing and summarising the sources. However, keep this to the minimum as comprehension is a low-level skill and you need to leave room for higher-level skills.

Advanced skill: contextualising the sources

First, to analyse the sources correctly you need to understand them in the context in which they were written. People in Italy in the Second World War saw the world differently from people in early twenty-first-century Britain. The sources reflect this. Your job is to understand the values and assumptions behind the source.

- One way of contextualising the sources is to consider the nature, origins and purpose of the sources. However, this can lead to formulaic responses.

- An alternative is to consider two levels of context. First, you should establish the general context. In this case, Sources 1 and 2 refer to the period in which leading Fascists, the King and army generals were plotting to remove Mussolini from power. Second, you can look for specific references to contemporary events or debates in the sources. For example:

Sources 1 and 2 both refer to the events of July 1943, when Italy was on the brink of invasion by British and US forces. Grandi, in Source 1, specifically blames Mussolini's poor leadership as a major cause of this defeat. The King, in Source 2, supports the claim that the war is lost, but also points out that the public, as a result of the war, 'hated' Mussolini. In the context of this defeat, both the leading Fascists, in Source 1, and the King, in Source 2, were seeking to end the war and maintain themselves in power. They knew the Allies would not make peace while Mussolini was still the dictator, and feared a popular uprising or even a revolution if the war went on any longer. Such a revolution might not only remove Mussolini but also destroy the Fascist Party and overthrow the monarchy.

Use context to make judgements

- Start by establishing the general context of the source:
  - Ask yourself: what was going on at the time when the source was written, or the time of the events described in the source?
  - What are the key debates that the source might be contributing to?
- Next, look for key words and phrases that establish the specific context. Does the source refer to specific people, events or books that might be important?
- Make sure your contextualisation focuses on the question.
- Use the context when evaluating the usefulness and limitations of the source.

For example:

Source 1 is valuable to a historian investigating the reasons why Mussolini fell from power because it shows how the Duce had lost the support of most of the key Fascist leaders including Grandi, and Mussolini's own son-in-law, Ciano. Mussolini's poor leadership is highlighted as a major reason for Italy's defeat in the Second World War and it is this defeat and the fear of allied invasion which prompted the rebellion by Fascist leaders. Moreover, Source 2 is valuable because it confirms the key importance of defeat in the Second World War as a cause of Mussolini's fall from power. The King also points out how Mussolini has lost all public support, another major reason for his downfall. Interestingly, the King in Source 2 suggests that he regrets Mussolini's downfall, whereas in reality he was involved in the plotting and was aware of Grandi's plans, in Source 1, to win a vote in the Grand Council seeking Mussolini's dismissal.

OCR A level History

Essay guidance

The assessment of OCR Units Y220 and Y250 Italy 1896–1943 depends on whether you are studying it for AS or A level:

- for the AS exam, you will answer one essay question from a choice of two, and one interpretation question, for which there is no choice
- for the A level exam, you will answer one essay question from a choice of two, and one shorter essay question, also from a choice of two.

The guidance below is for answering both AS and A level essay questions. Guidance for the shorter essay question is at the end of this section. Guidance on answering interpretation questions is on page 175.

For both OCR AS and A level History, the types of essay questions set and the skills required to achieve a high grade for Unit Group 2 are the same.

The skills are made very clear by both mark schemes, which emphasise that the answer must:

- focus on the demands of the question
- be supported by accurate and relevant factual knowledge
- be analytical and logical
- reach a supported judgement about the issue in the question.

There are a number of skills that you will need to develop to reach the higher levels in the marking bands:

- understand the wording of the question
- plan an answer to the question set
- write a focused opening paragraph
- avoid irrelevance and description
- write analytically
- write a conclusion which reaches a supported judgement based on the argument in the main body of the essay.

These skills will be developed in the section below, but are further developed in the 'Period Study' chapters of the *OCR A level History* series (British Period Studies and Enquiries).

Understanding the wording of the question

To stay focused on the question set, it is important to read the question carefully and focus on the key words and phrases. Unless you directly address the demands of the question you will not score highly. Remember that in questions where there is a named factor you must write a good analytical paragraph about the given factor, even if you argue that it was not the most important.

Types of AS and A level questions you might find in the exams	The factors and issues you would need to consider in answering them
1 Assess the consequences for Italy to 1920 of its participation in the First World War.	Weigh up the relative importance of the consequences of Italian participation in the First World War to 1920.
2 To what extent was Liberal weakness the most important factor in enabling Mussolini to create his dictatorship 1922–6?	Weigh up the relative importance of a range of factors, including comparing Liberal weakness with other factors.
3 'The most important reason for Mussolini's consolidation of his dictatorship in the years 1922–6 was Fascist violence.' How far do you agree?	Weigh up the relative importance of a range of factors, including comparing the use of Fascist violence with other issues to reach a balanced judgement.
4 How successful was Mussolini's foreign policy in the years 1925–40?	This question requires you to make a judgement about how successful Mussolini was in achieving his aims in foreign policy. You would need to think about aims such as:

- Making Italy 'great' – expanding Italian territory in Africa and Europe
- Making Italy 'respected' by the great European powers: Britain, France and Germany
- Making Italy 'feared' by other countries, such as in the Balkans.

Planning an answer

Many plans simply list dates and events: this should be avoided as it encourages a descriptive or narrative answer, rather than an analytical answer. The plan should be an outline of your argument; this means you need to think carefully about the issues you intend to discuss and their relative importance before you start writing your answer. It should therefore be a list of the factors or issues you are going to discuss and a comment on their relative importance.

For question 1 in the table (on page 171), your plan might look something like this:

- Heavy casualties – link to growth of nationalism and frustration with a 'mutilated victory'.
- Economic problems – inflation and working-class unrest. Link to growth of socialism.
- Disillusionment with Liberal governments – blamed for heavy casualties and economic problems, and for the 'mutilated victory'. A very important consequence as it enabled socialism to grow in strength and prompted the emergence of fascism.
- Growth of socialism – important as fear of socialism promoted the growth of nationalism and then fascism.
- Growth of nationalism – link to the 'mutilated victory' and hatred of socialism. Nationalism provided a breeding ground for fascism.

The opening paragraph

Many students spend time 'setting the scene'; the opening paragraph becomes little more than an introduction to the topic – this should be avoided. Instead, make it clear what your argument is going to be. Offer your view about the issue in the question – what was the most important consequence of Italy's participation in the First World War – and then introduce the other issues you intend to discuss. In the plan it is suggested that disillusionment with Liberal governments was the most important factor. This should be made clear in the opening paragraph, with a brief comment as to why – perhaps that disillusionment with Liberal governments led to the growth of both socialism and fascism. This will give the examiner a clear overview of your essay, rather than it being a 'mystery tour' where the argument becomes clear only at the end. You should also refer to any important issues that the question raises. For example:

There were a number of important consequences of Italy's participation in the First World War, including heavy casualties, economic problems and the rapid growth of socialism[1]. However, the most important reason was growing disillusionment with Liberal governments[2]. This was particularly important because it enabled the growth of the Socialists, which in turn prompted many middle-class and conservative Italians to begin to support the Fascists[3].

1 The student is aware that there were a number of important reasons.
2 The student offers a clear view as to what they consider to be the most important reason – a thesis is offered.
3 There is a brief justification to support the thesis.

Avoid irrelevance and description

A well-prepared plan will stop you from simply writing all you know about the consequences of the First World War and force you to weigh up the role of a range of factors. Similarly, it should also help prevent you from simply writing about the military events of the First World War. You will not lose marks if you do that, but neither will you gain any credit, and you will waste valuable time.

Write analytically

This is perhaps the hardest, but most important skill you need to develop. An analytical approach can be helped by ensuring that the opening sentence of each paragraph introduces an idea, which directly answers the question and is not just a piece of factual information. In a very strong answer it should be possible to simply read the opening sentences of all the paragraphs and know what argument is being put forward.

If we look at question 2, on the importance of Liberal weakness in enabling Mussolini to create his dictatorship 1922–6 (see page 171), the following are possible sentences with which to start paragraphs:

- Liberal weakness was certainly an important factor in enabling Mussolini to gain more power and to survive the Matteotti affair.
- Fear of socialism caused the conservative elites, particularly the King and wealthy industrialists and landowners, to look with more favour on the prospect of a Fascist dictatorship.
- Mussolini's own political skills enabled him to convince many Liberals and the elites that he could be trusted with increased power.
- Fascist violence deterred public protests and potential opposition from other political parties.

You would then go on to discuss both sides of the argument raised by the opening sentence, using relevant knowledge about the issue to support each side of the argument. The final sentence of the paragraph would reach a judgement on the role played by the factor you are discussing in the creation of the dictatorship. This approach would ensure that the final sentence of each paragraph links back to the actual question you are answering. If you can do this for each paragraph you will have a series of mini-essays, which discuss a factor and reach a conclusion or judgement about the importance of that factor or issue. For example:

Fascist violence was an important factor in enabling Mussolini to create his dictatorship[1], but mainly in the year 1924. Fascist blackshirts intimidated voters during the 1924 election and

helped rig the election result. Blackshirts were also prominent in the following months to deter public protests against the murder of Matteotti and to remind other parties of the dangers of resisting Mussolini's acquisition of more powers[2].

1   The sentence puts forward a clear view that Fascist violence was important in the creation of the dictatorship.
2   The claim that it was important in 1924 is developed and some evidence is provided to support the argument.

The conclusion

The conclusion provides the opportunity to bring together all the interim judgements to reach an overall judgement about the question. Using the interim judgements will ensure that your conclusion is based on the argument in the main body of the essay and does not offer a different view. For the essay answering question 1 (see page 171), you can decide what was the most important consequence of the First World War, but for questions 2 and 3 you will need to comment on the importance of the named factor – Liberal weakness or Fascist violence – as well as explain why you think a different factor is more important, if that has been your line of argument. Or, if you think the named factor is the most important, you would need to explain why that was more important than the other factors or issues you have discussed.

Consider the following conclusion to question 2 (on page 171): To what extent was Liberal weakness the most important factor in enabling Mussolini to create his dictatorship 1922–6?

Although the Liberals had several weaknesses, such as the rivalries between leaders such as Giolitti and Salandra, and were unable to agree on how to respond to evidence of Mussolini's involvement in the murder of Matteotti, Liberal weakness was not the most important factor in enabling Mussolini to create his dictatorship. It was Mussolini's political skills which were crucial as he was able to exploit these weaknesses, persuading a significant number of Liberals to vote for the Emergency

Decree law and then the Acerbo law of 1923, both of which increased his power[1]. Mussolini was also skilful in winning the support of the conservative elites for a dictatorship by exaggerating the extent of the Socialist threat and by claiming that only he, and not the Liberals, could crush this threat[2].

1 This is a strong conclusion because it considers the importance of the named factor – Liberal weakness – but weighs that up against a range of other factors to reach an overall judgement.
2 It is also able to show links between the other factors to reach a balanced judgement, which brings in a range of issues, showing the interplay between them.

How to write a good essay for the A level short answer questions

This question will require you to weigh up the importance of two factors or issues in relation to an event or a development. For example:

Which was the more successful of Mussolini's economic policies?

(i) Agrarian policies.

(ii) The corporate state.

Explain your answer with reference to both (i) and (ii).

As with the long essays, the skills required are made very clear by the mark scheme, which emphasises that the answer must:

- analyse the two issues
- evaluate the two issues
- support your analysis and evaluation with detailed and accurate knowledge
- reach a supported judgement as to which factor was more important in relation to the issue in the question.

The skills required are very similar to those for the longer essays. However, there is no need for an introduction, nor are you required to compare the two factors or issues in the main body of the essay, although either approach can still score full marks. For example, an introduction could be:

Mussolini's agrarian policies did have some successes. The Battle for Grain provided cheap tractors and machinery to farmers and helped to increase wheat production by over 50 per cent. Italy became less dependent on imports of foreign grain[1]. The Battle for the Marshes famously drained the Pontine marshes near Rome, increased the amount of cultivable land, built thirteen new towns, and reduced the threat from malaria[2]. Both of these battles were also propaganda successes for the Duce. He could claim to be modernising Italian agriculture, and pictures of him helping with the harvest or driving tractors contributed to the cult of personality[3].

1 The answer explains one of the successes of Mussolini's agrarian policies.
2 A second success of his policies is explained.
3 A further type of success is considered, and this could be developed and compared to the propaganda success of the corporate state. The answer could go on and explain the failures of Mussolini's agrarian policies.

Most importantly, the conclusion must reach a supported judgement as to the relative importance of the factors in relation to the issue in the question. For example:

Both policies had some successes, but it was the agrarian policies which had the more long-lasting effects on the Italian economy. The corporate state could only claim to be a short-term propaganda success. The corporate state did not transform Italian industry, or create a genuine partnership between worker and employer, thus ending class conflict. The employers kept their power and the workers simply lost their rights. The agrarian policies also had their failures, such as higher prices for bread and the neglect of citrus and livestock farming[1], but at least some of the claimed successes were genuine – the increase in wheat production and the amount of land under cultivation[2].

1 The response explains the relative importance of the two factors and offers a clear view.
2 The response supports the view offered in the opening sentence and therefore reaches a supported judgement.

Interpretations guidance

How to write a good essay

The guidance below is for answering the AS interpretation question OCR Unit Y250 Italy 1896–1943. Guidance on answering essay questions is on page 171.

The OCR specification outlines the two key topics from which the interpretation question will be drawn. For this book these are:

- Italy 1915–25.
- Fascist Italy 1925–43.

The specification also lists the main debates to consider.

It is also worth remembering that this is an AS unit and not an A level historiography paper. The aim of this element of the unit is to develop an awareness that the past can be interpreted in different ways.

The question will require you to assess the strengths and limitations of a historian's interpretation of an issue related to one of the specified key topics.

You should be able to place the interpretation within the context of the wider historical debate on the key topic. However, you will *not* be required to know the names of individual historians associated with the debate or to have studied the specific books of any historians. It may even be counter-productive to be aware of particular historians' views, as this may lead you to simply describe their view, rather than analyse the given interpretation.

There are a number of skills you need to develop to reach the higher levels in the mark bands:

- To be able to understand the wording of the question.
- To be able to explain the interpretation and how it fits into the debate about the issue or topic.
- To be able to consider both the strengths and weaknesses of the interpretation by using your own knowledge of the topic.

Here is an example of a question you will face in the exam:

> Read the interpretation and then answer the question that follows:
>
> 'The truth is that a critical mass of people in Italy did actively support fascism.'
>
> (From Nicholas Farrell, *Mussolini: A New Life*, Phoenix, 2004.)
>
> Evaluate the strengths and limitations of this interpretation, making reference to other interpretations that you have studied.

Approaching the question

There are several steps to take to answer this question:

1 Explain the interpretation and put it into the context of the debate on the topic

In the first paragraph, you should explain the interpretation and the view it is putting forward. This paragraph places the interpretation in the context of the historical debate and explains any key words or phrases relating to the given interpretation. A suggested opening might be as follows:

The interpretation puts forward the view that fascism was genuinely popular among a majority of Italians. The author suggests that fascism's appeal went beyond the wealthy and middle class and extended to the peasantry and the industrial working class[1]. Farrell is arguing that the Italian public were not simply blinded by Fascist propaganda or forced into acceptance of the regime by blackshirt violence, as some historians have suggested. Rather, most Italians were enthused by aspects of fascism which they believed had improved Italy[2].

1 The opening two sentences are clearly focused on the given interpretation, identifying the widespread appeal of fascism, but there is no detailed own knowledge added at this point.

2 The remainder of the paragraph sets the interpretation in the context of the wider historical debate about the wider appeal of fascism.

2 Consider the strengths of the interpretation

In the second paragraph, consider the strengths of the interpretation by bringing in your own knowledge that supports the given view. A suggested response might start as follows when considering the strengths of the view:

There is some merit to the extract's view as Fascist policies did generate significant public support[1]. Social policies, particularly the Lateran Agreements with the Catholic Church in 1929, persuaded many Italians that fascism was proving a success[2]. In foreign policy, the war in Ethiopia, 1935–6, was viewed by very many Italians as an outstanding success[3].

1 The answer clearly focuses on the strength of the given interpretation.
2 The response provides some support for the view in the interpretation from the candidate's own knowledge. This is not particularly detailed or precise, but could be developed in the remainder of the paragraph.
3 The final sentence points out a second reason for popular support.

In the remainder of the paragraph you could explain these factors in greater detail and show how policy successes were linked. For example, the war in Ethiopia was supported by the Catholic Church, and the regime contrasted its victory to the Liberal failure to conquer the country in 1896.

3 Consider the weaknesses of the interpretation

In the third paragraph, consider the weaknesses of the given interpretation by bringing in knowledge that can challenge the given interpretation and explains what is missing from the interpretation. A suggested response might start as follows when considering the weaknesses of the view:

However, there are a number of weaknesses in Farrell's interpretation[1]. It is true that the Lateran Agreements gained the support of the Catholic Church, which then urged Italians to support fascism, but the extract fails to point out that Fascist policies lost Catholic support later in the 1930s. Similarly, while the war in Ethiopia was popular, Mussolini's growing friendship with Nazi Germany alienated many Italians[2]. The interpretation also ignores the fact that many working-class Italians felt the regime offered them little and were certainly not active supporters of fascism[3].

1 The opening makes it very clear that this paragraph will deal with the weaknesses of the interpretation.
2 It explains clearly one weakness and provides evidence to support the claim. The evidence is not detailed and could be developed.
3 Although more detail could have been provided about why the regime lacked support from the working class, another major weakness of the interpretation has been identified, and this could be developed in the remainder of the paragraph.

There is no requirement for you to reach a judgement as to which view you find more convincing or valid.

Assessing the interpretation

In assessing the interpretation you should consider the following:

- Identify and explain the issue being discussed in the interpretation: the extent to which Italians actively supported fascism.
- Explain the view being put forward in the interpretation: the interpretation is arguing that a majority of Italians not only accepted fascism but genuinely supported the regime.
- Explain how the interpretation fits into the wider debate about the issue: whether the regime commanded genuine public support or ruled a people cowed by propaganda, fear and intimidation.

In other interpretations you might need to:

- Consider whether there is any particular emphasis within the interpretation that needs explaining or commenting on, for example, if the interpretation says something is 'the only reason' or 'the single most important reason'.

- Comment on any concepts that the interpretation raises, such as 'mutilated victory', 'corporate state', 'cult of personality'.
- Consider the focus of the interpretation, for example, if an interpretation focuses on wealthy and middle-class Italians, what was the viewpoint of the industrial working class? Is the viewpoint given in the interpretation the same for all areas of society?

In summary, this is what is most important for answering interpretation questions:

- Explaining the interpretation.
- Placing it in the context of the wider historical debate about the issue it considers.
- Explaining the strengths *and* weaknesses of the view in the extract.

Glossary of terms

Acerbo law Mussolini's July 1923 reform of elections to guarantee a Fascist victory.

Anarchists Oppose both a strong central government and capitalism, arguing that political and economic power should be held by workers and peasants, organised at a local level.

Annex To take over or seize a country.

Anschluss Literally meaning 'union', referring to the annexation of Austria by Germany, which had been prohibited by the Treaty of Versailles.

Anti-imperialist Opposition to expanding Italy's empire.

Anti-Semitism Hatred of Jews.

Anticlericals Those politicians, mainly Liberal, who opposed the claims of the Catholic Church that it deserved a privileged position within the Italian state. Liberals who were particularly anticlerical, and who demanded greater social reform, were known as Radicals.

Armistice Agreement to cease fighting.

Autarky Economic self-sufficiency allowing a country to operate without importing food or other key materials from other countries.

Authoritarian state A state with a strong central government that is able and willing to ignore parliament and suppress dissent.

Aventine secession Anti-Fascist MPs walked out of parliament in protest against Fascist violence, hoping that this would encourage the King to sack Mussolini.

Balkans Area of south-eastern Europe including Greece, Albania and Yugoslavia.

Ballot-rigging Fixing the result of an election by such illegal measures as destroying votes cast for opposition parties or adding fraudulent voting papers.

Battle for grain Fascism's attempt to make Italy self-sufficient in the production of grain, and thus bread.

Blackshirts Armed Fascist militia.

Blitzkrieg 'Lightning war' tactics employed by the Nazis very successfully in the early years of the Second World War. Involved co-ordinated use of aircraft, tanks and infantry.

Bolsheviks A group of very radical Socialists (often called Communists), led by Lenin, who seized power in Russia in 1917. They executed the Russian royal family and took control of all businesses.

Bourgeoisie The middle classes, owners of businesses.

Chamber of Deputies The lower, but most important, house in the Italian parliament – similar to the British House of Commons.

Civil service Civil servants advise government ministers on policy and ensure that government policies are carried out.

Collectivisation Seizure of private land by the state. The land would then be reorganised into state-run farms or distributed to groups of peasants.

Confindustria A powerful, conservative organisation representing big businesses.

Constitutional monarchy The king or queen is head of state but the prime minister is the head of the government. The monarch has the power to dismiss prime ministers but in practice leaves day-to-day politics in the hands of the prime minister and parliament. To stay in office and to pass new laws the prime minister needs the approval of the elected parliament.

Corporate state Mussolini's model for the economy whereby every industry would be part of a Fascist-led corporation that would sort out disputes between workers and management, and help to organise production, pay and conditions.

Coup d'état The violent overthrow of a government.

Cult of the *Duce* The promotion of Mussolini as the 'supreme leader' (*Duce*), the man who had saved Italy from socialism, and who was leading the country back

to greatness; a man whose creation, fascism, was admired around the world.

Depression   A period of economic stagnation that began in the USA and affected all European industrialised countries for most of the 1930s.

Duce   All-powerful leader. This was Mussolini's self-attributed 'title', which the regime encouraged people to use. It signified that he was not just prime minister, but also the effective dictator of Italy.

Economic sanctions   The banning of trade with an aggressor nation in an attempt to force that country to change its policy.

Entente powers   An alliance of Britain, France and Russia (Triple Entente).

Fascistisation   Mussolini's attempts to make ordinary Italians adopt Fascist ideas and a Fascist approach to life.

Free trade unions   Trade unions which represent the interests of workers, and which are independent of government control.

General strike   A strike involving millions of workers in a very wide range of industries. General strikes usually have a political motive, and are not just about pay and conditions of work.

Grand Council of Fascism   The supreme body within the Fascist movement, which discussed policy proposals and made all key appointments within the Fascist Party.

Hoare–Laval Pact   An Anglo-French attempt to find a compromise peace, giving Mussolini most of Ethiopia.

Irridentism   The demand that Italy seize from Austria those lands on its northern and eastern borders where a majority of the population spoke Italian.

Italian Social Republic   Mussolini's Fascist regime in northern Italy 1943–5.

Lateran Agreements   These comprised a treaty and a deal, known as a concordat, which officially ended the dispute about the role and status of the Catholic Church in the Italian state.

League of Nations   International organisation of over 100 countries created after the First World War and designed to help to prevent wars and end disputes between countries.

Leggi Fascistissime   Fascist laws which banned all opposition parties and organisations.

Liberal historian   One who sympathises with the Liberal regime, arguing that Italy, prior to fascism, was maturing into a stable, parliamentary democracy.

Liberal oligarchy   A regime controlled by a relatively small group of politicians, in this case Liberals, who formed a wealthy, educated elite.

Lire   The Italian currency from 1861 to 2002. (Singular: lira.)

Mare Nostrum   Literally 'our sea'.

Marxist historian   One who broadly subscribes to the views of Karl Marx, arguing that Liberal regimes are a guise for the exploitation of the working class and that such regimes will be overthrown once the working class realises and exerts its political strength.

'Mussolini made the trains run on time'   This phrase was coined by foreign journalists to suggest that the Fascist regime had somehow improved the efficiency of Italian industries.

Mutilated victory   The claim that Italy had been denied its rightful territorial gains in the peace settlement after the First World War.

National Fascist Party   Set up by Mussolini to unite the Fascist movement and to increase his control over local Fascist squads and their leaders.

National militia   Fascist squads were converted into a national militia, giving them legal status. This blackshirted militia was under Fascist Party control.

OVRA   Fascist secret police.

Partisans   Armed anti-Fascist groups.

Patronage   The use of appointments and promotions to reward support.

Personal dictatorship   A regime where a single person, rather than a team of ministers or a political party, holds total power. This individual is able to make their own laws and arrest opponents at will.

Polarising   Moving towards extremes.

Popolari Catholic political party founded in January 1919.

Press censorship Newspapers are no longer permitted to criticise the government.

Proletariat Industrial and rural working class.

Ras Local Fascist leaders, usually with their own Fascist squads.

Reactionary Hostile to parliamentary or democratic government, dismissive of individual freedoms and deeply suspicious of change.

Republicans Those who want to abolish the monarchy.

Revaluation Changing the value of a currency compared to another country's currency. (The Fascist government tried to increase the value of the lira against other countries' currencies.)

Revisionist A state that wanted to change the peace treaties signed after the First World War.

Roman question The political dispute over the role of the Catholic Church in the Italian state, including the territorial claims of the Pope over Rome, and the issues of civil and church marriage and divorce.

Satellite state A country that is very heavily influenced or virtually controlled by another state.

Socialist Socialists argue that the existing political and economic systems of Europe oppress the poor. They work to improve the political and economic status of the working class. Some believe that the existing political systems can be reformed peacefully, others argue that only violent revolution can bring about meaningful change.

Sphere of influence An area where Italy would be the dominant power.

Squadrismo The violent attacks of Fascist gangs, or squads.

Sudetenland An area of Czechoslovakia, bordering Germany and with a substantial German-speaking population. Hitler used this as a pretext to wage war against the western European powers.

Tariffs Taxes placed on imports of foreign products.

Trade unions Organisations, often Socialist, which seek to improve the pay and conditions of their members. Socialist trade unions represented several million factory workers and farm labourers.

Trasformismo Different political factions forming a coalition government regardless of ideological differences.

Triple Alliance Military alliance between Italy, Germany and Austria-Hungary signed in 1882.

Two-party system A political system, as in Britain, where there are two dominant and distinct parties competing for power.

Universal male suffrage The right to vote for all men over the age of 21, introduced in 1912.

Vatican City The area of Rome, comprising St Peter's, the papal apartments and the offices of the papal bureaucracy, which was ruled directly by the Pope and was completely independent from the Italian state.

War of attrition A war in which the commanders do not expect dramatic victories but hope to win by slowly wearing down their opponents over a period of months or years. High casualties are acceptable so long as the enemy's suffering is worse.

Further reading

General texts

Martin Blinkhorn, *Mussolini and Fascist Italy* (Lancaster Pamphlets, 1984)
Brief but useful introduction to the key issues in the study of the Fascist regime

C. Duggan, *A Concise History of Italy* (Cambridge, 1994)
Places Fascist Italy in its historical context

J. Hite and C. Hinton, *Fascist Italy* (John Murray, 1998)
Aimed at A level students. Contains a wealth of primary and secondary sources

Denis Mack Smith, *Mussolini* (Granada, 1983)
A very readable biography of the *Duce* from a highly respected scholar

Chris Rowe, *A New Roman Empire? Mussolini's Italy, 1922–45* (Nelson Thornes, 2010)
A level textbook, aimed at the AQA syllabus

Chapter 2

Martin Clark, *Modern Italy 1871–1982* (Routledge, 2014)
Highly informative on the problems of Liberal Italy before 1914, and on the impact of the First World War on Italian politics

Chapter 3

Alexander De Grand, *Italian Fascism: Its Origins and Development* (University of Nebraska Press, 2000)
This study argues that fascism grew as a reaction to the rise of the Socialists during and after the First World War. It stresses the importance of rural *squadrismo*

Philip Morgan, *Italian Fascism, 1915–1945* (Palgrave Macmillan, 2004)
The reasons for the growth of fascism during the post-war crisis 1918–22 are analysed

Donald Sassoon, *Mussolini and the Rise of Fascism* (HarperCollins, 2007)
Very readable analysis of the impact of the First World War and the crises which led to the rise of fascism

Chapter 4

R.J.B. Bosworth, *Mussolini* (Hodder, 2002)
Probably the most authoritative modern biography of the *Duce*. It clearly explains how Mussolini manipulated Italian politics in the years 1922–6, enabling the creation of his dictatorship

A. Lyttelton, *The Seizure of Power: Fascism in Italy 1919–39* (Routledge, 2004)
This respected work explains how Mussolini undermined liberalism in the period 1919–26

Chapter 5

R.J.B. Bosworth, *The Italian Dictatorships: Problems and Perspectives in the Interpretation of Mussolini and Fascism* (Arnold, 1998)
Examines the different interpretations of what fascism really meant to different groups of Italians in the period

R.J.B. Bosworth, *Mussolini's Italy* (Penguin, 2006)
Investigates the reactions of Italians to life under fascism, with fascinating quotations

N. Farrell, *Mussolini: A New Life* (Phoenix, 2004)
Controversial modern biography which stresses the extent of public support for Mussolini in the later 1920s and 1930s

Chapter 6

E. Tannenbaum, *Fascism in Italy* (Allen Lane, 1973)
An authoritative study. Argues that Mussolini was reluctant to introduce economic policies which would alienate big business

E. Townley, *Mussolini and Italy 1922–40* (Heinemann, 2002)
A level text with useful sections on the economy and the corporate state

Chapter 7

M. Koon, *Believe, Obey, Fight!* (Cambridge University Press, 2000)
A study of the impact of Fascist policies on Italian youth

J. Whittam, *Fascist Italy* (Manchester University Press, 1995)
Examines Fascist social policies and their impact on young people, women and the Church

Chapter 8

MacGregor Knox, *Mussolini Unleashed* (Cambridge University Press, 1982)
Stresses Fascist aggression and argues that Italy and Nazi Germany presented a 'revolutionary alliance against the west [Britain and France]'

Denis Mack Smith, *Mussolini's Roman Empire* (Longman, 1976)
Analyses the inconsistencies in Mussolini's foreign policy and why Italy fared so badly in the Second World War

R. Mallett, *Mussolini and the Origins of the Second World War* (Palgrave Macmillan, 2003)
Explains how Mussolini attempted to pursue his aggressive goals by exploiting Britain and France's fear of Nazi Germany

Chapter 9

P. Morgan, *The Fall of Mussolini: Italy, the Italians, and the Second World War* (Oxford University Press, 2008)
Detailed but readable account of the reasons for the fall of the *Duce* in 1943, and the civil war 1943–5

R. Moseley, *Last Days of Mussolini* (History Press, 2006)
A detailed but readable account of the final two years of Mussolini's life, during the Salò Republic 1943–5

Index

Acknowledgements: A&C Black, *G* by John Berger, 2012. ABC-CLIO, *Encyclopedia of World War II: A Political, Social, and Military History* by S.C. Tucker and P.M. Roberts, editors, 2004. Adams Media Corporation, *A Child in Confino* by Eric Lamet, 2010. Allen Lane, *Fascism in Italy* by E. Tannenbaum, 1973. Cambridge University Press, *Italian Industrialists from Liberalism to Fascism: The Political Development of the Industrial Bourgeoisie, 1906–34* by Franklin Hugh Adler, 2002; *Mussolini Unleashed* by M. Knox, 1982. Charles Scribner's Sons, *My Autobiography* by Benito Mussolini, 1928. Harper Press, *Sawdust Caesar* by G. Seldes, 1936. HarperCollins, *Mussolini and the Rise of Fascism* by Donald Sassoon, 2007. Hutchinson & Co., *My Autobiography* by Benito Mussolini, 1939. J.M. Dent & Sons, *Mussolini as Revealed in His Political Speeches (November 1914–August 1923)* by Bernardo Quaranta di San Severino, translator and editor, 1923. John Murray, *Fascist Italy* by J. Hite and C. Hinton, 1998. Lawrence & Wishart, *Selections from the Prison Notebooks of Antonio Gramsci*, Q. Hoare and G. Nowell Smith, editors, 2005. Longman, *Origins of the Second World War* by P. Bell, 1986. Macmillan, *The Road to War* by R. Overy and A. Wheatcroft, 1989. Manchester University Press, *Fascist Italy* by John Whittam, 1995. Novissima, *What Italy Owes to Mussolini* by M. Missiroli, 1937. Paternoster Library, The Mayflower Press, *My Autobiography* by Benito Mussolini, 1928. Penguin, *Christ Stopped at Eboli* by Carlo Levi, 2000; *Mussolini's Italy* by R.J.B. Bosworth, 2006. Phoenix, *Mussolini: A New Life* by Nicholas Farrell, 2004. Routledge, *Modern Italy 1871–1982* by Martin Clark, 2014; *Modern Italy: 1871 to the Present* by Martin Clark, 2014; *Mussolini and Fascism* by Patricia Knight, 2013. Vatican, *Non Abbiamo Bisogno* (*We Do Not Need*), 1931.